684.08 Vil
Vila, Bob.
Bob Vila's workshop

W9-BZE-537

JOHNSTON PUBLIC LIBRARY

I JOH 00 0 012250 2

DATE DUE

BOB VILA'S WORKSHOP

Also by Bob Vila

THIS OLD HOUSE

THIS OLD HOUSE
    GUIDE TO BUILDING
    AND REMODELING
    MATERIALS

BOB VILA'S GUIDE TO
    BUYING YOUR DREAM
    HOUSE

BOB VILA'S TOOLBOX

Designed by
    Marjorie Anderson
Photography by
    Michael Fredericks
Line drawings by
    Jeffrey Bellantuono

684.08
Yil

BOB VILA'S WORKSHOP

The Ultimate Illustrated Handbook for the Home Workshop

by

Bob Vila

William Morrow and Company, Inc.
New York

WITHDRAWN

JOHNSTON PUBLIC LIBRARY
JOHNSTON, IOWA 50131

Copyright © 1994 by Syndicated Multimedia Corporation

All rights reserved. No part of this book may be reproduced or utilized in any form or by any means, electronic or mechanical, including photocopying, recording, or by any information storage or retrieval system, without permission in writing from the Publisher. Inquiries should be addressed to Permissions Department, William Morrow and Company, Inc., 1350 Avenue of the Americas, New York, NY 10019.

It is the policy of William Morrow and Company, Inc., and its imprints and affiliates, recognizing the importance of preserving what has been written, to print the books we publish on acid-free paper, and we exert our best efforts to that end.

Bob Vila's Workshop was produced by Gallagher/Howard Associates, Inc. The photographs are copyright © 1994 by Michael Fredericks; the contemporary line drawings copyright © 1994 by Jeffrey Bellantuono. The period line cuts are drawn from public-domain catalogs of the nineteenth and early twentieth centuries. The photograph on page *xii* is copyright © 1994 by Christine Kitch.

Library of Congress Cataloging-in-Publication Data
Vila, Bob.
    [Workshop]
    Bob Vila's workshop : the ultimate illustrated handbook to the
home work shop / by Bob Vila.
        p.   cm
    Includes index.
    ISBN 0-688-11736-8
    1. Workshops.   I. Title.   II. Title: Workshop.
684'-08–dc20   94-8510
                                                                CIP

Printed in the United States of America

First Edition
1 2 3 4 5 6 7 8 9 10

I'd like to dedicate this book to the many young people who have picked up tools and gone on to apprentice themselves in the building trades, to the juniors and teenagers who have learned the joys of working on projects in their school and home workshops, and especially to my own teenager, Chris, who is just discovering his own talents.

workshop (work - shop) n. *Any space, room, or building, usually of small size, where manufacturing or handicrafts are carried out.*

ACKNOWLEDGMENTS

To start with, I must thank my collaborators on this book. They include Hugh Howard, who assembled the team and supervised the various steps in the project, as well as bringing his considerable writing skills to bear. Next comes Marjorie Anderson, our designer, and photographer Michael Fredericks, both of whom made major contributions to making this book the most attractive volume possible. Jeffrey Bellantuono's handsome drawings, too, make many points more clearly than words ever could. Jean Atcheson made a signal contribution to the process of getting the words right.

At William Morrow and Company, Inc., thanks go to Allen A. Marchioni, Susan Halligan, Lisa Queen, Larry Norton, and Scott Manning, all of whom helped find the audience for this book and for *Toolbox*; Adrian Zackheim, Michael Mouland, and Suzanne Oaks were a great help on the editorial end.

My appreciation, as always, to my co-workers at BVTV, Michael Ferrone, Jeanne Flynn, and Sheila Morris, for their help and cooperation.

At Sears, I must thank Andy Ginger, Robert Steck, John L. Royer, and Chuck Van Winkle at Hoffman Estates, and, at the Albany, New York, Sears store, Dan Daum.

Finally, there are the tradesmen and craftsmen who have shared stories and insights with me and my colleagues on this project and assisted in creating the workshop. Among them are Richard Ahlin, Michael Beecher, Richard Bennett, Ralph Bruno, Jerry Grant, Robert Haldane, James Krasawski, Pope Lawrence, Mark Lynas, Timothy Rieman, Bob Ryley, and Wayne Walker.

CONTENTS

Introduction *xiii*

INTRODUCTION

Grab hold of the word *workshop* and place it squarely in front of you. Now, close your eyes for a moment. What do you imagine?

How about the smell of freshly cut pine, with a fine mist of sawdust still lingering in the air?

Maybe there's a giant chestnut workbench, its ancient surface darkened with age and scarred with the effort invested in countless tasks well done. The table saw hums, perhaps, or the drill press rumbles, as one or the other does its work.

Tools are everywhere, and wood is stacked in tall racks. There's a broom leaning in a corner, too, even though there's very little evidence that much sweeping up has been done of late.

Actually, I have to admit I didn't have to imagine all this, since I *have* a workshop. But for those readers for whom a workshop is still no more than a fantasy, this book can help you realize that dream. Whatever the size of your dwelling, a home workshop can come out of a closet, or squeeze into your cellar or garage. It doesn't have to remain solely in the realm of your imagination. If you already have a workshop, I hope that in these pages I can help you make it even better.

Your particular workshop doesn't have to be a space the size of an airplane hangar; a great many repairs and even construction projects have been successfully launched from comparatively small spaces.

JOHNSTON PUBLIC LIBRARY
JOHNSTON, IOWA 50131

Workshops are a bit like clothing: They must suit the user, be appropriately tailored and fitted, and adapted to a range of uses. Just as your closet no doubt features dress clothes and casual, working outfits and some for lounging about, a workshop needs to be flexible, armed with tools for many tasks. Workshops can be large, freestanding structures or small spaces secreted within the confines of a house. I know of instances where stairwells or hallways can be almost instantaneously converted into workshops. The tools and work surfaces will be returned to their hiding places (usually in a nearby closet) almost as quickly as they appeared.

My father made furniture, renovated spaces, and fixed all sorts of things, and he did everything without a formal workshop. All he had was two toolboxes and a fold-up workbench. With them, it always seemed to me, he could solve any problem.

Critical to the efficiency of any workshop, large or small, is the range of tools found inside. Too many tools in a small workshop can overwhelm the space, but in general, more tools mean greater flexibility and the ability to do more jobs more efficiently. The mix of the tools is another factor, be they new or old.

I've always felt that there's a place in the shop for traditional, even antique tools, as well as the newest and cleverest of designs. For me, old tools represent a certain continuity. Just looking at them, let alone actually using them, I get an immediate sense of the past. Older houses that have some obviously original elements or furniture offer something of the same sensation. You have the feeling other people used these tools or walked those halls.

You know the old cliché "tried and true"? It applies to tools perhaps better than to anything else. In fact, a handmade and well-cared-for old try square was probably responsible for that turn of phrase being coined. The tool was used to test whether a piece was square: The verdict, most times, was that the workpiece was indeed tried and true.

New tools are appearing almost daily. The computer chip revolution is making its presence felt in the tool world thanks to electronic controls that are now available on tools as varied as routers, bandsaws, and heat guns. In general, these control mechanisms make tools more efficient and easier to use. Yet such technological advances are to be balanced with the pull of the past.

I can't remember how many times I've heard people say, "I remember the days when I could fix practically anything on my car with a pair of pliers and a screwdriver." That same observation, complete with the sentiment that something has been lost to the juggernaut of technical progress, is made by tool users, too.

For me, however, the bottom line is this: It's not such a great idea to get so mired in the past that you make your workshop endeavors more work than they have to be. Equally important, don't forget the tools and techniques of the past just because they aren't shiny and new.

Tools of today and yesterday can comfortably coexist in any workshop or toolbox. Many well-made tools don't wear out: Some seem to defy the wear and tear of time and work just as well or even better as the years go by. Hand tools, in particular, very often survive their users and get passed from one generation to the next.

Good design helps, of course. Stable woods like beech, rosewood, mahogany, boxwood, and hickory appear in the workshop in a variety of guises, from hand planes to hammer handles. Well-tempered steel is essential for chisels and other tools that require a finely honed edge. High-grade iron, fiberglass, plastic, and even stone all have distinct attributes that can be used to advantage in making, using, and maintaining tools.

A well-designed tool does more than employ the right material. Quality tools have a natural "feel" to them. Their heft is solid but not too heavy. They have a balance that allows them to employ gravity, as when the weight of a hammerhead helps drive the tool downward, or to defy it, as with a well-balanced screwdriver or chisel that can be put to work comfortably at almost any angle.

Some basic tools have been in use since ancient times, among them the level, the lever, and the screw. The earliest level was probably a trench filled with water; today, highly accurate spirit levels are found on key chains and tape measures, as portable and convenient as you could wish. A wrecking bar may be highly machined, but its leverage is often employed in much the same way that a caveman used a tree limb to lever a stone this way or that. Worm-drive mechanisms on some power tools and the helical flutes on many drill bits are true screw mechanisms, too, logical developments of Archimedes' imaginative thinking some two centuries before the birth of Christ.

The pulley, the wheel and axle, the inclined plane, the wedge – all are invaluable means of employing a minimum of force to accomplish the maximum amount of work. And each has its role to play in the workshop.

As does pure power, of course, in this era in which energy is everywhere. The advent of steam and then electric power transformed the workshop, first for the professional and then for the hobbyist. A modest investment today of a few hundred dollars equips the home workshop with a range of tools and options that Colonial tradesmen could never even have conceived. We may be learning to conserve energy but, at times, it seems as if it's our own calories we're husbanding, saving ourselves work by letting our power tools do the cutting and shaping.

Which brings us back, once again, to one of the fundamental questions this book attempts to address: Which tools do you need in your workshop, anyway?

SELECTING TOOLS

There are so many manufacturers, and so many kinds and types and models of virtually every tool, that the options may appear to be nearly infinite. Making the right choices can seem daunting in a marketplace where equivalent tools are sold for prices that differ, in some cases, by

500 percent or more. Whether your principal priority is to be true to your tight budget or to advance your personal quest for the best, the best tool to serve your needs isn't always evident.

Consider a few commonsense rules I've picked up over the years.

Start Sensibly. Invest first in the basic tools that you will need again and again. Wrenches and drivers, a drill and a circular saw, and other multipurpose tools probably should be on hand before sophisticated stationary power tools arrive. Make the decisions case by case: For example, a high-powered belt sander bought for one job is probably a poor investment, while a random-orbit sander that can be used for rough and finish work alike may get dozens or even hundreds of hours of use. Consider carefully what you really need, the options that are available, and buy the essentials first.

Add Equipment As You Go. When you set up your workshop you don't have to own every tool you'll ever need. A rarely used and expensive tool might better be borrowed or even rented for a special use. Many rental companies have a wide range of specialty and quite run-of-the-mill tools for a per-diem fee. If you only need the tool once (or once in awhile), the rental fees will probably be less than the purchase price would be. And no storage problem presents itself because the tool goes back to the renter when the job is done.

Using someone else's tool also enables you to discover if you like a certain brand or model, and may save you money when you come to buy one for yourself. If you didn't enjoy using the one from the rental shop or Dad's tool chest, keep shopping.

Once you know what you like and know what you need, don't hesitate to make the investment. You will discover (if you haven't already) that friends who borrow your tools grow less welcome, especially if they care less about your tools than you do. Return tools promptly and in the condition they were in when you took them home.

Buying Tools. The feel of a tool is part of its pleasure. The heft, the tactile sense of belonging that a quality tool gives of being an extension of the hand – that's what to look for when buying a tool, especially a hand-held tool like a plane or a chisel.

Now, you observe, that isn't so easy when buying from a catalog. And mail-order suppliers often have the best prices, right?

Keep in mind that some catalogs are less available – and sometimes less cooperative – when a tool breaks down and needs repair. Many professional craftspeople will tell you to seek out a fair, friendly, knowledgeable local dealer and develop a good working relationship early on. That's good advice. It may cost you money in the short run but over the long haul you will probably encounter fewer hassles.

Get the Feel First. Even if you can't or don't choose this approach, it's in your interest to find an opportunity to get the feel of a tool before buying it. Maybe it's at the store with the highest prices (ask if they're negotiable) or in a friend's workshop. But hands-on is important in making tool-buying decisions. If at all possible, put the tool to use, too.

At the very least, eyeball it. I can't tell you how many stories I've heard from people who have bought tools through the mail only to discover a tool was smaller than anticipated or too heavy or badly made in ways the buyer would have detected if he or she had been able to examine it firsthand. Don't be afraid to ask for dimensions.

When tool shopping, inspect the tools on display. Look for double-insulated bodies. Does the casting appear to be of good quality? Heavy-duty cords of reasonable length are often one indication of good-quality power tools. Does it look and feel sturdy? You may be surprised how much your own tool sense can tell you about a tool even if your inspection of it consists of little more than looking and lifting.

Beware of tools that, you're told, can do just everything! You see, they probably can't. There's a reason why a hammer is still a hammer and a chisel still a chisel many millennia after their invention. There's no reason to be afraid of innovation, but the best new tools tend to be refinements of earlier ones, not gimmicky new designs that are said to be capable of everything short of dancing and spitting nickels.

A Bargain Isn't Always a Bargain. Unfortunately, the cheaper a tool is, the more likely it is to be made of inferior materials, to have been badly machined or shaped, or have any number of manufacturing defects. Cheap chisels won't hold an edge and the motors on cheap power tools tend to burn out quickly. A penny saved buying cheap tools isn't a penny earned, but more like a penny wasted. Quality, brand-name tools of good repute earned their reputations: There's a reason why so many professionals buy American brands like Craftsman, Delta, Milwaukee, and Porter-Cable, and imported labels like Ryobi, Makita, and Bosch.

That isn't to say that the occasional worker in a workshop needs the best tools on the market. Rather, you should consider your needs, try to balance your investment with the dividends you can reasonably expect, and remember the old adage: You will, most likely, get exactly what you pay for.

Look for Flexibility. Buying fewer, more versatile tools is one good way to save money. Tools with attachments often make sense, such as a router that with a simple adapter becomes a biscuit joiner and also cuts mortises. Learn as much as you can about individual tools from sales catalogs, from friends and tradesmen, and even from salesmen in shops.

THE WORKSHOP AND THE TOOLBOX

This book is a companion volume to *Bob Vila's Toolbox.* The two books are intended to complement one another, so the tools described in each are largely exclusive of the other. By necessity there is some overlap, but in most cases a given tool is discussed in detail in one or the other book.

The tools selected for inclusion in *Toolbox* were primarily the portable ones we take with us to a work-site, whether it's an altogether new structure or a remodeling of the back bedroom. *Bob Vila's Workshop*, in contrast, looks at the tools that, for the most part, remain in the work-

shop. Some are large, like the table saw, some are smaller, like such benchtop tools as the jack plane. More than a few are quite portable and can be used almost anywhere, like the router.

For your convenience, we've incorporated a series of short entries in this book that sum up some of the recommendations in *Toolbox*. They're called *Tools from the Toolbox* (see pages 82, 105, 129, and 175) and are intended to remind you of some of the basic tools – wrenches, hammers, drivers, drills, and the rest – that have important roles to play in the workshop as well as at the work-site.

GETTING UNDER WAY

Before I talk at length about planning, building, and tooling up your workshop, let me tell you a story a stonemason friend of mine told me. It's about his getting started in his business. Even if you never plan to lay a single stone or make a dime from the products of your workshop, I think Ralph's experience is relevant.

Although his family had been bricklayers for two generations before him, he pursued other careers for a few years before deciding that masonry was what he wanted to do after all. His father and grandfather had served long apprenticeships, but he found himself making a career change, already into his thirties, with very little on-the-job experience.

So he went to work for wages that first summer for a brick mason in a nearby town. The man had been around awhile, having built just about every fireplace constructed within a twenty-five-mile radius over the preceding thirty years. He'd worked on rich people's houses, and he'd built stove chimneys in trailers. He'd done patios and barbecues and, well, he'd said yes to just about any masonry job that came his way.

My friend Ralph worked for him for several months, and took away with him two lessons. He learned countless tricks: The man knew every shortcut there was and had a clever solution to every fix he got into. On the other hand, my friend also learned that neither experience nor resourcefulness necessarily begets careful workmanship. The guy was a complete slob, who couldn't be bothered to tool a joint and level up a lintel. He did what had to be done, and no more. That most certainly wasn't Ralph's way, and he knew it from the first.

The moral of the story? If you have a chance to learn from a professional, to work with someone who has a body of experience, by all means do so. There's no better way to learn. And you should always pay attention to what's going on around you: Garner advice and recommendations when you can from books, magazines, television shows, and from idle conversations with strangers at the hardware store.

On the other hand, keep your own counsel. The experts know a lot – but your own good instincts are important, too. Use what you learn and what you know to do the best job you can.

BOB VILA'S WORKSHOP

P A R T   I .

CONTENTS

THE
WORKSHOP
SPACE

Not all workshops are the same. That's stating the obvious, but those six simple words sum up the biggest difficulty involved in the writing of this book, as well as the numerous decisions you face in deciding what your workshop is to be. You may be surprised and amazed to learn of the many directions you can go in designing, constructing, and equipping your shop.

I won't presume to tell you what you need, but I *can* tell you something of the priorities I had when I planned mine. I needed a shop that could be used both as a workshop and as a shooting set for *Bob Vila's Home Again.* The uses are not incompatible, but some imaginative thinking was required to serve both needs. For example, the windows are set high over the workbench, positioned carefully so that good natural light would illuminate work being done on the benchtop *and* so that we could point a video camera in to see the tools at work. It's a good shop that serves our needs well, big enough not only to build cabinets, but to squeeze in the cameraman, sound engineer, producer, and me, too.

Not everyone needs to think about camera angles, of course. And not everyone needs to worry about having the space to build cabinets, either. But the starting point, necessarily, is the work of defining the very nature of your own individual workshop-to-be. In the first chapter, then, we think through the plan; Chapter 2 concerns putting those good notions into effect.

If you are building a workshop from the ground up, the first thing you need are plans. And, guess what . . . even if you are adapting an existing space the first thing you need are . . . plans.

Chapter 1.

Thinking Through the Plan

There is no one perfect workshop plan: Each of us has different needs, depending upon whether we're cabinetmakers, occasional Mr. Fixits, or someone in between.

Home workshops can be freestanding shops, purpose-built structures of extravagant size. At the other extreme, a toolbox and folding card table can also constitute a "workshop." Most often, though, home workshops are modest spaces that put to use otherwise unused space in the house, cellar, garage, or an outbuilding.

Perhaps the key question to put to yourself is, "What is my avocation?" The layout, size, and equipment in your shop should evolve logically from your answer to that query, as each must reflect the nature of the work you will do there.

At one extreme, perhaps, is the homeowner concerned with occasional repairs around the house. For this, you need little more than a space to store tools in such a way that they are easily accessible. A cabinet or a closet would probably be quite adequate, making it possible to reach for the wrench and screwdriver without having to move the eight dusty boxes of books that got piled in front since the last time you needed a half-inch open-ended wrench. (Keep in mind, too, that the easier it is to get to the tools, the greater the odds you'll put them back where they belong and be able to find them with ease the next time you need them.) You probably don't even need a sawhorse, since the cellar stairs will suffice for the occasional saw cut.

At the other end of the spectrum is the woodworker making new kitchen cabinets. In that case, you need to have the space to lay out, cut, shape, and assemble large flat pieces of wood or plywood into bulkier boxes. Such complex projects require considerable time, too, which means that jobs in process will have to remain unfinished from one day (or weekend, or longer) to the next, while the glue dries or until your schedule allows you to return. If you are embarking on a second career as a woodworker, you'll need a high degree of organization, ample storage space for stock, and a miscellany of tools adequate to the nature of your work.

Somewhere in between is the home hobbyist teaching himself (or herself) toolcraft for reasons having little or nothing to do with the profit motive. In that case, the workshop doesn't have to be built (or equipped) in a day. A good plan, in fact, might well allow for a small collection of tools, in anticipation of other tools being added in the future as they are needed.

A dismantled bench, several tools, a few architectural elements in need of repair . . . all in search of a workshop, perhaps?

THE CELLAR SHOP

For most of us, the answer isn't a separate building, a closet, or even the garage. The single most popular alternative is right under your nose (and the rest of you, too, for that matter) in the cellar below.

Frequently, the space downstairs is unfinished. If the furnace is there, it's heated. Count two advantages already.

The separation from the rest of the house is hardly total, but there's at least some sound-proofing and a certain amount of the dust and dirt will be contained.

If there's a concrete floor, it's a solid, practical base for even substantial stationary power tools. A well-equipped shop needs a structure able to support heavy workbenches, fixed saws, and the other stationary tools. The floor surface must also be durable and not so precious that every scratch and mar will make you wince. And it probably needs to be resistant to solvents and grease.

It's true, cement floors are hard and cold, but otherwise they are just about perfect. You don't like the grayish color? The dust is hard to control?

Apply a concrete paint to seal the surface of the concrete. It'll cut down on dust and brighten the space, too, as paints are available in light shades and colors.

All of that's good news. On the other hand, dampness is a common problem in cellars. Make sure there is plenty of ventilation in yours if you plan to put your shop there, because moisture can ruin tools almost overnight. Condensation and minor dampness can often be addressed with a fan and a dehumidifier, but if the place frequently floods or has standing water in it, you will probably want to keep on looking for your workshop space.

What about access? Can you get a sheet of plywood down the stairs? You don't want to set yourself up to make the mistake of building a captive project, like a boat or a bureau that can never escape the basement. It happens.

What about other users of the space? Is there already a playroom for kids in your cellar, or a utility space with a washer and dryer? Noise, safety, and dust can become important matters when the other inhabitants might be inconvenienced by the arrival of a workshop. One common (and relatively simple) solution is a partition, but it isn't the magic answer in all cases.

Yet before we lose sight of first principles in talking of tools (that'll come later) we need to talk of exactly what the space options are and how they may best be used.

A rule of thumb . . . If you can get a sheet of four-foot-by-eight-foot plywood into your workshop without endangering life, limb, or any of your worldly possessions along the way, the access route is probably adequate. If you felt like a contortionist in making the trip, however, rethink your workshop site.

LOCATION, LOCATION, LOCATION

Perhaps you already know exactly where you will be locating your workshop. Maybe you already have a workplace in some form. If so, you may want to skip ahead a few paragraphs. But if your workshop is still little more than wishful thinking, read on a bit.

The most obvious place to locate a workshop in most homes is in the basement. Cement floors and walls are no particular disadvantage in a workshop, and cellars are often the last unclaimed space in a busy house. There's much to say about cellars (see above and facing page), but there are other possible settings, too.

Survey all your options before deciding where to set up shop. Among the alternatives might be a spare room, an attic space (is it tall enough?), the well beneath a stairway, the garage, a converted porch,

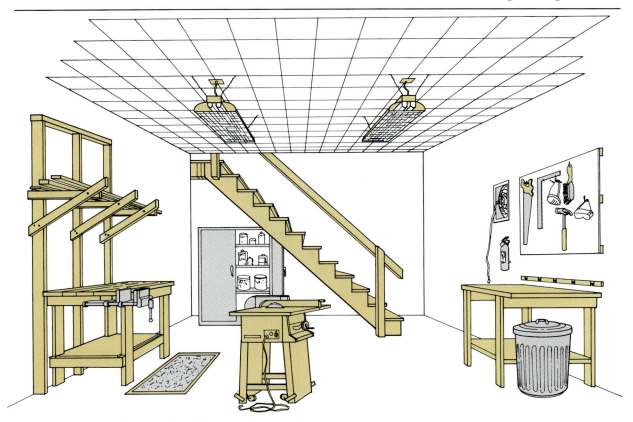

The cellar woodshop has a million different guises, but the basics are more or less standard. The ingredients typically are a workbench with a vise, a wood storage rack, a table saw, an assembly table, a tool rack, and a metal cabinet for storing finishes and other flammable materials . . . or whatever portion of these elements you can fit into your cellar space.

an outbuilding like a barn or a shed, a back hall, a closet, or even a piece of furniture like an old dresser or desk. For some kinds of workshops, a piece of the kitchen will do, say a single drawer and a borrowed piece of counter or cabinet.

Whatever the space being considered, think through its workshop possibilities from two angles. One approach is obvious: Will it work as a workshop? The other angle is just as important: Will it interfere with other activities in the house? Turning an empty and unused space into a useful space probably makes sense; adopting a corner of the kitchen as a paint shop is likely to inconvenience everybody else in your household.

But let's consider each of the options in a little more detail.

The Garage. The garage offers some inherent advantages. Most are well ventilated, relatively large, and can be turned into combination spaces (the car won't complain about being displaced now and again). But the garage utilities, like heat and electricity, might require upgrading, though if the garage is detached from the house, issues of noise and dirt and dust are probably moot.

Raw space is what you might call this cellar corner. Raw – and ready for transformation into a home workshop.

Typically, a garage workshop has a workbench built permanently into the end wall opposite the garage door. If they are mounted on roller stands, quite good-sized power tools can be easily maneuvered to the side of the garage so that the car can be brought in from the cold. Another advantage of a garage is the size of the broad, tall door; it makes getting almost any machine inside no problem at all. In many garages, the area over the overhead door is open to the rafters, lending itself to storage if the roof is pitched. If you have a garage, it just might be the best answer.

The Spare Room and Other Inside Options. An extra room is the right choice in some homes, but often the liabilities outweigh the potential gains. The comforts and conveniences are appealing, of course, since the room is probably heated and has electrical service and perhaps even good lighting, both natural and artificial.

On the down side, access is often difficult. That's a problem if you have to move in large machines and quantities of material. Hallways and doorways designed for domestic use just aren't industrial-sized. Noise can be a problem, too, in the interior of a house, as can dust and dirt. A second-floor room exaggerates all these problems, doubling or even tripling the exposure of both house and inhabitants to the dirt and noise pollution.

The bottom line, then, for a spare bedroom or other empty room in the main portion of your house is this: If your workshop activity is loud and takes lots of space, you would do better to find another spot. Woodworking will probably require significant and potentially expensive renovations, like soundproofing and a vacuum dust system. On the other hand, if the work can be confined to a tabletop and won't wake up a napping nephew in a nearby room, go for it.

A converted back porch has fewer of these liabilities, since access to it is easier. But you may need to add electricity, insulation, or make some structural changes to adapt it effectively.

The Attic. The biggest plus is that attic spaces are often unused except for storage. Unfortunately, the minuses are numerous.

Take your tape up top and measure the height of your attic. Even if you can stand up comfortably, will you be able to maneuver raw materials around? Or will you find yourself cutting down materials at an outside work station first?

Accessibility questions must be raised here, as well. Flights of steep stairs are risky and tricky when moving materials and heavy tools. You may find that the top of the house is prohibitively difficult to reach with equipment or supplies.

In this mid-nineteenth century engraving, a "country carpenter's shop" is reproduced. Perhaps in the days when handsaws and hand planes were dominant there wasn't quite the same volume of fine saw-dust to get everywhere (like into the sitting room next door). I doubt that today a workshop would be tolerated with such equanimity so close to the living spaces.

THE CLOSET WORKSHOP

For many occasional, around-the-house handypeople, a closet workshop is an easy answer to a multitude of headaches. One frequent complaint of homeowner-handypersons is tool inaccessibility: It's a pain to do even simple jobs if finding the right wrench or that small screwdriver requires ten minutes of rummaging around the bottom of a back closet packed with deflated footballs, widowed ski gloves, and stacks of empty paper bags.

Your problem-solving efficiency might increase a good deal if you follow this recipe: Find one underutilized closet, some scrap stock (to be cut into shelves), and add a dollop of organizational thinking. *Et voilà*, a workable workspace emerges.

An ordinary closet will do. Remove the closet bar first.

Design the workshop so that the shelves run the full depth of the closet: you won't be able to walk into it anymore, but the deep shelves will hold much more stuff. Make sure the battens that support the shelves are sturdy enough to bear the weight (nail or screw them to studs). Three-quarter-inch plywood works well for shelves if you don't have scrap at hand.

Plan the installation first: Your arrangement should take into consideration any toolboxes or carriers, large tools, materials, or other objects you plan to store there. Heavy objects are best stored near the floor (why lift heavy objects any higher than necessary?). Frequently used hand tools belong at waist or chest height for quick and easy access.

With the addition of a fold-out table on the door or attached to one of the shelves, there's even a bench available.

You can put the door to use for hanging tools, too. If it's a hollow core door, stiffen it with a sheet of half-inch plywood glued and screwed in place. Or replace it with a solid door.

Before you start installing shelves in the coat closet next to the front door, think about the location as well. The easier it is to close off adjacent spaces, the better. Just a single handsaw cut produces a surprising amount of dust; a power saw raises much more.

Speaking of power tools, remember that they require electricity. Is there an outlet near the closet? Preferably, it should be one that is wired for twenty amps, so as to accommodate the power surge that many saws produce.

Only you can identify which is the right closet in your home and the right arrangement within it for your needs. And I can't pretend to have addressed all the questions or possibilities here. One option I'd recommend for the adventuresome home handyperson is to enlarge the opening of the closet workshop, making it four or five feet wide instead of the typical two-and-a-half feet or less. If you add a folding workbench, maybe a portable table saw, and a few other elements, pretty soon it'll feel like a full-fledged workshop.

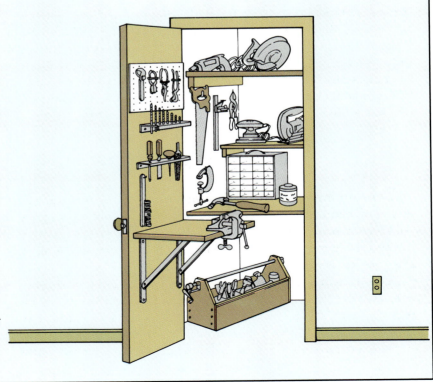

Now, how about the floor? Often the ceiling joists that support the attic (and the ceiling below) are undersized for workshop loads. If it's hot in the summer, you may have to install windows and vents. An exhaust fan may be necessary, too.

If you are lucky enough to live in a giant Victorian house with one of those grand, tall spaces beneath steeply pitched eaves, the attic may be just the place for your shop. But for most of us, it's not an option.

Barns and Outbuildings. A century ago, most householders were also farmers. They might have gone to work in town or at some other trade during the day, but about half of all Americans were at least part-time farmers. Many of the barns, sheds, and other auxiliary structures still standing around old farmhouses are survivors from that era.

Today, many barns and other outbuildings are long gone, but if such a "dependency" (as the preservationists like to call such peripheral buildings) has survived, it may be the perfect answer.

Before you arrange delivery of the tools for your new workshop, however, check matters out carefully. You'll need power, and very likely more than just one antiquated fifteen-amp line. Otherwise, you'll be forever going back and forth between the shop and your panel (or, worse yet, putting the building at risk of fire by overloading the line). Two lines, one of which carries twenty amps, are probably the minimum.

What about structural stability? And heat? Security may, too, be an issue, as unwanted visitors might just make off with valuable tools and materials if they are left unprotected.

The Nook or Cranny Approach. There's the closet model, of course (see facing page). But there are lots of small spots in the average house that could be adapted. For example: a fold-down worktable over a washer/dryer, concealing shelves bearing tools and supplies; under the stairs; stairwells and back halls are often large enough for small, self-contained tasks, but rarely offer enough space and flexibility to function as full-fledged workshops.

KNOW THY NEEDS

You may think you already know what you need. "Just a practical space, you know, enough for my table saw and to try out that antique combination plane Uncle Herb left me." But how big is that, really?

The following are some of the major concerns to consider in planning your workshop.

The Workbench. The primary work surface is key in any workshop, so important that an entire chapter is devoted to the subject later in this book (see page 43). For now, however, think about its size: How large is the bench to be? Will it be the only surface (aside from the tabletops on stationary tools) in the shop? Will you be standing when you work?

Converting a room to a workshop? If it's a spare bedroom or recreation room, consider the effect the transformation could have on the resale appeal of your house. Not every buyer will fall in love with your workshop. . . .

Will your bench have storage shelves or drawers beneath? Do you want access to it from the front *and* back?

The Stationary Tools. First comes the workbench, but your next concern, very likely, is a stationary saw of some sort, probably a radial-arm or table saw. You may also want a band saw. In a luxuriously appointed shop, there may also be a drill press, jointer, shaper, planer, and so on. Make a list of what you really need; make a second one of what you'd like to have.

How big are those items that must remain stationary? How much do they weigh? Top-of-the-line table saws weigh hundreds of pounds, as do many production-line-quality freestanding machines. For most homeowner shops, this isn't an issue, but keep it in mind if you're considering moving your Delta Unisaw up to the rickety second floor of that old chicken house out back.

Material Size. What's the longest piece of stock you're likely to need? Sixteen-foot-long one-by and two-by stocks are usual, though shorter lengths can be bought, too.

What's the widest sheet of rigid material you are likely to want to bring in? Virtually all plywood and other sheet stock is sold in four-foot-by-eight-foot sheets. You'll need to make room for them, or plan for cutting them down first.

Think ahead a bit to the projects you are planning to take on. What's the largest layout you'll need to do? Will it be laying out the face plate for a ten-foot wall of cabinets or using tweezers to apply decorations to tiny Christmas ornaments?

Materials Access. Where will the stock and other materials be arriving? A second-floor space far from the staircase and at the end of a twisting hallway doesn't make logistical sense. On the other hand, the front hall where unexpected guests may come knocking probably isn't the best choice either.

If the work you'll be taking on requires big machinery or produces finished products of large size, you may want to add a special door to accommodate the comings and goings of outsize items. Many professional shops have double, sliding, or garage doors.

Storage. How much stock are you likely to keep on hand? If you buy your wood rough cut and need to air-dry it on the premises, your demands are obviously much greater than the occasional workshop worker who buys what he (or she) needs on a Saturday morning with the expectation that the job will be done by sundown.

Material storage is divisible in most cases into three general categories: virgin boards or lumber, stackable on racks; oddball bits and pieces of stock, storable in bins or smaller racks; and miscellaneous hardware and other elements. Suitable racks, shelves, and cabinets belong in your plans, too.

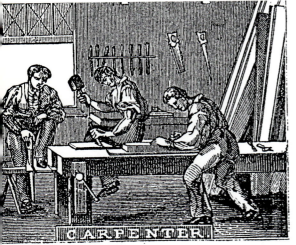

Taken from an 1857 book entitled Popular Technology; or, Professions and Trades, *this engraving portrays a shop that looks bare indeed in comparison to the workshop of today.*

THE END-WALL SHOP

This is the classic garage work area. The bench is fixed on the end wall and your car is still comfortably situated in its bay. Maybe there's a little storage space on the side walls or in the rafters overhead. The arrangement is practical, compact, and interferes not at all with the business of the house.

Then comes the transformation: With the car removed (even temporarily), the real workshop can reveal itself. Some two hundred square feet of space is suddenly open and available. You can design a fold-up worktable from the bench; one or more stationary tools on casters can be rolled out from the side walls. The garage door up front makes loading and unloading tools and materials a simple matter, with no twisting and turning to squeeze through narrow doorways. There's a reason why this is a popular option.

One handy space-saving trick useful in the garage workshop is a roller table. Its top can accommodate a benchtop table saw and other tools, too, while the tool (or tools) not in use on a shelf are stowed beneath. Prefabricated roller tables are available from mail-order catalogs, but some two-by stock, plywood, a set of inexpensive casters, and a few fasteners are really all you need to make one for yourself.

One caveat regarding garage workshops should be kept in mind: Not all activities that can be done there are truly compatible with one another. Woodworking is a dusty occupation, while most automotive mechanical work involves grease and oil. Fine woods can be ruined when brought in contact with petroleum products; many engine and motor parts just won't function when contaminated with sawdust and other grit.

Keep your shop clean to minimize the risk of such problems. And try to avoid interrupting one kind of work with another: Do the tune-up first, then make those birdhouses.

So often, it's mostly a matter of what you can squeeze in. This garage has a good, long workbench, with a fixed radial-arm saw on top and a shelf beneath. There's storage on the walls and in the rafters, and good lighting, too.

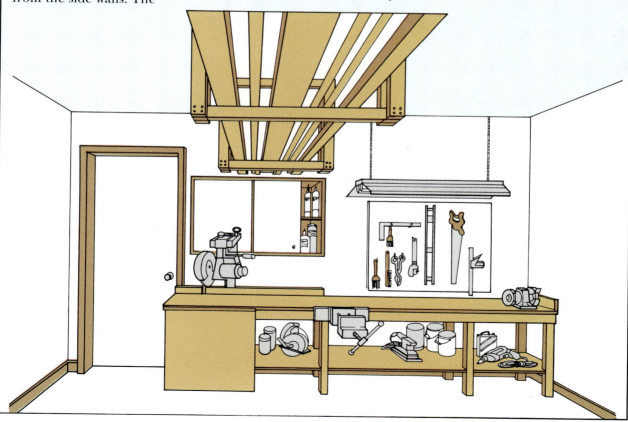

THE WORKSHOP DRESSER

This workshop dresser is used primarily as a sharpening station, and its vise for metalwork, in a larger shop. But a similar installation can be a workshop all on its own.

An old chest of drawers or desk can be transformed into a combination bench and tool cabinet. With the tools stowed away, it will take up no more space than it did in the days when it was used for clothing storage or as a home office. But when put to use, a compact workshop unfolds, like a pop-up scene in one of those clever children's books.

Organize your tools into the drawers. Hammers, pliers, and screwdrivers in one, perhaps, chisels in a second, and planes and saws in a third. Do it logically: The tools you need frequently go in upper drawers, heavier ones below. Add dividers to protect the fragile cutting edges of planes and chisels.

A great flat-topped oak desk makes a perfect benchtop; it may even accommodate a woodworker's vise on the front or side.

A benchtop table saw with separate stand (a Workmate will perform this and many other functions) can be stowed on top of the piece when not in use. If the surface is a comfortable height, you can even affix a radial-arm saw to its top. Saber-saw and router adapter tables can be fastened to the top of the piece as well, adding a built-in shaper and jig.

The Dust and Dirt Factor. Sawdust gets into *everything*. Most workshops produce rubbish and waste; the closer your workshop is to living areas, the greater the likelihood that you'll spend more time cleaning up or, worse yet, justifying the mess you are making to others in the household inconvenienced by it.

Other Considerations. You may not have the luxury of choosing which way(s) the windows face, but solar orientation can help to keep the shop warmer in colder weather and lighter all year round. If your workshop is to be a place where you spend a great deal of time, you may even wish to have a view. The well-known woodworking teacher and writer Tage Frid, for example, has a breathtaking view of a babbling brook from the window of his Rhode Island shop.

Climate control can also be an issue. The attic or cellar is often unbearably hot or cold. Dampness is a concern, of course, both for your tools and for the workpieces. A damp cellar can be the cause of paint or finishes that never seem to dry, warped or even moldy stock, and rusty tools.

If you do any painting or finishing work, ventilation becomes crucial. Proper precautions need to be taken when flammable or even potentially toxic materials are used.

Before embarking upon workshop creation or transformation, you'll need to translate all your answers to these questions into a floor plan. For example, if you use standard sixteen-foot stock, you'll need at least one dimension to be a minimum of sixteen feet long, and probably longer for ease of doing cutoff work on long pieces. A table saw will need a certain amount of space at the front and back of the table, and is probably best located at or near the center of the room. But before you start laying out the shop, let's talk a little more specifically about some of the layout options available to you.

When incorporating a workshop into your household, especially if there are young and curious hands in the house, make sure the powerful saws and other machines are secure. Many models come with special switch locks. Use them, or, if your tools aren't so equipped, go the old-fashioned way: Unplug the stationary tools when you leave the shop and put all portable ones well out of reach. And don't forget about chisels, saws, utility knives, circular sawblades, and any other edged tools. Stow them safely away.

THE LOGIC OF LAYOUT

A landscape designer friend of mine tells a story about the college he went to. During his years there, the university embarked upon an ambitious building plan, adding several large structures around the main quad: a dorm, a chemistry lab, and a couple of others. The look of the place, which had remained unchanged for a century, was suddenly transformed, as glass and steel modernist structures were interspersed with the earlier ivy-covered stone Victorian-Gothic.

The streetscape wasn't the only thing that changed. The patterns of use of the quad itself were also affected, as more people were moving in more directions. The long-established roadways and paths no longer served the traffic.

The planners did an interesting thing, my friend recalls. Instead of commissioning a hugely expensive study to try to predict the new patterns that would result from the opening of the new buildings, rather than devising an anticipated program and laying out a new scheme, the university's brain trust decided to let the students and faculty, the lifeblood of the university, shape their own arterial flow.

Sure enough, the approach worked. A semester after the buildings were completed, a definite crisscross of paths emerged.Only then were the landscapers hired to come in and memorialize it: They paved the paths, then planted grass and shrubs, *off* the beaten paths. A pretty clever move, I thought.

THE FREESTANDING WORKSHOP

There's no reason why your workshop can't be easy on the eyes, outside and in. This one was created in order to write and research this book. We trimmed it out to reflect many of the vernacular Greek Revival homes and other structures common to the area in which it is located. Old doors and windows bought at salvage add to the old-timey feel of the place.

If you're serious about working, you may want to consider building a special structure, or converting an existing one, to serve as a workshop. It's expensive, of course, and may require building permits and electrical inspections and added property taxes to pay but there's no better way to get exactly what you want than to design a workshop to your needs and tastes. And it'll keep the sawdust out of the kitchen and the rest of the living space in your house.

If your shop will be equipped with a range of stationary power tools, you'll probably require a minimum of six or seven hundred square feet of space (roughly twenty by thirty, perhaps twenty-five by thirty). That's enough for equipment, some storage, and working areas.

In researching and writing this book, we decided to design a workshop that fulfilled some of these basic criteria. The result was the workshop space that you see throughout this book. It is not a dream workshop, really; that, I'm afraid, would have to be the size of a gymnasium and have a million dollars' worth of equipment. But it's sizable, with an unobstructed rectangular working area seventeen by twenty-nine feet.

It's an all-purpose shop, though the emphasis is clearly on woodworking. It faces south, with bright light coming from the east and west, too. The windowless north side has a large closet and utility space.

The ceilings are tall, nine feet, to be exact. Working with an eight-foot piece of stock is no problem at that height, requiring much less of that tedious bending and twisting to maneuver pieces of wood or plywood. The lighting is recessed: We lost a little brightness in the process (largely compensated for by the use of floodlight bulbs) but eliminated the need for guards.

Much was learned in constructing and using our workshop. We made some mistakes. The cedar ceiling, for example, looks great, but it has become apparent that light hard

The workshop interior, complete with woodstove, shaper, benches, hanging tools . . . and plenty of unfinished jobs to do.

surfaces are better than dark wooden ones. The ceiling seems to absorb rather than reflect light, which is a disadvantage. There simply is no such thing as too much light in a workshop, because the better the illumination the more accurate the work can be.

But we made some good decisions, too, many of which you will find in these pages. The woodstove serves a double duty, burning up unnecessary scrap and keeping us warm. The wood floor is warm, and easy on the back and legs. The walls are white, unpainted plaster (a skim coat on top of plasterboard). They have proved durable and easy to patch after butts and bangs delivered by workpieces being maneuvered into position. The windows on the east and west walls are aligned; this makes the shop seem much larger when we're planing or ripping sixteen-foot lengths of stock, as we can simply extend them in and out the windows.

One thing to keep in mind about building a new workshop (as opposed to, say, moving a bench into your garage and putting it to work) is that, with new buildings, in most communities, there are building code requirements. Even for workmanlike structures the strictures may be many and stringent. Find out local requirements ahead of time and amend your plans, if necessary, to conform with them.

Seeing the forest for the trees is a perennial problem, whether the trees have been milled into lumber or stand tall and true in the forest.

Now, maybe you can do the same thing in your workshop. You can move your benches, tables and tools, and storage units around as you devise better work flows. But as is so often the case, what works in academe might not be the best approach in the workaday world, namely in your workshop.

For one thing, the rearrange-it-later approach may simply mean that once you're set up, the haphazard plan becomes the permanent plan, thanks to sheer inertia (it is a pain to move furniture, after all, especially when some of it is as heavy and awkward as workbenches and stationary tools). For another, too little advance planning may mean you buy a power tool that's too big for your space.

So I, for one, would recommend a certain amount of advance planning. Even if the layout you devise evolves over time (and it almost certainly will), you'll probably find the workshop a more efficient place to work right from the start if you think it through as thoroughly as you can beforehand.

I'm guessing you'll find it to your advantage to consider the issues that follow in your planning process.

Stationary Tool Space. Tools take up two kinds of space. First, there's the square footage required by the tool and its stand, whether it's in use or waiting patiently for its next opportunity to show its stuff. With a big table saw, that can represent a dozen or more square feet; a drill press requires roughly from three to five square feet.

Second is the *operating space* around the machine. When the table saw is used to cut a piece of four-by-eight-foot plywood, the tool space increases geometrically, as the thirty-two-square-foot sheet of stock is pushed and pulled through the blade. Even if you're not planning on using your table saw to cut plywood, you need to allow ripping and crosscutting space. This means that in front of and beyond the blade you need distances at least as great as the length of the longest board you'll need to rip; and that you'll require space for cutoff work on either side of the saw.

The bottom line, then, is that in most cases the logical place for the table saw is at the hub of the workshop.

If you have a fixed-in-place cutoff saw (a radial-arm, miter saw, or sawbuck, for example), it can, unlike the table saw, be conveniently positioned against a wall. Don't set it in a corner, however, as you'll need space on either side of the blade. Figure into your plan a two-

It's a board's-eye view of the workshop. In fact, the distance from the prow of that piece of pine to the workbench on the far wall is about fifteen feet . . . but when you are ripping a long piece of stock, a big workshop seems suddenly to shrink.

foot-deep, three-foot-wide space for the saw itself and tables or other supports flanking the tool. Allow enough space directly in front of the saw for the operator to be able to comfortably line up and operate the saw.

The band saw has spatial requirements similar to those for the radial-arm saw: the tool can be positioned with its back to the wall, with operator space at the front. The most area will be required on either side of the saw.

In many workshops, band saws and drill presses are not used constantly, so they can be set back out of the way. Jointers and shapers can also sometimes be set back out of the midway, but keep in mind that the more trouble they are to reposition, the less useful they'll be. Remember, too, that while jointers and shapers take up relatively little floor space, you need to allow space on either side that is at least the length of your longest workpiece: a four-foot workpiece needs about a ten-foot space (the tool, plus four feet on either side), eight-foot pieces closer to twenty. The longer the pieces to be joined or shaped, the greater the space required on either side.

Tabletop versus Freestanding Tools. When purchasing some power tools (the list includes the jointer, shaper, sander, and even some models of table and band saw), you may decide to opt for benchtop models. A single bench can then serve, alternately, a range of purposes. Make-ready time is increased significantly, of course, as not only the blades, fences, miter gauges, and the rest must be set but the machine itself has to be positioned and powered. But for the small shop, the infrequently used tool may be quite easily stowed on a shelf out of the way, opening up more space for other tasks.

Partitions. If you are planning to introduce your workshop into an existing space in your house, you may find it necessary to construct a partition to separate the dust and dirt of the workshop from, say, the laundry room with which it is to share the cellar. Or, for safety reasons, from the children's play area.

Within the workshop itself, you may deem it necessary to subdivide the space for a painting and finishing area.

Natural Light. Natural light is best, so any windows that offer illumination to the space should be put to good use. If you have little sunlight in your shop, locate your workbench so that its work surface gets whatever there is. Even the best eyesight is made better by good light, so the close work to be done on a benchtop benefits from the natural light.

Another thing about windows: As we have learned in our workshop, they can make a small shop seem bigger than it is when long workpieces being ripped or planed begin with one end out one window (or door), are run through the machine, and extend out another window.

For a serious workshop, you will probably need a minimum of two major freestanding tools: One will be a cutoff saw (radial-arm, miter saw, sliding miter saw, or equivalent), the other a table saw. Plan your shop around these two workhorse tools.

Artificial Illumination. The same rules apply: Good light is essential, and if isn't natural light, it will have to be artificial. Don't put your safety at risk by working in poorly lit or shadowed areas: If you can't see what you're cutting or shaping, you just might cut or gash yourself. (See also *Lighting*, page 28.)

Plumbing. You don't need plumbing, you say? Then what about washing up not only paintbrushes but yourself after a particularly dirty job? A utility sink is a very handy convenience to have near at hand.

Temperature and Moisture Control. If your workshop is to be located in a portion of your house that is already comfortably warm, this will not be an issue. But if you're converting a barn or shed or an unheated space, especially if you live in a climate where winter temperatures make for cold hands, you'll need to devise a heating strategy. In some climates, air conditioning is a virtual necessity in hot weather.

Is your cellar damp? If so, you may have to correct that problem before installing your tools and lumber supplies. Insulate pipes to prevent condensation. Make sure your gutters outside keep rainwater running away from the house. Cracks in the cement floor or walls should be filled with hydraulic cement; a high water table may necessitate a sump pump to collect water at a low point and pump it out. Any or all of these circumstances may also require a dehumidifier. In any case, dampness is unacceptable where power tools are to be used because of the risk of electric shock.

Egress. A door that leads directly outside is best (avoiding corners and hallways); a double-wide door is better still. The closer the door is to the outside world, the less stuff to be tracked in from without.

Electricity. It's a rare workshop today that doesn't need electricity; most need multiple receptacles of high amperage (20 amperes or more). Are there plugs available or will you need to add new lines and circuits? If you need to add wiring, when laying it out keep in mind that there's no such thing as too many outlets in a workshop. The fewer (as in, ideally, zero) extension cords the better; they're safety hazards. A good minimum is to have receptacles set at no more than six-foot intervals around the perimeter of the room, and, if possible, flush-mounted floor plugs in the central area.

If a poured cement floor prohibits the installation of plug receptacles flush to the floor and you elect to surface-mount a plug, protect the exposed feed wire. A piece of one-by-four stock with a groove cut in its underside and its top edges chamfered, will pose little more tripping risk than a threshold. However, paint its protective covering a bright color to remind you and any other visitors to your shop of its presence.

A receptacle or circuit that is overloaded is a hazard, in particular one fused beyond its limits. Power tools, especially heavy-duty saws,

If you must use extension cords, make sure they are rated to handle the power your tools need. Keep them short, too, or the voltage drop that will occur as a result of a long cord will cause the motors on your saws and other tools to overheat. Which can, eventually, cause the motors to burn out.

require lots of amperage, and you may need to add a circuit or two to serve the increased demand in your workshop space. Some tools require 220-volt service, so you may want to install a special plug and line to power that high-powered table saw. (See also page 27.)

DRAWING A FLOOR PLAN

Now that your head is swimming with the challenges presented by your machines, the limitations of the available space, and your numerous needs and desires, it's time to translate it all to a floor plan. Preparing this piece of paper can prove to be an important discipline in thinking about your workshop.

The first plan you make may well change – indeed, you may revise the plans many times – but the discipline of putting it on paper will compel you to ask yourself questions, to search out information, and to make adjustments.

We talked in *Bob Vila's Toolbox* about making drawings using an inexpensive drafting board, T square, triangles, and the rest. For laying out a workshop floor plan, even less is required: a couple of sharp pencils and some graph paper will do. And a tape measure to determine the sizes of the machines, etc.

Do it to scale. Take the largest dimension of the space and determine how to most efficiently fit it on your graph paper: ½ inch to the

The tools are quite simple: the T square, a couple of triangles, a compass, a pencil, a board, some tape. That's all you need. And, yes, a bit of imagination. . . .

foot will allow for a fourteen-by-twenty-foot shop, for example, on a standard $8\frac{1}{2}$ x 11-inch sheet. A scale of $\frac{1}{4}$ inch to the foot will accommodate larger spaces.

Outline the Area First. Begin with the perimeter of the space. Indicate the windows and doors (include the swing of the doors, too). If your space is to be shared (with the furnace in your cellar, for example), draw in the fixed elements around which you must work. These include plumbing lines, stairways, columns or piers that support the house, chimneys, appliances such as hot-water heaters, freezers, washers, and dryers. If your workshop space will double as a garage, be sure to identify the floor space that will, at least some of the time, be occupied by your vehicle. In a garage, you may also need to allow for garden tools, lawn mower, and other yard care equipment. And bicycles, perhaps?

Position the Tools. For purposes of discussion, let's assume that your shop will be used primarily for woodworking. That being the case, you'll likely try your hand at a bit of joinery, maybe make a cabinet or two, and almost certainly take on the kinds of projects that we all seem to confront now and again, like fixing toys or windows or chairs or other things from around the house.

You'll certainly need a workbench, some kind of work surface on which to perform all kinds of tasks, starting with layout. You'll need cutting tools: ideally, a cutoff saw (perhaps a radial-arm saw) and a table saw (for ripping and just about everything else). If you plan to fix or make objects larger than a breadbox, you will probably need another work surface, a work or assembly table with a broad top. Space for other tools and material, supplies, and other tools is necessary, too, but the primary points of orientation will be the workbench, table saw, cutoff saw, and worktable.

The workbench will go against a wall, preferably in front of a window. The cutoff saw goes against a long wall, with enough space on either side of the blade to cut long pieces of stock to almost any length. The table saw and worktable are set in the middle of the room; the worktable may even do double duty, functioning as an extension table to the table saw, as well. The floor plan suddenly emerges.

Measure your workbench (if you have one; if not, decide how large a workbench you need). Measure the top of your table saw, too. Draw the outlines of the workbench and table saw to scale on a separate sheet of graph paper and cut them out. For tools or work surfaces you don't yet own, use the dimensions given in tool catalogs to guide you through the planning process. You may find that your initial choices are too big, or, if you're lucky, that more space is available than you thought.

Like checkers on a game board, these representations can be moved around. Put the table saw at center; put the other tools along the walls (see the individual entries for the table saw, band saw, shaper, and the rest later in this book).

makeready (make-red-ee) n. *Final preparation of a machine for running. The term is most commonly used in the printing business, but in other industries as well.* Syn. Setup.

See that window over my shoulder? That is one of the shoot-in (with the camera) or look-out (at the camera) openings we built over the workbench in my television shop.

Go with the Flow. In considering where the tools should go, keep in mind that the arrangement of the workshop should be an organic one: The sequence of tools should follow the life of the process. Say you generally start with raw stock. The first step probably involves rough-cutting the large sheets or lengths of material from the lumberyard into workable pieces. Thus, your cutoff saw (the one you rely upon for cutting stock to length) probably belongs in a location that is convenient to your storage racks.

Perhaps more cutting follows: The table saw or the band saw are probably next. Perhaps a shaper, jigsaw, jointer, and drill press are involved in further station stops, followed, perhaps, by the sander. An assembly table follows. The workbench may be required at one or several points in the process, depending upon how much shaping is done by hand.

In your mind, walk through the operations involved in the work you will do in your workshop, and translate the logic to your plan. It may be a circle around the table saw at center; it may be **U**-shaped, or an in-and-out ell. Find an approach that works for your shop and your work, and you'll find that you can save countless footsteps.

Don't Forget the Elevations. Elevation drawings take time, but they, too, can help you think through the process. Draw each of the walls of your shop, incorporating windows and doors, benches and tables, bins, racks, shelves, and anything else you want (or that you have to contend with, like the furnace, water heater, and the rest). Heating, cooling, and ventilation equipment, ducts, or pipes must also be drawn in.

Oh, and one other thing: Don't get so involved in moving furniture ("The jointer will go here, the sanding station, er, over there . . .") that you forget to leave yourself some empty space. You need areas where there aren't any tools: Some floor space will be required not only for you to walk around, not only for operating the machines, but for assembling the objects you are making or working on.

Saving Space. *Freestanding tools on rollers can quickly and easily be maneuvered out of the way, clearing space for other tools. Good candidates are the drill press, band saw, jointer, and sanding station.*

THE PLANNER'S CHECKLIST

In laying out your workshop, have you considered the following:

Existing Utilities. What about the fixed equipment or appliances that encroach upon the perimeter space, such as the furnace, hot-water heater, washer/dryer?

The Workbench. How big is it?

The Table Saw. Is there enough space on all sides for presenting workpieces both for ripping and crosscutting?

Band Saw. You can put its back against the wall, but don't forget to leave operator space at its front and space on either side for workpieces.

Drill Press. Like the band saw, the drill press can be set out of the way, against the wall. But

you'll need work space in front for you and for the stock being drilled or shaped.

Jointer, Shaper, and Sander Stations. Each of these needs to have space to approach from and to go to. And operator areas, too.

Assembly Tables. Don't skimp here. This work can be painstaking; it requires good light and care. Give yourself some elbow room.

Chapter 2.

Putting a Plan to Work

In the first chapter, we talked of possibilities. We examined the options that you might, or might not, have, and asked some questions about the challenges one or another of the potential workshop spaces posed. I made a case, as well, for putting on paper a sketch or two of the likely layout your shop might take.

Now it's time to refine the plans a bit, to add some shadings to that rough penciled sketch on the graph paper. In this chapter, we will discuss in some detail issues such as lighting and wiring requirements, specifications for doors and exhaust fans, along with a bit about noise pollution and fire prevention. I'll offer a couple of sample layouts for workshop arrangements. And we'll discuss a few tools, too, including the shop vacuum and fire extinguisher.

So let's get to it, it's time to work on the workshop.

The space is light, equipment-filled, and (needless to say) cluttered with work to do.

ELECTRICITY

Power tools swallow up power the way dogs consume their food: in great, huge gulps. Most tools have two kinds of demand, one being the surge at starting (because of the energy required to get them up to speed), the other being the power required to run them continuously. The bigger the tool, the bigger the gulps. The electrical entrances in most homes are adequate to handle all the basic tools your home workshop is likely to include, but the existing wiring in the cellar or garage or wherever may not be up to the demand.

Check the situation out with care: How many plugs are there? Are they all on the same circuit? What is the rating of the circuit(s)? What else is serviced by those circuits? If the kitchen, utility room, or any sensitive equipment such as computers or facsimile machines are on the same line, you'll need to add new lines.

You will need ample, conveniently located receptacles. For small shops, at least one 20-ampere line (for the tools) and one 15-amp line (for the lights) are recommended. If your needs are such that two power tools will ever be running simultaneously, two 20-amp lines are probably in order, though for some hand-held power tools (electric drills and small sanders, for example) a 15-amp circuit is sufficient.

Some large machines require 240-volt current, among them certain table and radial-arm saws.

The bigger the shop, the more likely a subpanel in the shop itself will be worth the investment. A large feed line run from your main panel delivers the power to the auxiliary panel; there, circuit breakers control the separate lines. One advantage of a subpanel within the shop is its sheer convenience when a breaker cuts off power to a line (and it happens, from time to time). When the breakers are right in the workshop, resetting them is an easy step or two away.

If you have no electrical experience, however, the job of installing such a system should be left to a licensed electrician. Even if you know what you're doing, consult with the local wiring inspector to be sure your work meets local wiring and safety standards. Select a subpanel with a minimum of four breakers.

Most new power tools today are made with double-insulated bodies, but properly grounded receptacles are still a must. A sensible precaution is to use ground-fault-interrupters. They will automatically cut off power in the event of a grounding failure. One GFI receptacle at the head of an existing line is sufficient (you needn't replace all the plugs on the line, as one GFI will protect the whole circuit). Another option is to install GFI circuit breakers at the panel to protect the line. If ever any water is present in the workshop, GFIs are not an option, they are a must.

Floor outlets are preferable for stationary machines located in the middle of the shop, because they avoid extension cords lying in wait to trip you up. When the floor beneath is wood frame, floor plugs are relatively easy to install; when it's poured concrete, a raceway installation is possible, in which the plug and the line running to it are surface-mounted with metal or plastic channels used to protect the wiring. The raceway is about a half-inch square, and must be used with matched switch and plug boxes. Electrical supply houses carry fittings for raceway installations. Protect the raceway with wood chamfered to resemble a threshold; paint it a bright color, too, to draw the eye to it and reduce the risk of tripping.

If you are thinking of buying a production-quality stationary power tool – maybe it came out of an old factory or commercial woodshop nearby – check out its power requirements first. Many such tools require three-phase power or 660 volts, neither of which is to be found in the average home. Unless you are launching a business, you're probably better off staying with quality tools intended for consumer use.

LIGHTING

At a minimum, you need a conveniently located switch at the entrance that powers up the main lighting. Most likely, this means overhead lights that illuminate the entire space. Don't try to get away with less than you really need: Inadequate lighting is unsafe, an open invitation to accidents and injuries.

Localized light is probably necessary, too, perhaps at certain individual machines or over worktables, especially those where close detail work is to be done. Goosenecked, clamp-on lights are practical solutions for some machines, but we'll get back to that in a moment.

Overhead Lights. Fluorescent lights are a cost-efficient and effective solution to lighting the shop as a whole. They provide broad areas of

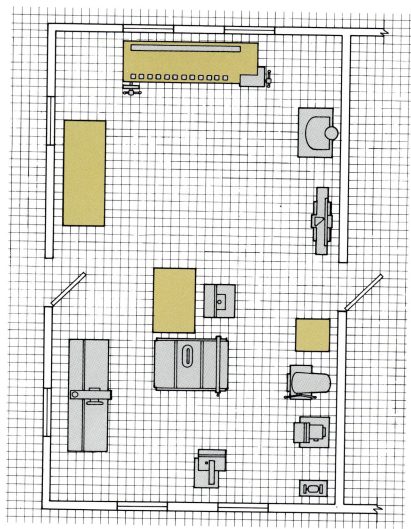

This floor plan resembles that of the workshop where most of the pictures in this book were taken. That's an antique woodworking bench at top. Moving clockwise, there's a woodstove, jointer, toolbox, drill press, sanding station, and grinder along the wall. A band saw is at the bottom, a radial-arm saw on the left, and an assembly table at top, left. In the center of the room is the table saw and a router table. Quite a complete setup, from which much good work can be done.

light for less electricity than is required for traditional incandescent bulbs. Fluorescent shop fixtures also offer the advantage of being self-contained; their metal housing protects the guts of the device (the transformer or "ballast" and the internal wiring). When suspended from light chains, they can be moved up or down (or even to different sites) easily and safely, without exposing the wiring, merely by adjusting the links on the chain. Buy fluorescent fixtures in which the lamps are shielded with a guard, protecting them from being struck by swinging boards and other objects in the shop.

Recessed incandescent fixtures are another option. On the face of it, there are several disadvantages: They are more expensive to install and to run; they take more time, trouble, and skill to install; and, in the end, the light is more localized and there's less of it. But some people just don't like fluorescent light and the recessed fixtures do protect the bulbs. If it's important to you, go with the incandescent fixtures, but be sure you install enough of them.

Fluorescent lighting fixtures are easy to install, inexpensive to run, and provide a good deal of generalized light, especially over the likes of benchtops and other work surfaces.

If your incandescent fixtures are surface-mounted, shield the bulbs. Hardware cloth is one option; another is inexpensive cages (they resemble those on droplights). They snap onto the base, limiting the flow of light only slightly. Again, they serve to protect the bulbs from workpieces inadvertently swung in their direction.

Area Lighting. Localized lighting may be fluorescent or incandescent. The design and configuration of local lamps varies enormously: An old desk lamp may suffice in one application, while a goosenecked lamp may be required in another. Lamps with clamp-on bases are handy in a variety of applications, as are jointed-arm lamps that allow the light to be positioned specifically for individual jobs, especially with specific stationary machines.

The trusty old droplight we talked about in *Toolbox* has more than a few uses, including those ad hoc moments when, on hands and knees, we find ourselves trying to find that damn lock washer that fell beneath the bench.

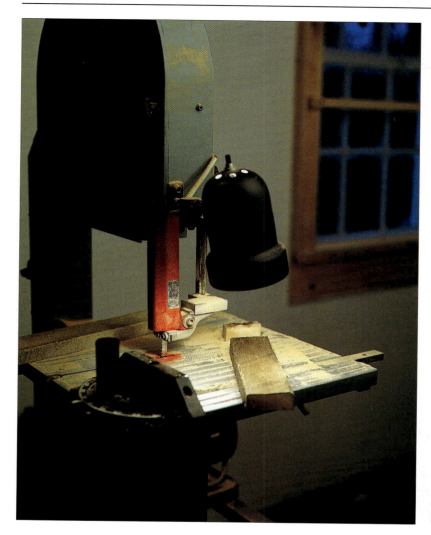

No matter how effective the overhead lighting, some tools just get in their own light. A band saw, with its slight blade and narrow kerf, is much easier to use accurately when the cutting edge is brightly illuminated. The bench grinder is another tool that is easier to use with a tool-specific light, perhaps one with a gooseneck that can be adjusted.

NOISE POLLUTION

Noise is an occupational hazard in any shop where power tools are used. But a hazard it is, and strategies must be employed to minimize the discomforts and risks it poses to you and to the peace of your household. The problem is twofold: You need to control both the noise within the shop and the din that escapes to pollute nearby rooms and spaces.

Noise Without . . . Two modes of sound transmission require your attention: one, through the air and, two, as transmitted through walls, ceilings, or floors.

The first is relatively easy to address. A good, tight door with weatherstripping added can lessen the volume traveling from one room to the next. But limiting the conduction of sound through walls usually requires more complicated renovations.

SHOP SPECS

Consider some of these issues as you plan your workshop.

Doorways. Standard household doors are often as narrow as thirty-two or thirty-four inches; in a shop, a minimum of thirty-six inches is more like it. Wider, even double doors make moving in machinery and stock and moving out millwork easier.

Stairways. As wide as possible is the rule: certainly no less than thirty-six inches (if you have any choice), and forty-two inches is better yet. The steps should, ideally, fit the standard formula, being not too steep (risers more than eight inches tall tend to be a bit trippy). Wide treads of ten or more inches make carrying tools, materials, and finished work a bit less hazardous.

Ventilation. If you need a ventilation fan (and you will if you do any spray painting or much finishing work), here's the formula for determining the size you need. Calculate the number of cubic feet in your shop (width times length times height), then divide by four (e.g. a 10-foot-wide x 20-foot-long x 8-foot-tall space = 1,600, divided by 4 = 400 cubic feet). Many standard kitchen exhaust fans will move some 400 cubic feet of air per minute (CFM), but larger fans are available for larger spaces.

Be sure if you ever use contact cement, solvents, or other materials that produce flammable fumes that the fan is equipped with an enclosed motor.

Heating and Cooling. Your shop should be not too cold, but also not too hot. Somewhere in the sixty- to sixty-five-degree range is probably best (warmer is not ideal, because you want to work with some protection and perspiration will tempt you to shed the safety gear).

In a cellar, a nearby furnace will probably suffice. A small space heater is an option in a space that is warmed to some degree by another source. An electric baseboard heater is relatively inexpensive and easy to install but expensive to run for long periods. Some models come with a built-in thermostat, others require a separate wall-mounted control.

In other spaces, you may need to provide another source of heat. A traditional one is a woodstove, an especially efficient approach in cold-climate woodshops. The supply of fuel in a woodshop usually keeps pace with the need (when you're at work on a project, the scrap provides you with heating BTUs; when you're not at work, you don't need to heat the place anyway). Woodstoves require special precautions. When spray painting, or using strippers or other chemicals with flammable fumes, be especially careful with the stove and use an exhaust fan. You may want to heat the shop first, let the fire die, then do your work.

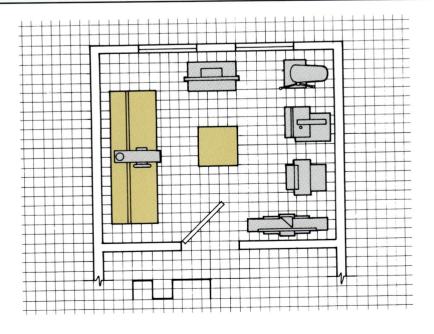

How many tools can you fit into a small shop? In this twelve-foot by ten-foot space are a radial-arm saw (left), a shaper (top), and a drill press, band saw, planer, and jointer (right, top to bottom). All but the radial-arm saw are on casters, so that each tool can be moved into position for shaping or cutting long workpieces.

Be vigilant about keeping the vicinity of the stove clean. Sawing, sanding, and other tasks launch sawdust into the air. A little sawdust and a hot coal that escaped the stove undetected spell instant danger. Be sure to follow the local fire codes when installing a stove (clearances below, beneath, and behind the stove, as well as spark protection in front of any openings). Make sure you have proper fireproof materials or insulation around the stove fittings. A proper chimney may be most important of all.

One source of heat is a wood-stove. You burn your scrap and sawdust (I think that's a workshop corollary to the law about conservation of matter that we learned in high school physics).

In this shop, we added an antique mantel for character. There's no fireplace behind it, just a sturdy, safe, and inexpensive stove chimney made of concrete donut block.

Applying acoustic tile to a ceiling can limit the sound traveling from a cellar workshop to the rooms above. When the problem is sound traveling through the floor to living spaces below, the floor of the workshop can be modified. A layer of sound-absorbing fiberboard can be laid on the floor; attach furring strips and plywood and vinyl flooring atop that (see illustration, following page).

New walls can be double-studded, using two-by-three studs between two-by-four plates and sills (or two-by-fours between two-by-sixes). Stagger the studs on opposite sides of the wall so that the wallboard and supporting framework on each side of the wall is independent from its mate on the other. This way, the sound is not conducted straight through the wall.

. . . And Noise Within. Sound inside the shop is an important issue: too much sound can be literally deafening, short and long term. Over time, loud tools will produce actual hearing loss; in addition, too much noise also causes fatigue. In short, sound can be dangerous both to your hearing and to your safety.

Place pads beneath the feet of power tools. Purpose-made anti-vibration pads of neoprene can be used, as can layers of leather, cork, or felt.

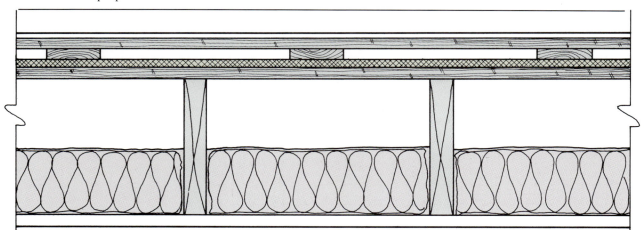

A soundproofed floor is like a double-decker sandwich. In this particular installation, from top to bottom, the layers are vinyl sheet flooring, three-quarter-inch plywood, furring strips, a layer of fiberboard, the existing plywood and floor joists, insulation, and the finished ceiling below.

Wearing protective hearing devices is the first and most obvious strategy (see *Protective Gear*, page 135). There are other options, too. To muffle vibrations, use rubber pads as mounts for benchtop machinery. Rubber or cork feet on stationary tools can also help.

Some flooring is quieter than others. Vinyl sheet flooring is relatively inexpensive, easy to clean, and absorbs some sound. A thin underlayment (building or rosin paper or a purpose-made product from the floor store) will also help.

When purchasing machines, ask friends, local contractors, or even the salespeople about the loudness of the models you are considering. There are table saws that hum and others that positively scream; some routers are distinctly more deafening than others.

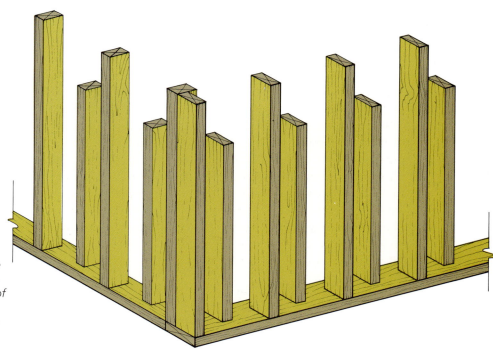

Double-studded walls prevent the direct transmission of sound. The sound-deadening characteristics of such a wall can be further enhanced by weaving insulation between the studs.

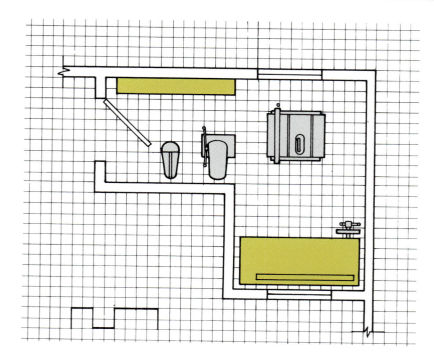

Here's another small shop – its largest dimension is about twelve feet, with each ell roughly five feet wide. It features a workbench, table saw (with windows behind and in front of it for ripping long stock), a jigsaw, and a drill press.

FIRE PREVENTION

It hardly needs to be said, but you should of course do everything you can to reduce the risk of fire in your workshop. Fires are not only dangerous and expensive: Big ones are also frightening in a way that few domestic events can match. Fire is one of Mother Nature's ways of reminding us of her raw and immeasurable power.

A few simple precautions are in order. For one, consider at the planning stages what you will do with flammable materials. Liquids such as solvents, paints, and finishes, for example, should be stored in a metal cabinet away from the furnace or any other source of heat. Make sure the top of each can is tightly closed. If you ever use gasoline for cleaning parts or other tasks, use it outdoors or in a well-ventilated space separate from the house. Don't store gasoline, benzene, and other inflammable solvents in your home.

In planning and, eventually, in working in your shop, you must consider the risk of fire – and how it can be minimized. In woodshops, in particular, the dangers are considerable, because of the omnipresent sawdust. If your shop is within the walls of your house, a tight, fireproof door is a sensible precaution. A double layer of gypsum wallboard on the cellar ceiling or garage dividing wall (it may already be in place there, as it is code in many areas) will act as a fire barrier.

But the simplest and easiest precaution you can take is to install a smoke detector. It's an inexpensive, yet highly effective way of alerting us to the presence of a fire, often before our own senses can detect it. The loudness of a smoke alarm is undeniable – and when there's a fire, that's good news.

Some smoke detectors can be fooled by dust and steam. But when sensibly located they perform an essential service when a fire occurs and are no inconvenience when nothing is burning.

The fire extinguisher has been around for awhile, but today's models are cheaper, easier to use, and highly effective. Along with the smoke detector, one or more fire extinguishers also belong in your shop.

Smoke Detector. There are several types of smoke detectors, and the best choice for a workshop is the photoelectric variety. It detects smoke entering the device when it deflects a beam of light, and, unlike the ionization detector, the other common design, is less likely to be triggered by only a minor amount of smoke in the air.

SWEEP-AWAY TOOLS

Safety and convenience are certainly served by keeping the shop clean. You may even find that a broom-cleaned space is a pleasure to come back to.

In any case, you'll need a broom, a dustpan and brush, and a short-handled workbench brush. A shop broom with a wide brush works wonders in a large shop, though a traditional flat broom suffices nicely, especially in a smaller space. Don't be tempted to add your sweepings to the pile under the table saw; it accumulates quite fast enough on its own. Bend down a moment, dustpan in hand, and get the dust up.

A whisk broom or other workbench brush is invaluable when doing benchtop work with the likes of planes, chisels, or routers. A flick of the broom now and again, on or around the workpiece, makes

examining your progress much, much easier.

Shop Vacuum. A shop vacuum is a useful investment for the workshop of some size. It will make cleaning up sawdust and miscellaneous debris easier, of course, but the good ones have the power to pick up glass and even shards of concrete. Some convert to blowers, too.

Unless your shop is very large, don't buy a giant shop vac. A sixteen-gallon model is prob-

ably large enough. Be sure to buy a wet/dry machine. It will prove its worth for cleaning up spills and minor floods – in the house and workshop alike.

Whether you're scraping a door, sawing boards, or cleaning up after a finishing job, one or another of these cleanup tools will surely come in handy.

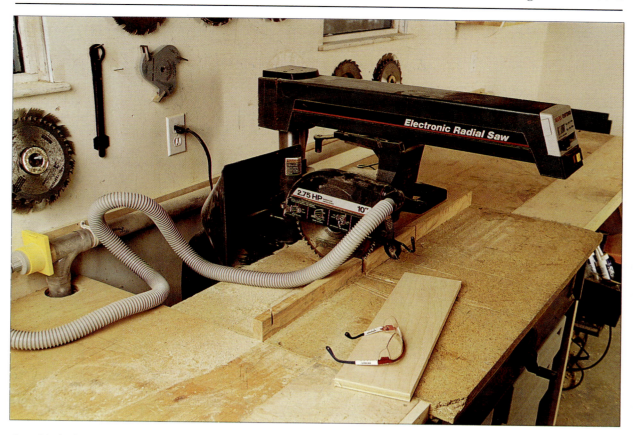

An added advantage of the shop vacuum is that it can be adapted for use as a small-scale, portable, but quite effective dust collection system. Many stationary power tools are manufactured with exhaust ports to which a vacuum hose can be affixed. Turn on the tool, start the vacuum, and the work that follows raises much less dust. If you intend to use your shop vacuum for such a system, a larger-capacity machine (perhaps thirty-two gallons) may be in order .

The perennial complaint in workshops, however, is that even photoelectric detectors are fooled by the presence of particulate matter such as sanding dust or sawdust.

To minimize the likelihood that yours will sound its screaming warning (and provoke you, on the third or fourth false alarm, to disconnect it, thereby defeating the whole purpose), be sure to locate the smoke detectors according to the manufacturer's instructions (which usually means away from corners).

Equally important, keep in mind that the detectors should be as far away as possible from sawing and sanding stations.

If your shop is located out of hearing range from the rest of your home, link the smoke detector to another similar device inside the house or to a central alarm system.

Fire Extinguisher. Buy one. Or even two. That's my first piece of advice. Next, make sure the fire extinguisher you buy is marked ABC

Remember about oil and water: They don't mix. That's true when you have a grease or oil fire, too. Water won't put it out, and may even spread flaming material. Don't douse a grease fire with water, because you may end up getting burned by the steam and boiling water the fire spits back at you.

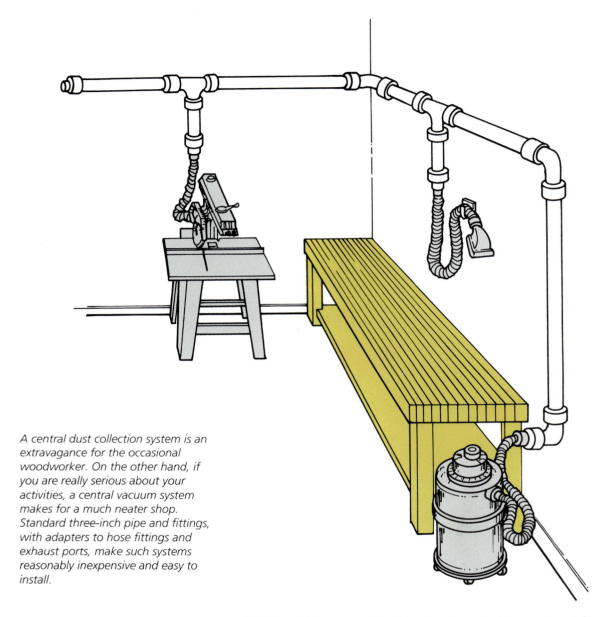

A central dust collection system is an extravagance for the occasional woodworker. On the other hand, if you are really serious about your activities, a central vacuum system makes for a much neater shop. Standard three-inch pipe and fittings, with adapters to hose fittings and exhaust ports, make such systems reasonably inexpensive and easy to install.

or BC. The letters mean that it's a dry chemical fire extinguisher, and is effective against all three major classes of fires. (Class A is burning ordinary materials like wood and paper; Class B, flames fed by grease, oil, or other flammable fluids; and Class C, electrical fires.)

Choose a convenient spot to locate the fire extinguisher, preferably near the entrance. Don't shove it into a corner, or beneath a tool stand or table. Set it at a level that can be reached by adults and not-quite-grown-ups alike. Many models come with brackets designed for the purpose. If you often work with paints or solvents, buy two fire extinguishers and locate the second one over the bench or table at which you do most of the finishing or cleaning work.

A sprinkler system is also an option; if you have plumbing skills, it needn't be prohibitively expensive. Heat-sensitive sprinkler heads will release a spray of water when set off. Take care, however, when maneuvering lengths of stock about the shop: a good hard bang with a one-by-four will deliver an immediate shower. A basketlike guard is a good idea, though no guarantee of protection.

Spontaneous combustion is another way of saying that where there's smoke there's fire. Rags soaked in linseed oil, some kinds of stain, and certain other chemicals will generate heat as the oil molecules oxidize and can suddenly ignite without a spark. When finishing tasks produce such rags, hang them to dry where the air flows freely or stow them in a closed metal container until they can be properly disposed of.

P A R T   I I .

CONTENTS

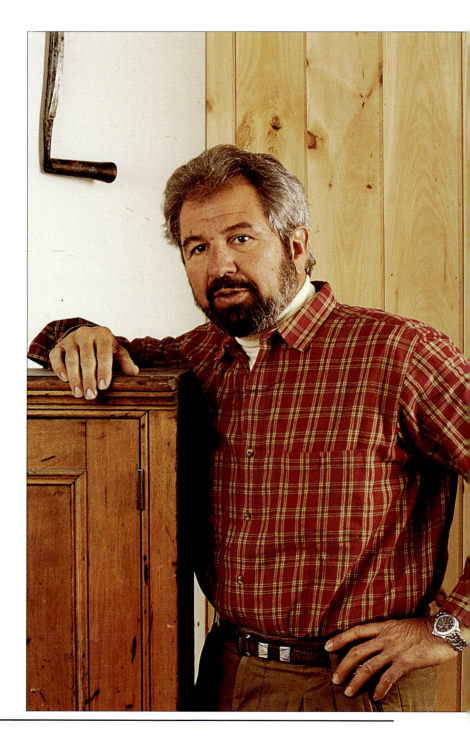

THE
WORKBENCH

There's something elemental about working with tools. I think that's part of their appeal. It's as if somewhere in our genetic makeup there's a connnection to an ancestor who was a master carpenter or shipbuilder or wheelwright. A trip to the workshop awakens in us a sense of belonging there amid the sawdust, scrap, and shavings.

Nowhere in the workshop is that sense of history to be felt more distinctly than when you stand before a traditional workbench. Sure, benches have changed in a hundred little ways since some caveman first adapted a ledge in his domicile for using his favorite sticks and stones to fashion or shape weapons or household implements. But more than a few elements of an all-purpose home workbench today would be recognizable to woodworkers of the near and distant past.

If it is the bench itself that bears the strongest imprint of time – in Chapter 3 we will talk about benches of all sorts – there are wonderful simple benchtop tools that also have long traditions. The bench hook, the shooting board, the vise, and bench dogs all make life easier in the workshop, as well as improving the finished product. We'll discuss them and their history in Chapter 4.

I'm comfortable in my workshop, whether I'm talking to the camera or putting tools to good use.

Chapter 3.

The Basic Bench

This long bench has seen much use, in this shop and the others it inhabited in earlier lives.

The workbench is to the workshop as bases are to the game of baseball: Without a proper bench at which to work, you'll be like a base runner with no place to go. But unlike baseball diamonds, the shape, proportion, and size of workbenches are infinitely variable.

If there's one constant in benches of today and of yore, it's their very diversity. A good bench is a bench that suits its user's needs, that helps the worker accomplish his or her tasks faster, better, or with a higher degree of safety. Which means, in short, there is no one model that suits everybody.

In ancient times, the woodworker's bench consisted of a plank or split log with four splayed legs. Descendants of those benches are manufactured today, usually with a top of hardwood slabs glued together. The norm nowadays is four straight legs supporting the bulk above, often with braces and a shelf below. Despite the improvements, the linkage to Greek and Roman antecedents is still evident.

Workbenches have flat tops, though sometimes at the rear there is a cavity called a tool well that contains tools and components (and prevents them from falling off). One advantage of having the well set into the top of the bench is that, even with a variety of objects in the well, a large sheet of material can still be laid flat over the entire surface of the bench; the contents of the tool well offer no interference.

The front edge of a woodworker's bench is usually lined with square holes positioned at regular intervals. These holes hold bench dogs and holdfast clamps in place for securing workpieces (see *Bench Dogs*, page 62, and *Holdfast Clamps*, page 64). Beneath the top of the bench, some cabinetmaker models feature single storage drawers, others several drawers and even cupboards incorporated into a caselike base.

At the rear, many benches also have a slot cut in them for tools. Tools in use like chisels and drivers can be temporarily slid into the slot, and the handles protruding from the benchtop are easy to reach.

As simple as its elements are, the workbench is more than a tabletop with legs, a well, and a few holes. Virtually everything in the workshop comes to rest on the bench at some point, even if only between operations at other stations. Planning and layout, cutting and shaping, assembling and finishing – all can be, and often are, performed on the benchtop. The better the design, and the better suited its size and configuration to your labors, the more efficient a tool it will be.

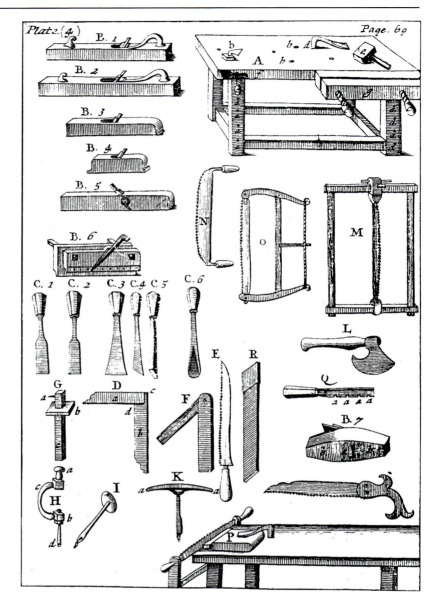

The first book published in English that described the tools of everyday trades was Mechanik's Exercises or the Doctrine of Handy-Works *by Joseph Moxon, printed in 1678. This plate from its chapter on joinery illustrates the workbench, planes, saws, and other tools – a surprising number of which haven't changed a great deal in some three and a quarter centuries.*

So what sort of bench do you need? Consider the questions that follow if you're not sure.

Size and Shape. What do all benches have in common? Each has a work surface on the top that's essentially flat. Otherwise, workbenches tend to be as varied as the uses to which they are put.

I've seen antique cabinetmakers' benches that are sixteen and seventeen feet long, more than three feet wide, and supported by a dozen drawers and doors – and that weigh as much as a felled oak tree. In contrast, jewelers' cabinets seem to be on a dollhouse scale, with tiny tools to match. For most of us, however, space limitations preclude the biggest, and the smallest are just not big enough.

A good size is five to seven feet long and two to three feet wide.

Permanent or Portable? This is a distinction that decides much about your bench choice: Is it to remain stationary or must it fold, roll, or otherwise make itself scarce between jobs? Large, heavy benches are more stable and, in general, more adaptable to different jobs (sometimes several at once). But the bigger the bench, the more hassle involved with stowing it.

What Height Is Right? Old benches tend to be lower. People were shorter then, that's part of the explanation. But another factor is leverage: When tools are powered by human muscles alone, leverage and gravity are invaluable allies to be enlisted. A lower work surface allows for more pressure from above.

If you have a choice of bench heights, as you will if you elect to make your own bench, you might find it expedient to make it the same height as your table or radial-arm saw. That way its surface can be used as a table extension to support long boards being cut.

One traditional rule of thumb for benches is that they should be approximately the height of their user's hip joint. In practice, this generally means in the range of thirty-three to thirty-six inches.

The subject of the next chapter is the surprising range of benchtop accessories, some of which can help make your bench more useful. Jigs and dogs and stops and clamps, among other elements, are essential to most benches, as are vises. Before buying or building your bench, read ahead and decide what your needs are for devices that will hold your workpieces firmly.

Draw Yourself a Picture. As with your workshop as a whole, a simple drawing of your workbench can help you think through your needs, and determine the materials required, should you elect to make your own. Again, graph paper makes the task easier.

You may even want to put yourself in the picture. If your workshop space already exists, find a large piece of cardboard, wallboard, or plywood that's about the size of the workbench top you envision. Find a couple of stools or chairs, perhaps a few books, and turn them into stanchions to support the "benchtop." Is it too big for the space? Is it large enough for the tasks you envision will be performed upon it?

Once you decide upon the right shape and size, decide where the vise will go. Or will there be two vises? And whether you'll have one set of dog holes or two. Think it through, then go back to your graph paper.

If you opt for a bench with drawers or cabinets built into its base, don't forget the toe spaces: Leave a space roughly three inches deep and four inches wide at floor level for your toes, just like kitchen cabinets. The absence of a toe space means you'll be forever kicking the face or sides of the cabinets which is irksome and, with tools in hand, potentially dangerous. And you'll have to lean over farther to reach the back of the benchtop.

BENCH CONSTRUCTION: DOS AND DON'TS

Making a bench isn't especially difficult if you have some basic skills and a good basic tool kit. However, there are a few simple guidelines that may help you to execute your plan.

Benchtops. Hardwood is desirable. Solid hardwood is preferable to glued-up stock, but either will do. If you are to have holes for bench dogs and holdfasts, hardwood may even be essential. Maple, a common choice, is durable and plentiful.

Massive Members Mean Stability. A good workbench is rigid: If it shifts when you are hammering or sawing, it's not stiff enough and you're wasting energy. Generally, rigidity means using large-dimension (two inches or thicker) hardwood stock.

Mortise and Tenons Add Strength . . . The best benches are joined with mortise and tenon joints where the legs connect with the benchtop and where the stretchers link the legs.

. . . and Bolts Are Best. Carriage or machine bolts are preferable to nails because, over time, the wracking pressures that are inevitable in pushing and pulling on the benchtop will loosen the nails, producing wobble. Lag screws are next best. When assembling the top, glue will help, too.

A solid benchtop can be made of stock glued and clamped; shape the tool tray first, and cut one member at intervals to allow for bench dogs.

THE WOODWORKER'S BENCH

This is perhaps the most familiar configuration for a woodworker's bench. Its top is of hardwood and is usually two or more inches thick (antique benches were often shaped from one tree, new ones are glued and assembled from thick strips). There are two vises, one at the tail, another at the front. Holes for bench dogs probably line the front of the bench and maybe the back as well. A tool well may be built into the rear or one end. Typically, four legs support the bench, often with a shelf connecting them that adds stability as well as storage space.

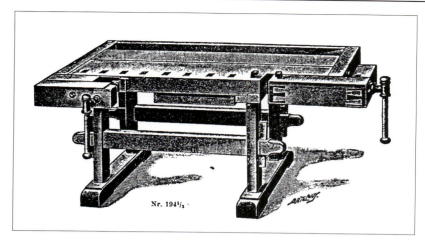

This line cut comes from a turn-of-the-century Austrian tool catalog. Sometimes referred to as a European-style bench, this woodworker's bench is also quite standard on these shores. Virtually identical models are found in contemporary English and American catalogs.

Note the tail and front vise (both with wooden jaws, though with steel screws and other components), the row of bench dogs along the front, and the tool well at the rear. The stretchers beneath offer solid support for a shelf.

THE CABINETMAKER'S BENCH

A small cabinetmaker's bench, ideal for a small workshop. The drawers, shelf, and cabinet provide easily accessible storage, and the benchtop has two vises (at the tail and face) along with a tool well at the rear.

The top of the cabinetmaker's bench resembles that of the woodworker's bench. There are vises, usually one at the tail and one at the front. Holes for bench dogs punctuate the front of the bench, aligned with the tail vise. Sometimes there are bolts or collars for holdfasts.

What distinguishes the cabinetmaker's bench is the casework below the working surface: drawers and cupboards that are used to store tools and supplies. New ones tend to be more expensive than traditional woodworker's benches (the casework involved in drawers and cabinets requires much added time and materials). Old ones are rare enough that they are hard to find.

A good cabinetmaker's bench is an excellent option for the small-scale workshop where the bench is expected to perform multiple duties. The benchtop provides the work surface, the space below efficient storage for a good many tools.

This is an all-purpose bench, one that gets used as a work station. Depending upon the work being done, a drill press, jointer, or fixed sander gets located on its work surface. Sometimes it's cleared off for use as an assembly table. It would have a woodworker's bench vise added with little difficulty as well. Note the electrical boxes conveniently located on each leg, and the deep shelf for setting tools not in use.

THE BACKBOARD BENCH

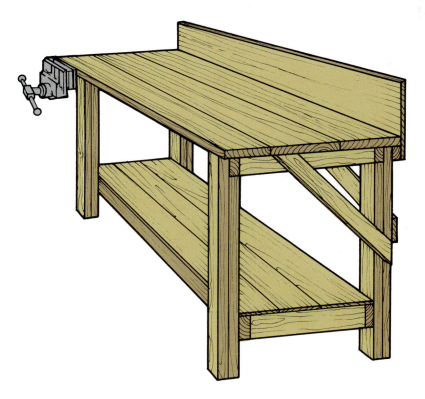

The basic backboard bench: This straightforward design relies upon two-by-four stock for the legs, stretchers, and other framing elements, and one-by stock for the braces, top, lower shelf, and backboard. A few screws, a minimum of cutting, and the bench is made.

This simple, sturdy bench is little more than a long, tall table. It has a board across the back (to keep tools and supplies from tumbling off) and a shelf beneath. The backboard bench is probably the easiest to construct, and is best suited to all-purpose work. If you anticipate that your bench work will consist more of making repairs than of fabricating new objects from wood or other material, this bench is probably your best choice.

An engineer's vise can be mounted on the benchtop, providing assistance for all sorts of basic fix-it work around the house, from plumbing to electrical. You may elect to install a wood vise, too, either on the front or on one end. Typically, the front vise is set above or near the front left leg, while the tail vise is set at the right end.

PORTABLE BENCHES

If you're working out of a closet, a portable bench may be the answer. Commercially available benches like the Workmate offer surprising flexibility, including three different heights, a variety of means of clamping, and the capacity to collapse quickly and easily into a suitcase-sized bundle (see *The Portable Workbench* in *Bob Vila's Toolbox*, page 210).

I suppose this is a sort of half-breed, a cross between a backboard bench and a machinist's bench. Manufactured in the 1880s, this durable, if boxy, design would certainly assist in a wide variety of tasks.

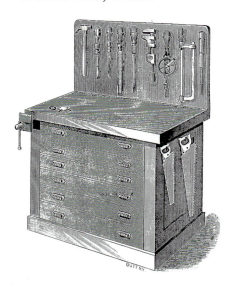

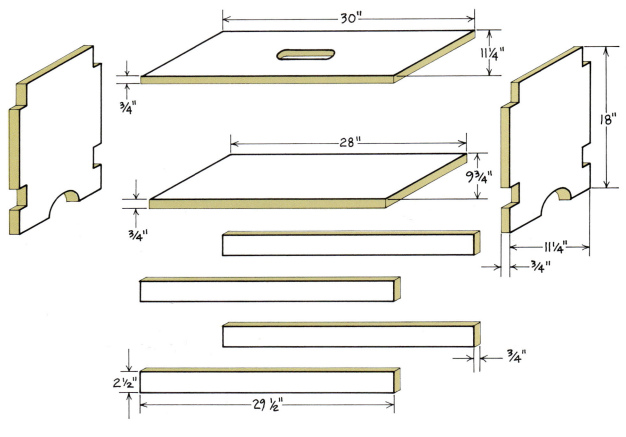

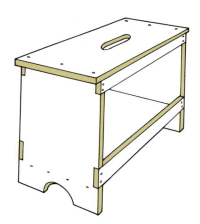

The top, sides, and shelf are made of standard one-by stock, either one-by-ten or, better yet, one-by-twelve-inch dimension boards; a single eight-foot length will do. A ten-foot-long, one-by-three furring strip will suffice for the horizontal side boards.

Cut the pieces to length. Use your saber saw to cut out the carrying slot in the top and, if you wish, a decorative cutout at the base of the end-pieces. Glue and screw the assemblage together.

The finished product . . . simple yet handy indeed.

Another option is to make one to suit your needs (and storage limitations). You might try one along the lines of this little box bench, a tried-and-true variety. It doubles as a short bench and tool carrier, with its work surface on top, carrying slot, and shelf below. If the sizes specified don't work for you, don't hesitate to vary the design.

The portable bench at work. It's simple to make, and then goes willingly wherever you need it.

WORKTABLES

Unless your workshop is too small to accommodate any work surfaces beyond the workbench, a worktable should have a place on your floor plan.

If there is room for it, make yourself one using a full sheet of three-quarter-inch plywood. It's economical to make and large enough to be used for many varying tasks (some of them at the same time, meaning that you don't have to move everything off every time you change gears).

Build into its base electrical plugs, preferably on all four sides. Utility boxes set into each of the four side supports will prove their worth immediately. A shelf beneath (or even some drawers or cupboards) will be useful, too; among other things, you can stow the drill or saber saw or finishing sander, all ready to go. Depending upon the nature of the work you do, you may want to set up permanently a bench grinder, stationary belt or disk sander, or one or another of your tabletop stationary tools. Think it through first. Leaving one side entirely clear for assembly and other tasks is a good idea, too.

If you plan to paint or do a great deal of gluing on the top of the bench, you may want to purchase an inexpensive sheet of quarter-inch-thick masonite or hardboard. It's replaceable at minimum cost when the accumulation of paint or glue or other unwanted material begins to be a problem. Tack it down with small brads.

Don't forget how handy sawhorses can be. They can be portable benches, either alone or in pairs with a sheet of plywood placed on top. Even in large, carefully organized workshops sawhorses are always a welcome option for many jobs, from cutting sheets of plywood to supporting large case pieces during gluing.

This reproduction counter was made by craftsman and Shaker authority Tim Rieman. Most likely, an original Shaker piece of this configuration would have been used as a tailoring counter, but it's a practical design for a multitude of jobs, with its long, broad work surface and ample storage below.

Setup Table. For assembling cabinets, a low-to-the-floor setup table may prove to be a very handy addition to your workshop furniture. It should be about half the height of a normal workbench (perhaps fifteen to twenty inches tall). It can be a permanent fixture; a portable table that's hung from the wall or ceiling when not in use; or just a flat surface like a solid old door or piece of plywood set on a simple frame. Three feet by six feet is a convenient size. You may wish to add electrical plugs and casters, too.

The Glue Bench. If you find yourself doing a great deal of gluing, whether it's cabinets or chairs, casework or millwork, you may find a simple-to-construct work surface called a glue bench invaluable.

Most often the glue bench looks like a big drawer on legs. The top of the bench is recessed a few inches (typically, six to eight), with the boards around its perimeter forming a long, narrow cavity. The boards support the object to be glued, and the bed of the drawer contains the supplies, like glue, scrapers, and the rest. The clamps can be stowed beneath the bench or, better yet, conveniently at hand on a wall rack nearby.

THE WORKSHOP DOLLY

No fine craftsmanship here, or even fancy stock. Simple two-by-fours, four casters, some wood screws, and it's done. (You can even skip the lap joints, if you wish.)

Buy four casters, pick over your scrap pile, and find a few wood screws. With those supplies in hand, you can save yourself a lot of backbreaking labor moving large objects around your workshop.

A simple dolly is really just a platform on which cabinets, dressers, or other workpieces can be set. They can be moved from one area to another to be worked on (or simply gotten out of the way).

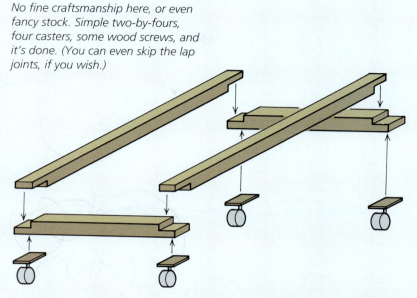

This rugged dolly can make moving even that heavy and awkward toolbox a great deal easier.

Chapter 4.

Outfitting the Bench

Whether your workbench has a working surface the size of a sheet of plywood or one that more nearly resembles the school desk you had in third grade, you will probably need one or perhaps several of the array of devices that have been specially adapted for bench work.

These tools are often referred to as "bench furniture." This grouping includes not only vises, but holdfasts and dogs, bench hooks, and shooting boards. None of them actually performs an operation like cutting or planing or shaping or fastening. But each is used to grip workpieces firmly in place so that they can be manipulated in the production process.

At the top of the list are the vises. They are built-in clamping tools that can make a great many jobs easier. Having both hands free to hold the plane, router, or other tool can make for a marked increase in precision and safety. You may be familiar with the several kinds of vises, or perhaps you think that they're all the same. They are not, any more than all handsaws are the same. Leg, tail, shoulder, face, engineer, and other vises will be discussed in the pages that follow.

Bench dogs, stops, and holdfasts are next. These perform what you might call supporting roles, in many cases, to the vises. There are time-proven varieties and newer designs and innovations, some of wrought iron, others of wood, and still others a combination of both. Whatever their age and raw material, these tools are invaluable, especially to woodworkers, once again enhancing the care and accuracy with which tools can be applied to the workpiece.

The bench hook and its near relation, the shooting board, make me wonder at the cleverness of their inventors: they're so simple, so practical, yet so useful. So, without further ado, let's go on over to the benchtop.

Two vises, bench dogs of various designs, several holdfasts, a bench hook, and a shooting board all inhabit this photograph and the workshop in which it was taken.

THE VISES

A vise, according to its dictionary definition, consists of two jaws for holding work and a mechanism, usually a screw device, that opens and closes those jaws. That's a rather broad definition, but then vises are a rather diverse lot.

For convenience, vises are loosely categorized by the position on the bench they usually assume. Vises of a design suited for the right-hand end or "tail" of the bench are of a rather different shape from

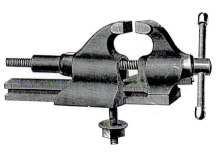

Called a "heavy chipping vise," this old-fashioned tool looks quite streamlined. Its weight? A hefty one hundred and sixty-nine pounds.

those typically found attached to the front or "face" of the bench. Yet, as is true with most tools with long histories, not all vises fit neatly into simple subdivisions.

You see, some of the vises attached to the front of workbenches aren't truly face vises, like the leg vise and shoulder vise. And the engineer's vise traditionally is set neither on the face nor on the tail of the bench, but actually on the benchtop.

The bottom line? Most woodworkers will find a face vise invaluable; almost as many would quickly learn to love the advantages of a tail vise if they don't already. The sturdy engineer's vise is essential for anyone who works with metal – which includes almost every woodworker, by the way, when it comes to sharpening, and dealing with all sorts of hardware and other components.

Each vise has some specialized advantages, but you'll have to make the call. And speaking of making, you're luckier than your ancestors only a century or so ago. There are many kinds of vises in a myriad sizes on the market today. If you wish, you can make your own but, unlike your great-great ancestors, you don't have to.

The Face Vise. Face vises are designed specifically for holding wooden workpieces while such operations as drilling and sawing are performed.

This wooden face vise has steel mechanics, but its jaws are wood.

The traditional material is wood. A wood face vise consists of a movable front jaw that is mounted to a broad, square beam that slides in and out of a matching channel. While the beam keeps the jaw steady and properly aligned, the jaw is driven by a wooden bench screw. The whole mechanism is fastened to the benchtop from below.

Modern variations of the wooden face vise are often called woodworker's vises. Also mounted flush to the bench front, these are all metal (except for jaw liners of wood that prevent the damage that would result if the metal jaws were tightened directly onto wooden workpieces; see page 62).

Woodworker's vises are designed to be attached to the underside of the front of a woodworking bench. The vise's constituent parts include a pair of iron jaws, while its other components – its slides, drive, screw, and handle – are usually steel. Like wooden face vises, the inner jaw is fixed, while the outer jaw is operated by turning the handle centered on the front of the tool. Clockwise motion will tighten the screw mechanism, drawing the jaws together; a counterclockwise motion will open the jaws. These vises are usually located over or near a leg (to avoid putting unnecessary force on the benchtop) and are fastened with lag screws or carriage bolts.

Hybrid face vises combining wooden and metal elements are sold, and many woodworkers who elect to make their own benches fabricate matching vises, often using a mix of off-the-shelf metal drive elements with shop-made wooden jaws and attaching points such as blocking and guides.

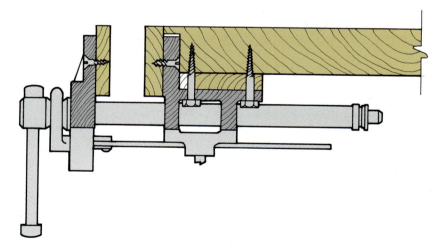

If you are attaching the vise to the bench, install it so that the top of the jaws is flush with the top of the workbench and the fixed jaw is let into the front edge of the worktop. In this case, a rabbet has been routed into the face of the bench.

Woodworker's vises come in almost any size, with jaws ranging from six inches wide to ten inches or more, with a maximum opening capacity ranging from roughly four to as many as fifteen or more inches. The size you need depends upon the size of the stock you will be likely to use for most of your projects.

When edge-planing long, wide stock, the face vise alone isn't up to the job of clamping the piece firmly in place. A front-mounted holdfast is one traditional option (see page 64), but another solution is to use the vise in combination with a bar clamp, as pictured here.

If you elect to buy a factory-made woodworker's vise, you will probably need to line the jaws in order to protect your workpieces from the mars and dents that unlined iron jaws will cause when clamping wooden workpieces. To do so, affix jaw liners through the holes provided in the face of each jaw. The liners should be of nominal one-by stock (actual thickness, three quarters of an inch). If you work exclusively with softwoods, pine liners will suffice. However, you may wish to use a more durable hardwood liner.

The front jaw probably has threaded holes designed to accommodate flathead machine screws; you will need to countersink the screwheads so that they are set slightly into the wood liner. You can use wood screws driven from the face of the inner jaw into the face of the workbench.

The End Vise. Built into the end of a bench (almost always the right-hand end), the end or tail vise, as it is also called, can be used to clamp workpieces to the bench between its jaws. The flush-mounted end vise uses the benchtop as the inside jaw, and the bench screw drives the movable jaw tight against it.

The end vise is a much more flexible tool than might at first appear. It is distinguished from other vises in that a rectangular hole is cut into its top, and that hole is aligned with a series of other holes along the front of the benchtop. A workpiece to be shaped or cut is set along the front of the bench, flush to a bench dog set into the "dog-hole" in the vise (see *Bench Dogs*, page 62). The other end of the piece is then butted to another dog inserted through the dog-hole nearest to it and quicker than you can say, "Tighten her up," the tail vise transforms virtually the entire benchtop into a giant vise. For that reason, the tail vise, with its ability to hold work between bench dogs, is one of the hallmarks of a cabinetmaker's bench.

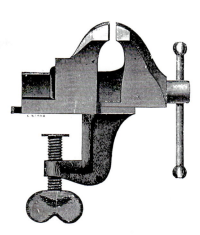

If you don't have the space for a fixed bench and vise, a clamp-on vise may be the convenient resource you need. Essentially just a small-scale, portable vise, with a pair of jaws tightened with a screw device, it is distinguished by its method of mounting: a clamp, with screwdrive and thumbscrew, that adapts to table, bench, and countertops. This model happens to be almost a hundred years old, but similar contemporary models are made for both wood- and metalworkers.

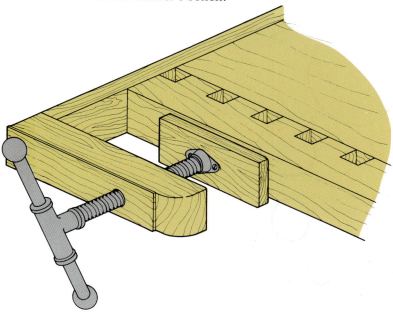

Another variation on the theme of vises is the shoulder vise. It sits at the left end of the bench in the position usually occupied by a face or woodworker's vise. It is distinguished, however, by the fact that both its jaws are fixed.

That may sound paradoxical – if neither of the jaws moves, how can the vise clamp anything? – but there is a movable clamping board that, driven by a screw and tommy bar, clamps rather in the way your shoulder and upper arm move to hold a piece of plywood against your rib cage. (No doubt that's why it's called a shoulder vise.) Northern Europe has a long tradition of using shoulder vises.

The Leg Vise. This antique vise was probably an American innovation. Today, it's relatively rare, having been largely superseded by the woodworker's vise. That doesn't mean it isn't a worthy tool; on the contrary, it's a simple, strong device that is probably the easiest of vises to make from scratch.

Usually set onto the front left-hand end of the bench, the leg vise has long jaws, the rear one, most often, being the leg of the bench. The outside jaw is the one that moves, and it is generally made of large-dimension hardwood stock. A screwdrive, located above the midpoint of the vise's length but below the area of the clamping

In a small shop, there simply isn't room to set up a station for every activity. The grinder is one tool that isn't used every day, yet must be accessible for sharpening and other miscellaneous tasks. A space-saving solution is to mount it on a piece of board and then to add a ledger strip beneath it. Position the ledger between the jaws of a vise and, with a turn of the drive mechanism, it's a stationary tool, all ready to go.

surface, adjusts the opening of the jaws. Occasionally, the bottom of the outside jaw is merely hinged to the bench leg, but this means that the jaws of the vise will not be parallel (except when closed), and the thicker the stock, the weaker the bite of the jaw. To avoid weakening what is otherwise a very efficient design, most leg vises have an adjustable screw or beam at the foot that keeps the jaws parallel.

Leg vises were favored by coach-builders and wheelwrights in the past, but still have a range of uses in their (admittedly) rare appearances in today's woodshops.

*If you have an **L**-shaped tail vise on your bench, treat the rear jaw respectfully. Don't clamp objects at its extreme end, and do heavy-duty clamping with the front jaw or another vise altogether. Misusing the rear jaw can cause the rest of the vise to twist out of alignment.*

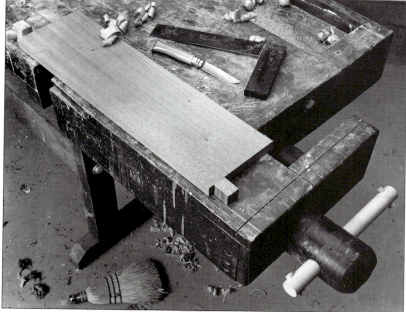

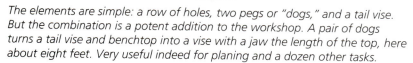

The elements are simple: a row of holes, two pegs or "dogs," and a tail vise. But the combination is a potent addition to the workshop. A pair of dogs turns a tail vise and benchtop into a vise with a jaw the length of the top, here about eight feet. Very useful indeed for planing and a dozen other tasks.

The Engineer's Vise. This heavy-duty device is mounted on the benchtop, bolted to its surface. It weighs as much as an anvil and, in fact, may even function as a hammering block now and again as many models have a flat surface behind the jaws designed for use as an anvil. The engineer's vise is also called a machinist's vise, or sometimes a mechanic's or railroad vise.

The iron jaws of an engineer's vise will mar wooden workpieces on contact. For occasional crossover use, you might try jaw liners like these (one's on the rear jaw, the other standing in front of the vise).

The primary purpose of a machinist's vise is to grab hold of things and to hold them steady in its rough jaws, freeing up both your hands so that you can bend, shape, hammer, cut, drill, or perform any number of other operations. The jaws of the vise usually have a machined face that can easily scar wood. Some models these days are sold with reversible jaws that are smooth on one side and serrated on the other. If you have frequent need of a metal vise and only occasional need for a wood vise, you may buy jaw liners. Many machinist's vises also have pipe jaws located beneath the main, flattened jaws.

The base on many machinist's vises swivels, accommodating a variety of workpieces presented at different angles.

BENCH DOGS

The only thing canine about a bench dog is that, in a sense, it's like a tooth protruding from a jaw. A bench dog is a peg or post that, when positioned in an opening in a benchtop, serves as a fixing point for a workpiece. Dogs are most often used with a tail vise, with one dog set into the vise, and one into the benchtop (see photograph on page 61). The vise is tightened to hold the wood tightly between the two dogs. A single dog can also be used when planing, but the user must then concentrate not only on the action of the plane but on maintaining balance so that the piece doesn't shift during the planing process.

Bench dogs or stops, as they are also called, are made of wood, steel, or iron. They may be wedge-shaped or may have a wide, protruding lip at the top to hold the dog in place. Some commercially made wooden dogs have a metal spring attached to one side enabling the dog to be set at various heights. The protruding lip may be smooth or have a

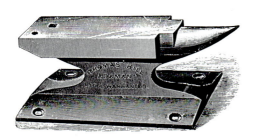

Here are three types of bench dogs. In the foreground is the traditional wooden dog; at the rear is the so-called bench puppy. Both designs are set into matching holes drilled or chiseled through a benchtop.

In between them is an aluminum stop which has to be let into a wide but shallow mortise in the benchtop. When not in use, the aluminum stop sits flush into the benchtop; when needed, a turn or two of the set screw at center lifts the stop above the plane of the benchtop. Teeth in the raised edge then hold the workpiece.

milled face (crosshatched like that of a framing hammer) or teeth cut into it.

Many woodworkers feel more comfortable using wooden dogs. Planes do slip, from time to time, and it only takes one collision between plane iron and metal dog to waste an hour's working time, turning the woodworker back into a machinist, grinding and sharpening the nicked blade.

A rather elaborate turn-of-the-century cabinetmaker's bench stop, revealing the mechanism that is mortised into the benchtop to keep the dog in place.

Sitting It Out. *Some bench jobs, especially those that take patience, precision, and a steady hand, are better done sitting down. If you are working at a bench designed for stand-up work, a normal chair just won't suffice.*

A bar-sized stool or chair may be the answer. Lots of designs are available, from tall director's chairs to traditional all-wood Windsor or captain's chair designs.

jig (jig) n. *A mechanical device used to maintain the correct position between a workpiece and the tool being used to cut or shape it.*

A catalog drawing of a holdfast. It is described as consisting of a "Wrought Iron Pillar, Screw and Handle, with Malleable Iron Shoe and Arm."

HOLDFAST CLAMPS

Holdfast clamps they're called; some people call them holddowns. Whatever the name used, the purpose of these pieces of bench furniture is the same: to hold material fast and flat to the workbench while it is being worked.

Hold-down devices come in a variety of configurations. The classic iron holdfast is shaped like an inverted **L**. The leg of the **L** is set into a hole in the workbench top or through a hole in one of the sturdy timber legs of an antique bench; the base of the **L**-shaped holdfast, which often has a slight crook in its neck, rests on the workpiece. The holdfast is then struck with a hammer, driving it into the benchtop (or bench leg), wedging both itself and the workpiece firmly in place.

A more modern variation is a holdfast clamp with a screwdrive. This variety usually has a collar set into the benchtop to accommodate its shaft, though it may also bolt to the benchtop. An arm with a steel screwdrive and T bar then can be used to fasten workpieces securely. These holdfast clamps are removable, their fasteners sitting flush to the work surface.

The holdfast family, including two **L**-shaped holdfasts (front and rear) with clamps for affixing work; a traditional **L**-shaped holdfast that requires only a few raps with a mallet and leverage to hold the work; and a lightweight toggle clamp. The most expensive option, the iron holdfast at the front, is the most flexible, as it is set into a collar that is drilled and counterbored into a benchtop; more than one collar can be located and the holdfast moved from one to another.

Another variety is an adjustable screw-driven clamp. A shaft is fixed to the bench, often on the front, through a collar that allows the shaft to be pushed in or out, adjusting the gap between the arm of the clamp and the workpiece. The screwdrive beyond the elbow of the holdfast levers the arm to tighten (or loosen) the piece.

Sometimes more than one holdfast is necessary, especially on larger benches. Often they are used together with a woodworker's vise, also mounted on the face of the bench.

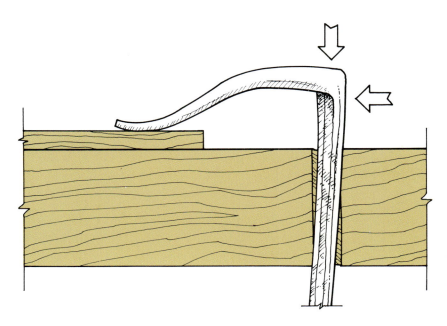

The holdfast is wedged to the benchtop with a hammer or mallet blow on the head; it's released with a rap at the back. The flex in the gooseneck helps to hold the workpiece against the benchtop.

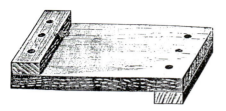

THE BENCH HOOK

If simple pleasures appeal to you, you will enjoy using the bench hook. This tool makes securing and then crosscutting a piece of stock as easy as one, two, three.

The bench hook could hardly be less complicated, consisting of two small blocks of wood (called cleats) that are joined on opposite sides and opposite ends of a piece of board. The blocks are fastened with the grain running perpendicular to the board.

Obviously, a bench hook isn't a hook at all (it isn't curved, and wasn't bent, either). But one of the blocks on the contraption does hook over the front edge of a bench or other work surface.

The bench hook, in place. Using it is just as easy as it looks.

A bench hook makes holding a piece to be cut much easier. It's set up the moment you set it in place (unlike a vise which always requires adjustment) with one cleat flush to the front of the benchtop. You then position the workpiece to be cut tight to the other block. By holding the piece against the top cleat with one hand, you will also be holding the bench hook tight to the front of the bench. Step three is to reach for your saw and make your cut.

(Note that if you use a Japanese-made saw with a bench hook the position of the hook must be reversed, because Japanese saws cut on the pull stroke.)

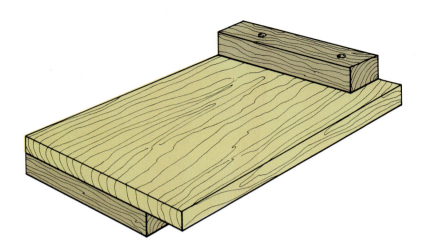

The size is mostly a matter of choice. The bench hook pictured here happens to be ten inches wide, fifteen inches long, and have two eight-inch cleats. Note that the cleats stop shy of the right-hand edge; that prevents your saw from cutting into the benchtop as you complete your cut. If you are left-handed, however, shift the cleats to the right.

THE SHOOTING BOARD

When using a shooting board to plane end grain (for which the tool is especially well suited), be sure you hold the workpiece tight to the stop, allowing the workpiece to protrude only slightly. This prevents splitting of the end grain.

A block plane, with its cutting iron set at a low angle, is perfect for such end-grain work.

THE MITER BOX

A simple miter box made of wood (usually beech) or plastic, like this one, is an inexpensive way of making sure the finish cuts you make with your handsaw – both forty-five-degree miter and ninety-degree cuts – are true.

Lining them up perfectly without a miter box is tricky, and when it comes to fitting the pieces together, the miter box more than proves its worth.

In the compact workshop, the miter box has one signal advantage over the powerful miter saw that has become the rule for most professional carpenters these days: It weighs only a few ounces, is smaller than a shoe box, and can be set up on your bench, ready to go, in about the time it takes to pull a handkerchief from your back pocket.

The tool has been in use for centuries, in more or less the same configuration – an open-ended wooden box, with slots cut into the sides to guide the saw. Elaborate versions are available with infinitely adjustable angles and ball bearings and metal superstructures, and they're worth the money if you find you use a miter box frequently. For its occasional convenience, however, I'd recommend having a basic model within easy reach. They're handy for molding work, frame-making, and a multitude of other ad hoc cutting tasks in the workshop. (For a more detailed discussion of the miter box and its uses, see *Toolbox*, page 49.) Don't forget to rest the piece to be cut atop a piece of scrap wood. That will greatly increase your miter box's life expectancy.

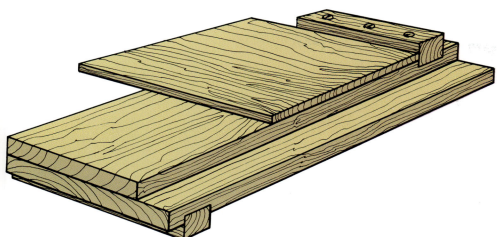

This shooting board is made from two twenty-inch-long boards, one of one-by-ten stock, the other of one-by-eight. They are put to use as the baseboard and fence, respectively.

For strength, the cleats can be let into dadoes, though this is not essential. The top cleat should align precisely with the right-hand edge of the fence.

Keep in mind that when assembling a shooting board, you must use an accurate square for aligning the top cleat. If it isn't perpendicular to the fence, the tool will be useless for most work.

A near relation of the bench hook (see page 66), the shooting board is also a jig used to hold workpieces firmly in place. But in this case, the operation is not cutting but planing.

This device consists of two boards two feet or longer and roughly six inches wide. They are fastened to one another, with one edge of the upper board set parallel but perhaps two inches back from the outer edge of the lower board. A block of wood is fastened perpendicular to the top board near its end to act as a stop.

To use the shooting board, clamp it between two bench stops on the benchtop. Position the workpiece flush to the stop and so that the edge to be planed protrudes slightly over the channel, or rabbet, formed by the two boards. You can then slide your plane along the rabbet with its iron held precisely square to the workpiece.

CONTENTS

HAND-HELD TOOLS

Having gotten this far, you will have thought through much of your workshop. You know how big it is to be, the layout of the place, and have allowed spaces for the freestanding tools that you'll need.

If you are lucky, a rich uncle left you all the tools you will ever need to do the work you plan to do. More likely, you resemble the rest of us, and you know full well you're not yet fully equipped. Not that anyone ever really is, now that I think about it. New tools seem to appear almost daily and, as one's skills improve, different tools become necessary (or, at least, desirable).

Maybe you need more tools, maybe not . . . but in the chapters that follow we'll talk about some of the basic hand-held tools that can be useful in the home workshop, and how to use them well and safely. From laying out to planing to cutting and shaping, lots of tools are out there for you to put to good work.

I admit, it's more work. But for some jobs, the satisfaction of working with a hand plane is irreplaceable.

Chapter 5.

Measuring and Marking Tools

There are big-picture people and detail types. You know what I mean: Would you rather look at a giant photograph of Chartres cathedral or examine a slide of one of its stained glass windows? Is a tape measure accurate enough for you or does a micrometer feel perfectly natural when you hold it in your hand?

Actually, you don't have to answer these questions or even make any choices. But if you are a meticulous worker, if you get your greatest pleasure from the fine details, then the tools in this chapter are right up your street. If, on the other hand, gauges and the like don't really interest you, it is still worth paying close attention. They are more important than you may realize.

No project can get under way before it's laid out, with the lines transferred from the plans (or the image in your mind) to the material you will be using to make your project. So we'll go now to measuring and marking tools, including marking gauges, the panel gauge, mortise gauge, calipers (inside, out, and Vernier), micrometer, and depth gauge.

None of these tools is hard to use, and even you big-picture types may well learn to respect the ingenuity of their inventors and the shortcuts to good work that they offer their users. And for the detail-oriented among you, there's some pure pleasure here.

Quality measuring and marking tools, like the several sets of calipers, the profile gauge, and the combination square pictured here, make layout easy to do accurately.

MARKING, CUTTING, AND MORTISE GAUGES

These simple tools – the marking, cutting, and mortise gauges closely resemble one another – haven't changed much in generations (no doubt the old cliché about not fixing things that aren't broken applies here). For marking off straight lines parallel to the edge of a workpiece, for certain cutting tasks, and for laying out mortises and tenons, these tools are unsurpassed, as they are fast, efficient, and easy to use. You'll master them in a matter of minutes.

Each consists of a shaft or beam (it's usually square in section) along which slides a donut-shaped stop called a stock. The stock is locked in place with a thumbscrew threaded through its side that presses a brass shoe against the beam. The stock, preset in this fashion to a specific position, acts as a fence when butted to the workpiece.

These gauges are usually made of hard, stable woods like beech, mahogany, or rosewood, and occasionally of steel. Some particularly

That's a mortise gauge on the lower left (note the two pins) and a marking gauge at the top. The small blade and wedge are inserted in the hole in the shaft of the cutting gauge.

mensuration (men-sir-a-shun) n. *The act or process of measuring. E.g., "Who can believe that they who first watched the course of the stars, foresaw the use of their discoveries to the facilitation of commerce, or the mensuration of time?" From Samuel Johnson's* The Rambler, *1751.*

handsome models have brass strips let into the face of the stock, which add an ornamental touch to the face as well as reinforcing it.

The Marking Gauge. Also known as a butt marking gauge, this tool has a bradlike steel pin or spur fixed near the end of the beam that scribes the workpiece as the stock is pushed along the edge of the piece. The pin helps make this the accurate tool that it is, as a scribed line is thinner than a pencil line.

The marking gauge is especially useful for marking out a number of identical pieces. Using the marking gauge will save measuring time (you set it once, then mark as many pieces as you wish) and helps ensure that the pieces will be the same. Marking gauges are usually between eight and ten inches long.

Let me offer a few hints for using the tool. First, when marking with the grain, make two light passes rather than a single harder one. Second, keep the pin sharp by filing its tip. Most marking gauges have a scale inscribed onto the stock, so, third, check the scale periodically to be sure the spur hasn't bent, making the scale inaccurate.

The Cutting Gauge. Instead of a scribing pin, the cutting gauge has a flat blade wedged into a mortise in the end of the beam. In all other ways, the cutting and marking gauges are identical.

The cutting gauge is also used for marking, especially when laying out cuts across the grain, because the sharp blade cuts the grain instead of tearing it. The cutting gauge can also used to cut veneer and thick strips of woods when worked from both sides.

Keep the blade of the cutting gauge sharp. An occasional honing is all that is necessary, but if you let the tool dull, your cut lines will be more like tear lines and the tool will be of little use in veneer work.

The Mortise Gauge. On first glance, the mortise gauge looks identical to the marking gauge. In fact, it *is* a marking gauge, a purpose-made tool for marking out mortise and tenon joints. But instead of having a single pin at one end of its stock, it has two, one of which is adjustable along a track in the gauge's beam. The stock is also adjustable, making it possible to lay out cuts for both the mortise (the mouth, or opening) and the tenon (or tongue, which fits into the mortise).

A mortise gauge – note the two scribing pins along the stock, one of which adjusts by sliding it in the groove.

CALIPERS

Calipers and their near relations, the compass and dividers, have been in use at least since Roman times. While their designs are of a certain age, they have by no means outlived their usefulness. The transferring of measurements is their primary job, especially in situations where applying a rule to a workpiece is difficult (as with curved workpieces, for example).

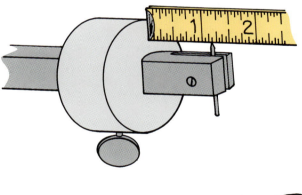

A marking gauge can easily be set from a rule butted to the fence, and the desired dimension aligned with the steel pin (top). In scribing a line with the gauge, cock the tool away from you and push in the same direction.

The Panel Gauge. *This handsome tool is a panel gauge, essentially a large-scale marking gauge. It accomplishes the same kind of jobs a marking gauge does (drawing lines on workpieces parallel to a straight side), but is used specifically on panels or wide boards.*

Once the distance from the marking pin to the fence is set from a rule or other workpiece, the panel gauge is used two-handed, with one hand at the headpiece, the other at the marking point.

This particular gauge has its headpiece fixed in place with a captive wedge. Note also the inlay work; it's a handsome, hand-crafted tool that some craftsman took pride in producing.

Calipers range from relatively small (a few inches in height) to quite large (some tradesmen of the past used calipers three feet or more in height). They may be of wood or iron, but usually are of steel. Generations of toolmakers and craftsmen have made them for specific purposes, ranging from the tiny ones for precision jeweler's work to giant ones that are employed at foundries.

Some designs have a threaded rod at the head that opens or closes the calipers; others, called firm-joint calipers, have a single rivet or other fastener that holds the hinge tightly, yet loosely enough to allow the calipers to be opened and closed. Still others, called spring calipers, have a steel spring rather than a hinged joint.

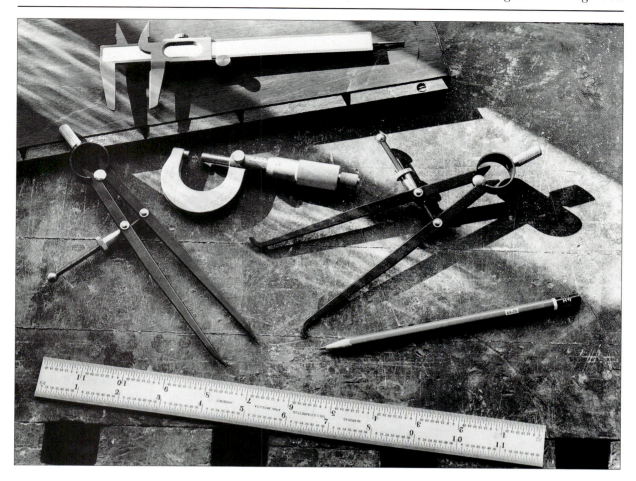

Inside calipers, also called straight calipers, are used to measure inside dimensions. Their legs are straight, with feet that point outward. Most *outside calipers* look bowlegged, with rounded legs that toe in. They are used to measure the outside diameter of pipes or the progress of a turned leg or other work on a lathe.

The legs of a pair of calipers are spread or brought together in order to match a dimension being measured. The calipers can be set to a given dimension from a rule, scale, or pattern, then used to check the workpiece being shaped. They can also be employed in the reverse process, adjusted so that the feet drag slightly when drawn over (with outside calipers) or inside (inside calipers) a workpiece. Then the distance between the feet is measured with a rule.

Slide Calipers. At a glance, there is something of a resemblance between slide calipers and a monkey wrench. Both have a fixed jaw at the head, with a lower jaw that slides along the tool's spine. The lower jaw in a pair of slide calipers may have a nut that clamps it in place, rather than the worm drive of a monkey wrench; the calipers also have a scale along the slide that indicates the space between the jaws. Slide calipers are generally small, most having the capacity to measure workpieces a maximum of somewhere between three and twelve inches.

That's a micrometer at center, a tool used for fine machine-shop measurements. At left is a pair of outside calipers, at right inside calipers, and at the top is a pair of slide calipers, all of which can be very handy in a home workshop.

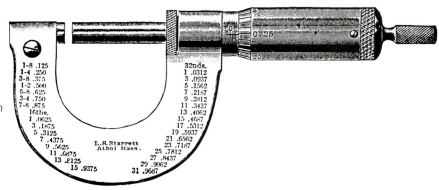

The machinist's micrometer, as illustrated in an 1895 catalog. Today, the basic elements remain the same.

design, when the edge of the tool is pressed against a piece of molding or another irregular shape, the tool will conform exactly to that shape. It is especially useful when dissimilar materials are being joined.

Space is always at a premium in the workshop, so shelves and window-sills and hooks and hangers of all sorts get put to use. I find that for tools that are used frequently, a designated hook or even just a nail works well. This highly accurate bench rule hangs conveniently just about anywhere. And it's light, thin (reducing the risk of parallax), and usable as a straightedge, too.

The plastic blades of the contour gauge are pressed over the face of a molding or other irregularly shaped surface to be matched (top); then its opposite edge is used to draw a copy of the profile on the stock to be cut. The gauges are sold in a range of sizes.

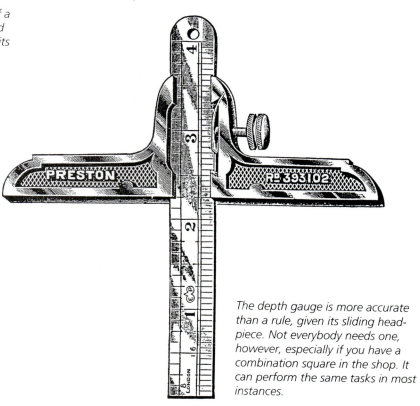

The depth gauge is more accurate than a rule, given its sliding head-piece. Not everybody needs one, however, especially if you have a combination square in the shop. It can perform the same tasks in most instances.

TOOLS FROM THE TOOLBOX

In the companion volume to this book, *Bob Vila's Toolbox*, much space was devoted to some basic tools that are as essential in the workshop as they are at a work-site. While space doesn't allow me to say it all again, a few key tools and considerations bear discussion here.

Tape Measure. When it comes to marking and measuring and laying out, the tape measure has a thousand different uses. For your workshop, make sure that you have at least a three-quarter-inch-wide, ten- or twelve-foot-long tape. I find a small (six-foot-long, half-inch-wide) pocket tape goes with me most everywhere.

Try Square. A try square helps mark offcuts, identify what's square (and, equally important, what isn't), and belongs on your workbench at all times. There are numerous designs to choose from, but probably the most versatile is a combination square.

Torpedo Level. It's small, portable, and invaluable for a great many leveling-off or plumbing-up tasks about the place.

Bevel Gauge. Angle cuts, anyone? This is a tool that takes the guesswork out of matching an existing angle; it's inexpensive, easy to use, and useful indeed.

That's a combination square at center, with a try square (left) and a bevel gauge above it. There's a torpedo level, two tapes, and a zigzag rule. A toolbox full of such basic tools is just as handy in the workshop as at the work-site.

TEMPLATES

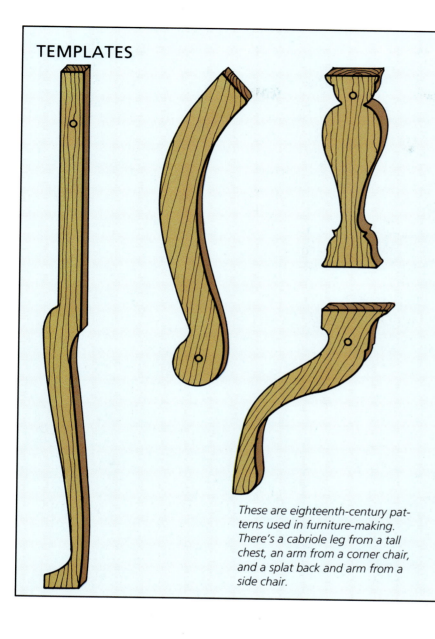

Templates are patterns or models used in the making of specific pieces, usually those with curved lines or irregular designs and shapes. If, for example, you are making a set of chairs with shaped seats, legs, or back splats that are supposed to match, templates can be used as patterns to ensure that all the chairs have matching elements.

The template is laid down on the raw stock and the pattern is traced; then the workpiece is cut to match the master. Such patterns can be made from cardboard, plywood, hardboard, or scrap stock around the workshop. They save considerable layout time and produce more consistent, accurate results.

The word template is also used in reference to the guides used with routers. Cut with a saber, jig, or band saw, the template can be just about any shape. Don't forget, however, that you must allow for the distance between the bit and the baseplate of the router.

These are eighteenth-century patterns used in furniture-making. There's a cabriole leg from a tall chest, an arm from a corner chair, and a splat back and arm from a side chair.

Chapter 6.

Hand-Held Planes

I have a tool-collector friend who usually is one of the world's most positive people. He always thinks of the glass as being half full, he tolerates even loud and obnoxious children with smiles and interested nods, and has bought into the notion that good things happen to good people. One kind of behavior, though, makes even John cranky.

He hates "knowitalls." Especially one who launches into a boring lecture at the first opportunity, telling him things he already knows, or, worse yet, things that he knows better than Mr. Knowitall, thank you very much. Even so, patient old John always keeps his cool until the self-appointed expert is out of earshot. More than a few times, though, I've heard John mumble after such an encounter, "Those who can, do; those who can't, *they just talk about it!*"

Now what's that got to do with shaping tools, you ask? To my way of thinking, that key shaping tool, the plane, is the one by which a woodworker is to be judged. Or, to put it another way, paraphrasing John, those who plane, do; those who can't, well, they're just fiddling about.

Planes are touchstone tools. The device itself is deceptively simple: a blade mounted in a body that functions as a handle. But there are planes and then there are planes, just as there are woodworkers and then there are craftsmen.

Some planes are intended to make wood flat; until the Industrial Revolution introduced machine planers in the early nineteenth century, a hand-held jack or smoothing plane was the only way to remove the roughness in wooden stock left by the rough-and-ready saws of the day. Other planes are used for introducing curves into wood (molding planes), still others for shaping slots and grooves (rabbet and plow planes).

But the bottom line is this: The hand plane, along with some other shaping tools like the spokeshave, wood files, and, to get modern for a minute, the router and its wealth of bits, make precise and intricate shaping of wood possible. And they separate the knowitalls from the doitalls.

That's a rounder plane at center (it was once the easiest way to make a handle for a rake or other hand tool). But there's also a variety of other planes including (starting from top, left, and moving clockwise) a jointer plane, a large wooden hollow, an iron bullnose, a wooden smoothing plane of the so-called coffin shape, a standard metal jack, a pair of molding planes, a shoulder plane, and, atop the rounder, a block plane.

BENCH PLANES

Bench planes are a loosely linked category of flat-bottomed planes. The cutting irons are usually set at a forty-five-degree angle ("common pitch"), though for hardwoods the angle traditionally has been a bit

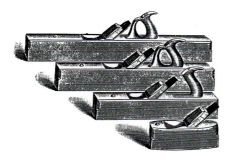

The full lineup of bench planes, including (top to bottom) jointer, fore, jack, and smoothing planes, from a pre-World War I tool catalog.

steeper, perhaps fifty ("York pitch") or fifty-five degrees ("middle pitch"). The bench planes, along with the smaller block planes, are used for surface smoothing and squaring. Other planes perform special types of shaving work, such as shaping moldings or rabbets.

Metal bench planes all have the same basic elements. There's the main body of the plane, with its handle at the rear and a knob up front. Within the frame is a sloping cavity into which the plane iron is inserted. The plane iron, consisting of a blade and cap, is fastened to the frame with a lever device. The blade does the cutting, the cap deflects the chips upward. The cap is screwed to the blade.

The bottom of the frame is called the sole. The opening in the sole is the mouth, the front the toe, the rear the heel. An adjustment nut or wheel raises or lowers the blade and a lateral adjustment lever shifts the blade from side to side.

Wooden bench planes are simpler than their metal brethren, generally box-shaped, and square in section. A handle extends upward from the rear of the plane. Just forward of center, the plane iron is held in place with a wooden wedge, with the bevel of the blade facing downward. The bodies of wooden bench planes tend to be made of American beech. The cutting irons can be single, but more often are capped. They are mounted bevel down, as in metal planes.

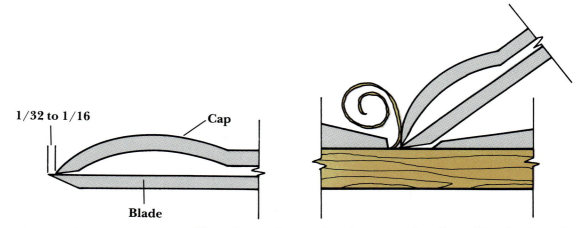

1/32 to 1/16
Cap
Blade

When setting up a plane, screw the blade cap iron between a thirty-second and a sixteenth of an inch shy of the blade's tip. This setting is important: too little clearance will cause shavings to jam, too much will produce chatter. The shavings should curl off smoothly.

The subgroupings under the general heading of bench planes include the jointer, jack, and smoothing planes. These planes are similar in design but differ in scale. The jointer is the largest, typically more than twenty inches long. The smoothing planes are the shortest, usually seven to nine inches long. The jack planes are in between, typically a foot to fourteen inches in length. All are to be found with both wooden and metal bodies. (The name fore plane, though now largely out of use, probably refers to planes of a size between the jack and jointer planes, typically eighteen inches long. I add the "probably" because some experts argue that fore and jack are really different names for the same plane. Apparently, though, one common application for the fore plane was to shave down or smooth the edges of windows and doors. An eighteenth-century source insists that it got its name from its

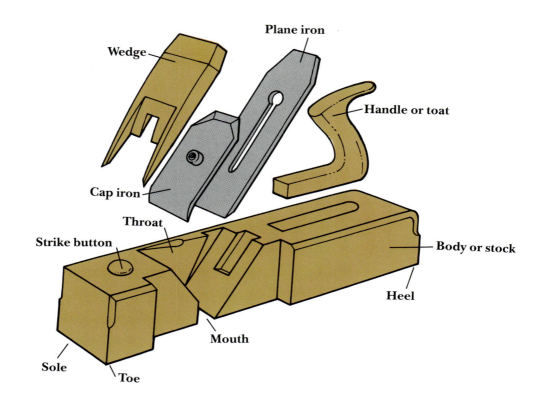

Wedge

Plane iron

Handle or toat

Cap iron

Throat

Strike button

Body or stock

Heel

Sole

Mouth

Toe

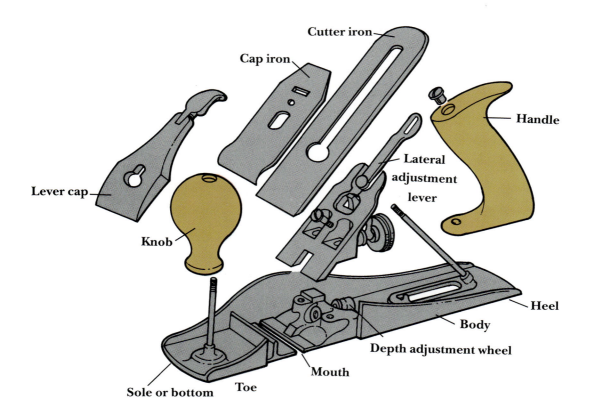

Cutter iron

Cap iron

Handle

Lever cap

Lateral adjustment lever

Knob

Heel

Body

Depth adjustment wheel

Sole or bottom

Toe

Mouth

Large jointer planes are not easy to handle so it was not uncommon for their users to mount them sole up, in order to present the workpieces to them rather than trying to wield the great heavy plane. This drawing, from an early twentieth-century French catalog, is of a cooper's long jointer plane set up in just such a fashion.

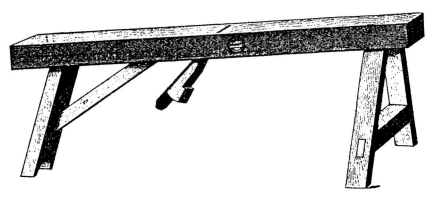

place in the smoothing process: "It is called the Fore Plane," asserts Joseph Moxon in his *Mechaniks Exercises,* "because it is used before you come to work with the *Smooth Plane* or with the *Joynter.*"

Jointer Planes. Sometimes called try, trying, or long planes, these are handsome and substantial tools. Wooden jointer planes tend to be very long, often twenty-eight or thirty inches and occasionally longer. Iron jointer planes are typically shorter, in the twenty-inch to two-foot

One chore – and I mean chore – that is made to seem very easy indeed by a jointer plane is planing the edges of a door. Get the door horizontal, edge up, perhaps in a sandwich of two pieces of scrap clamped with two big bar clamps. Then put the plane to work, making sure that its sole is precisely parallel to the door edge, especially at the beginning and end of the stroke. It will true, as well as smooth, the edge.

range. The metal jointer plane's body is much lower, too, with a closed wooden handle that stands proud of the base.

Adjusting a metal jack plane is usually done by means of an adjustment screw, which makes fine adjustments simpler than on wooden models.

Jointer planes were – and are – used to true the edges of long boards before they are joined to one another. They were once also used to smooth wide stock, though that task is rarely assigned them today.

Jack Planes. These are essentially smaller versions of the jointer planes, made up of the same elements in essentially the same proportion. Jack planes are used for sizing lumber and boards, but they are really all-purpose planes that can be used for almost any planing job.

Smoothing Planes. The wooden version of this smallest of the bench planes has no handle, and is sometimes referred to by the rather ominous name "coffin plane" (there is a certain resemblance, thanks to the curvature of the smoothing plane's sides). The shape fits comfortably into the hand.

The plane iron, too, is curved, almost imperceptibly convex at its tip. This slight curve suits the plane to the task its name suggests, smoothing boards (were it absolutely flat, the corners at the edge of the blade would catch the stock being smoothed).

Planes, like chisels and any other tools with finely honed edges, must be stored properly. They should be stored on their sides, with the plane irons out of harm's way (namely, not at risk of colliding with any metal surface). An alternative is to withdraw the iron into the frog of the plane, but this necessitates resetting the blade each time you use the tool, which makes this option impractical for the frequent plane user.

Think of this photo as a visual essay on the history of the smoothing plane. There's a coffin plane at left, the classic shape for most (though not all) wooden smoothing planes. At right is a metal smoothing plane, the type that has been the rule for most of this century. In the middle is the transition plane, the combination wood-and-metal-bodied smoother. This one dates from ca. 1895.

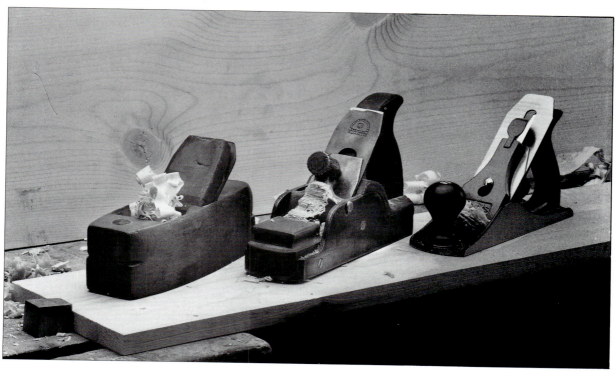

MAKING PLANE ADJUSTMENTS

Trying to use a plane with a cutter that's out of adjustment is like driving a car in the wrong gear: You may be able to make some progress with it, but the task is ever so much harder than it has to be. Planing with a properly adjusted plane should be a pleasure.

If you suspect your plane may be out of adjustment, hold the plane upside down. Sight down the length of the sole as you would the barrel of a gun. You should see the expanse of the sole broken only by a fine dark line where the plane iron protrudes ever so slightly through the mouth of the plane.

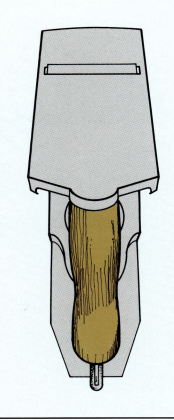

If you can't see the plane iron at all, it's retracted into the body of the plane and won't cut anything. If the plane iron sticks out too far, the plane will be very hard to push and it will jam quickly with thick shavings or even chunks of wood. The line you see should also be even from side to side; if it isn't, then the blade is crooked, and its corners will tend to gouge into your workpieces.

Larger planes often have double blades. The second iron keeps the cutting iron stiff and helps cause the shavings planed from the wood to curl up and out of the plane's throat. The relative position of the second iron to the first is adjustable, regulating the thickness of the shavings (see page 86). The second iron is most often set about a sixteenth of an inch back from the cutting iron.

Metal Planes. Setting the cutters in most metal planes is relatively easy. There are mechanical aids to help reset the blade, both laterally and for depth.

Begin by getting the blade square to the plane's sole. A lever is attached to the mechanism (called the frog) that supports the blade. When the lever is shifted from side to side, the angle of the cutting edge also shifts in relation to the sole. Sight down the sole, then reset the blade so that the

Holding the plane upside down, examine the mouth through which the cutter iron is to be seen. The bevel of the iron should just protrude and should be parallel to the plane's sole.

shadowy line you see squares with the plane's bottom.

Some planes allow you to adjust the mouth, the rectangular opening in the sole through which the blade appears. For finish planing on hardwood a narrow space in front of the blade is best; at the other extreme, rough planing on softwood is easiest with a wider mouth. A setting about midway between will allow the plane to be used for the widest range of jobs.

Next, experiment with the knob or nut at the rear of the frog that drives the adjustment screw. When you turn this knob, the cutter protrudes farther from (or withdraws within) the plane's mouth. Set the plane so that the cutter just barely peeks out from the sole, then run the plane along a length of scrap stock. Back off or advance the adjustment screw and retest until the tool is working to your satisfaction. Keep in mind that there's a very fine line between taking too little (which means that any planing job takes more strokes) and too much (when you risk tearing the grain with cuts that are too deep). Practice, as our grandmothers liked to say, makes perfect.

Wooden Planes. Adjusting a wooden plane is both easier (there are fewer parts to be concerned with) and more difficult (it takes a light and careful touch). With a wooden plane, the first rule is: If it ain't out of whack, don't fix it. Try a stroke or two on a piece of scrap board before fiddling with the plane's adjustment. If the tool doesn't work to your

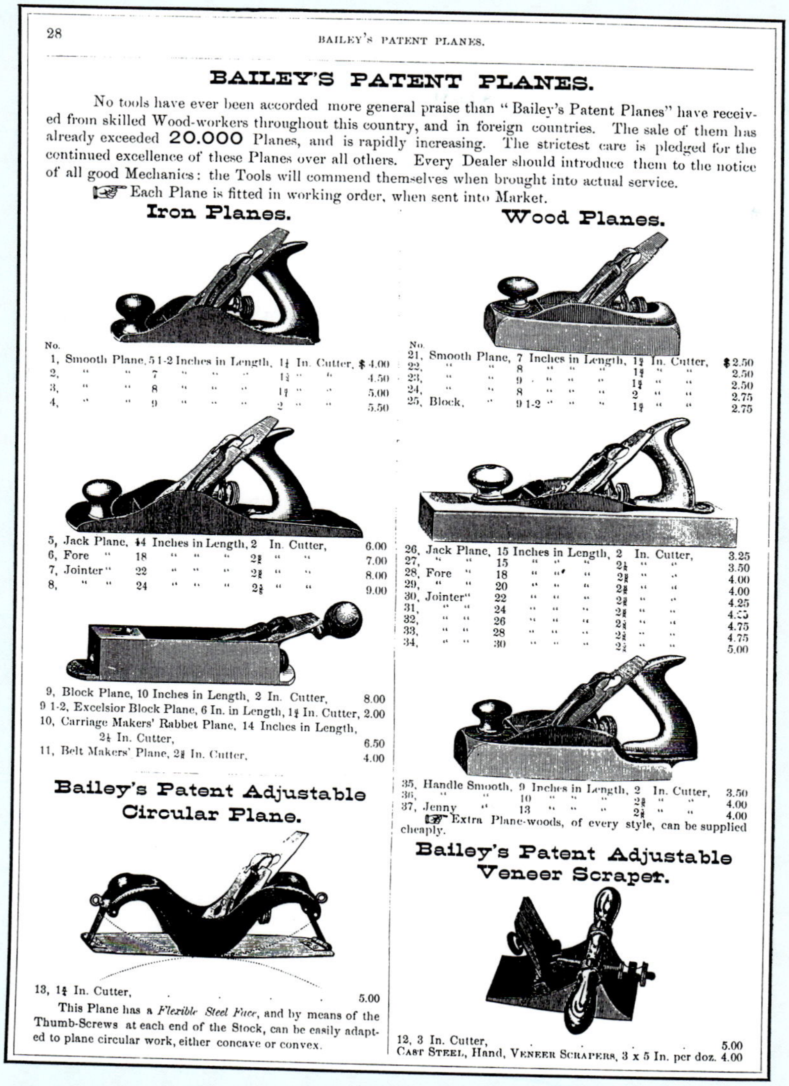

28 BAILEY'S PATENT PLANES.

BAILEY'S PATENT PLANES.

No tools have ever been accorded more general praise than "Bailey's Patent Planes" have received from skilled Wood-workers throughout this country, and in foreign countries. The sale of them has already exceeded 20.000 Planes, and is rapidly increasing. The strictest care is pledged for the continued excellence of these Planes over all others. Every Dealer should introduce them to the notice of all good Mechanics: the Tools will commend themselves when brought into actual service.

☞ Each Plane is fitted in working order, when sent into Market.

Iron Planes.

No.
1, Smooth Plane, 5 1-2 Inches in Length, 1¼ In. Cutter, $4.00
2, " " 7 " " " 1½ " " 4.50
3, " " 8 " " " 1¾ " " 5.00
4, " " 9 " " " 2 " " 5.50

5, Jack Plane, 14 Inches in Length, 2 In. Cutter, 6.00
6, Fore " 18 " " " 2⅜ " " 7.00
7, Jointer " 22 " " " 2⅜ " " 8.00
8, " " 24 " " " 2⅝ " " 9.00

9, Block Plane, 10 Inches in Length, 2 In. Cutter, 8.00
9 1-2, Excelsior Block Plane, 6 In. in Length, 1¾ In. Cutter, 2.00
10, Carriage Makers' Rabbet Plane, 14 Inches in Length, 2⅛ In. Cutter, 6.50
11, Belt Makers' Plane, 2⅜ In. Cutter, 4.00

Wood Planes.

No.
21, Smooth Plane, 7 Inches in Length, 1¾ In. Cutter, $2.50
22, " " 8 " " " 1¾ " " 2.50
23, " " 9 " " " 1¾ " " 2.50
24, " " 8 " " " 2 " " 2.75
25, Block, " 9 1-2 " " " 1¾ " " 2.75

26, Jack Plane, 15 Inches in Length, 2 In. Cutter, 3.25
27, " " 15 " " " 2⅛ " " 3.50
28, Fore " 18 " " " 2⅜ " " 4.00
29, " " 20 " " " 2⅜ " " 4.00
30, Jointer " 22 " " " 2⅜ " " 4.25
31, " " 24 " " " 2⅜ " " 4.[illegible]
32, " " 26 " " " 2⅝ " " 4.75
33, " " 28 " " " 2⅝ " " 4.75
34, " " 30 " " " 2⅝ " " 5.00

35, Handle Smooth, 9 Inches in Length, 2 In. Cutter, 3.50
36, " " 10 " " " 2⅜ " " 4.00
37, Jenny " 13 " " " 2⅜ " " 4.00

☞ Extra Plane-woods, of every style, can be supplied cheaply.

Bailey's Patent Adjustable Circular Plane.

13, 1¾ In. Cutter, 5.00

This Plane has a *Flexible Steel Face*, and by means of the Thumb-Screws at each end of the Stock, can be easily adapted to plane circular work, either concave or convex.

Bailey's Patent Adjustable Veneer Scraper.

12, 3 In. Cutter, 5.00
CAST STEEL, Hand, VENEER SCRAPERS, 3 x 5 In. per doz. 4.00

By 1872, when this advertisement for "Bailey's Patent Planes" was published, the buyer already had a choice between wooden- and metal-bodied planes.

satisfaction, only then should you adjust it.

Wooden planes have fewer parts than metal ones, usually just the solid wood body, the iron blade, and a wooden wedge that holds the iron firmly in place. If the plane isn't cutting deeply enough, set the plane sole down on a piece of scrap stock. Then tap the end of the plane iron with a mallet, striking it gently. Test and, if necessary, tap again. A few trials will tell you when the plane is properly adjusted.

If the blade protrudes too far, you will need to free the blade and the wedge. For a large (jointer or jack) plane, this can be done by holding the plane vertically and thumping its heel on a solid wooden surface such as a benchtop. If there's a strike button on the plane's top, rap it while holding the plane with its toe in the air. Striking the heel of a smaller, smoothing plane with a mallet while holding the plane iron and wedge will do the job, too. These blows should be delivered firmly but gently, and repeated as necessary to loosen the plane iron and wedge. The blade on a molding plane can be released by tapping the notch in the wedge with the mallet.

Reposition the blade in the plane, with the bevel at least an eighth of an inch shy of the mouth. Reset the wedge firmly, tapping it tight with a few gentle mallet strokes while holding the iron tight to the frog.

If the blade isn't set square to the sole of the plane, a tap or two to one side or other on the portion of the iron that protrudes above the wedge should align it. Then set the depth as described above.

Keep the Iron Honed. Whenever you have the blade out of a plane, inspect the edge carefully. If there are any nicks or the blade has dulled, sharpen it. Get into the habit of honing your plane blades periodically. The time required will probably be a great deal less than that consumed by trying to work with the tool when it's too dull to do its job. (See *Some Sharpening Shortcuts*, page 164.)

To keep your metal planes in good working order, occasionally wipe them with a rag dampened with machine oil. This will prevent rust, as well as keep the moving parts lubricated.

The moving filletster plane may just be the culmination of the wooden planemaker's art. On the one hand, it is little more than a simple, flat-bottomed plane designed for cutting rabbet joints. On the other, the filletster comes with design refinements that make it easier to use and that produce more precise results than simpler, earlier planes.

Note that the plane iron is set at an oblique angle; this serves to draw the plane into the stock as it is used, as well as making it possible to cut cross-grain rabbets. A fence on the sole can be adjusted (using two set screws) to vary the width of the rabbet being cut.

There's also an adjustable depth stop. The height of its shoe is set by turning the metal thumbscrew on the top of the plane. Finally, there's a spur tooth that protrudes at the shoulder of the plane's sole to help prevent grain tearout.

Yet there's nothing complicated about the filletster (or fillister, as it's known in England), and it's easy and satisfying to use.

MOLDING PLANES

For woodworkers with old-time tastes, using a molding plane is like drinking a vintage port. The planes are not for everyone, but for those who favor them they offer a unique satisfaction.

Tool-world modernists argue, "Who needs 'em? My router'll do everything they can."

The traditionalists' rejoinder is along the lines of "Maybe you think so, but I'll take the quiet of my workshop and the crisp lines of my moldings any day."

I think there's room for both kinds of tools in a workshop, though I must admit that when it comes to production work, the molding plane is obsolete, without question. But if you haven't run a molding or two, seen the thin shaving curling out of the plane, and felt the tautness of your forearm muscles after driving a hand plane . . . well, I guess you don't know what you're missing.

Molding planes are used to cut wooden moldings. The planes themselves have bodies of wood, often of beech, birch, hornbeam, boxwood, or even oak, with iron or steel blades. The plane irons are held in position by wooden wedges.

To woodworkers of generations past, this array would represent little more than a sampling of molding planes. They needed dozens and dozens, including hollows (top left), beads (top right), flat-bottomed (bottom right) and side rabbets (bottom left), and planes with complex profiles like those at center.

The sole of the plane body reveals everything about a molding plane: Its profile is the reverse of the shape that the wood on which it is used will take. The iron is ground to the same profile, though the cutting edge extends only partway from the right-hand side (on most planes) to the left. The right-hand side is a rebated groove, while the remaining portion of the stock acts as a fence and depth gauge to guide the planing process.

Another, subtler guide is found on the toe of many molding planes. It is an incised line that is, in essence, an instruction to the user as to how to position the plane. Called a spring line, it should be kept perpendicular to the workpiece, even if this means that the stock of the molding plane will not be. To ignore that line is, in most cases, to flatten the profile of the molding almost beyond recognition.

The craftsman of yesterday had a wide array of molding and related planes. Among them were purpose-made tongue-and-groove planes for shaping the edges of boards; these planes were sold in matched sets. There were hollows and rounds, planes with soles (and matching

If your plane digs too deeply when you are planing with the grain, check the blade: Does it protrude so far that it's biting off more than it can chew? If this isn't the problem, you may be going against an angular grain. Turn the piece around one hundred and eighty degrees. Try again . . . isn't that a bit easier?

PUTTING A HAND PLANE TO USE

Very few workshop tasks can be as satisfying as putting a plane through its paces. There you are, just you and, say, a molding plane, standing over a board fixed in place on the workbench. Your first stroke is gentle, even tentative, as you establish the line you will follow. After a few more passes, your stroke now strong and sure, the profile begins to appear. Pretty soon, there's a molding there, a bead or an ogee or a quirk ovolo.

Whatever the planing task before you or the type of plane to be used, there are some constants. One is balance: Get positioned so that you can use your weight and the strength in your shoulders and upper body. This isn't work for the lower arms alone. The workpiece should be clamped at a comfortable height in front of you.

Most planes work best two-handed, with the left hand guiding the plane at the front, the right driving from the rear. You may also find that positioning the front hand so that the fingertips or the heel of the hand just brush the stock may help guide your stroke.

Trueing an Edge. Use the longest plane you have, preferably a jointer or jack plane. The longer the plane, the less it will exaggerate any existing troughs and crests cut into the

edge. Clamp the stock to be planed in a vise, then set the plane at the end of the piece. Work with the grain. Before pushing the tool along the length of the board, apply some pressure at the front of the plane to be sure the sole sits flush to the piece (rather than on an incline, with the toe lifted above the piece). Likewise, be sure the heel sits flush to the board as the plane reaches the end of the planing stroke, shifting some of your weight to the back of the tool. This prevents "dipping," in which more wood is planed from the ends than from the center of the stock.

Lift the plane at the end of the stroke, and carry it back to the starting point. Don't drag it backwards. Plane irons get dull quickly enough without unnecessary wear and tear.

When you check for flatness in planing, look for light visible beneath a straightedge. In this case, the job is far from finished.

Check the flatness of your work with a straightedge as you go along. A steel framing square will do.

Smoothing Flat Stock. This is a two-step process if you are using unplaned stock or if the workpiece consists of glued-up pieces. For hardwoods, begin by planing diagonally to the grain, perhaps at a forty-five-degree angle, more with some hardwoods. Use a long-soled bench plane like a jack or, for a large workpiece such as a tabletop, a jointer plane.

The iron must be set to plane very fine shavings (thicker shavings will tend to tear the grain). Work from side to side, planing one way and then the other, until the surface is level.

When smoothing glued-up stock (note the glue line at center), work across the grain; the harder the wood, the steeper the angle you use (for softwood, about forty-five degrees, working up to almost ninety on some woods). As you can see with this mahogany, the raised edge at the glue line is gradually disappearing. Don't forget, you can work both ways, from one side, then the other.

Cutting a Rabbet. This may seem to defy reason, but the rabbet is most easily started at the forward end of the workpiece. Use short strokes at first, gradually moving farther back on the piece. If the plane you are using has a depth stop, work until it contacts the workpiece and stops the planing. If the plane has no depth stop, work to a line you have left with a marking gauge (see *Marking, Cutting, and Mortise Gauges*, page 73).

After the preliminary smoothing has been completed working across the grain, plane with the grain to produce the final planed surface. If the stock to be planed needs only minor smoothing, you can take a one-step approach, and plane only with the grain.

A century ago, a well-equipped woodshop would have contained a full set of planes called hollows and rounds. A hollow plane has a concave iron while a round has a convex one. Sold in matched pairs, hollows and rounds were, and are, used for shaping and trimming as well as making moldings. Frequently, an ogee or other complex molding profile would be shaped using both hollow and round planes. A full set of hollows and rounds consists of eighteen pairs of planes, ranging from an eighth of an inch to an inch and a half at sixteenth-inch increments.

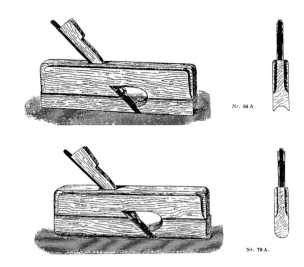

Nr. 84 A

Nr. 79 A.

A DECORATIVE TOUCH

The workshop you see on page 16 is decorated with Greek Revival pilasters, flush columns that punctuate the front (and side) elevations. They are not fabulously expensive, made-to-order decorations; they were made on site using standard one-by and five-quarter boards, a miter saw, and two bead planes.

That's a half-inch bead at the base of the capital (of five-quarter stock), a three-eighths-inch bead on the trim piece across the top. The shaft of the pilaster (made of one-by-eight boards) is trimmed with three-eighths-inch beads, too. And, as you can see, it all goes together easily.

Since the whole building was to be painted with oil paint, the wood is all common, full of knots to be sealed, in this case with an shellac-based sealer. We used a pneumatic siding gun to fasten everything. When painted, the finished product looks a bit impressive, yet properly vernacular for its setting.

blades) shaped, respectively, in concave and convex profiles. A set of bead planes was *de rigueur* in almost all woodworking shops in the waning days of the preindustrial age. (A bead molding, semicircular in section, was a pleasing way to finish a joint between two parallel pieces of wood, as in wainscoting or door panels.)

Those planes were just the foundation for the extraordinary variety of planes that were made in the eighteenth and nineteenth centuries, planes responsible for the wonderful moldings found in early American homes. The ogees (moldings with an **S** curve) and the ovolos (quarter-round), and dozens of other profiles and combinations give antique houses much of the character we so admire today.

That's a bead plane, together with the pilaster capital (facing page). You can see the nailers beneath the capital (above, left), which disappear as the capital is added (center). The last touch is a very simple curved decoration added in the broad valley between the pilaster pieces (right), giving the whole column the look of having an single exaggerated flute at its center.

RABBET PLANES

One of the most common wood joints is the rabbet. Consisting of a rectangular slot at the edge of one piece into which the edge or end of another fits, rabbet joints are strong, yet are also simple to make, especially when you consider the array of planes and other tools that will cut the rabbet itself.

Technically speaking, not all the planes I'm describing in this subgroup are rabbet planes; but because they all cut rabbets, I've simplified things a bit and lumped the plow plane, bullnose plane, filletster plane, and shoulder plane into one category.

rabbet (RAB-et) n. **1.** *A channel or recess cut from the edge of a workpiece, especially one that is to receive another member.* **2.** *A joint formed by the rectangular groove cut into one workpiece to receive the end of another.* **syn** *rebate (primarily British).*

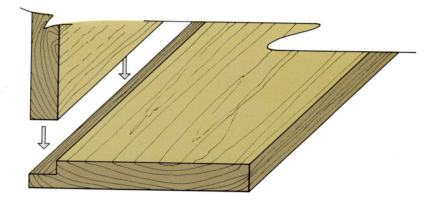

How many kinds of planes are there? The short answer is a hundred or more. In addition to those varieties discussed here – each of which is still available and in more or less general use – there are banding, boxmaker's, cooper's, fore, mast and spar, panel, snipe, table, and planemaker planes. And lots, lots more.

Rabbet Planes. A rabbet plane is, by definition, a plane designed to cut rabbets (also known as "rebates," particularly in Great Britain) in the edges or ends of workpieces. To enable them to do so, the plane iron is milled to a size slightly greater than the width of the plane body. This means that the cutting surface extends beyond the sides. Typically, they are about ten inches long, with cutting irons of an inch and a half in width.

Some rabbet planes have a second frog for bullnose work at the toe of the plane. This works well for stopped rabbets, grooves that end abruptly before the end of the workpiece, requiring planing close to the end point.

Some rabbet planes also have a spur that is lowered when the rabbet is cut across the grain. This eliminates tearout, as the spur slices the wood fibers to be planed before the plane iron reaches them. You must keep the spur sharp, however, by honing it occasionally.

A variation of a standard rabbet plane, one that comes with a guide fence and depth gauge, is called a filletster plane (see page 92). The depth gauge is fastened with a set screw or thumbscrew on one side and can be adjusted to various depth settings. A guide fence is attached to the base with screws.

Sharpening irregular shapes like the irons for molding planes or gouges for carving requires irregularly shaped stones called slipstones. These small-scale stones fit in the palm of your hand, and are applied to the tool.

Slipstones are used for honing. They come in a variety of shapes: in section, they may be circular, triangular, square, or conical. In this photograph, an Arkansas slipstone is being worked back and forth on the bevel of an iron from a beading plane. After the bevel has been honed, the burr raised on the back of the iron will be honed off on the fine black stone.

Store slipstones, like all sharpening stones, with care; though made of stone (man-made or artificial) they are fragile, and break and chip easily.

Plow Planes. Plow planes cut grooves and rabbets, plowing out stock along the grain of the wood; not surprisingly, they are also known as grooving planes. The tool features an adjustable fence that sets the distance from the edge of the wood, and a depth gauge to alert you when you have planed the stock to the preset depth. The fence is adjusted by moving a key or releasing a wedge.

Antique models have all-wood bodies, with fence arms of threaded wooden stock. More recent plow planes have wooden handles but cast iron stocks, with a variety of adjustments. On antique plow planes, the plane iron is held in place with a wooden wedge; on more modern

This plane, as billed in a 1914 catalog, has a boxed fence, boxwood screw arms, and eight irons. All for the then rather grand total of $6.60.

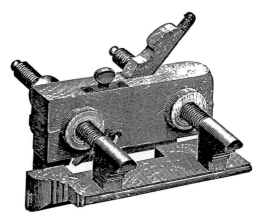

metal-bodied plow planes, adjustments are made with a steel screwdrive. Typically, the blades are set at about a thirty-five-degree angle.

Bullnose and Shoulder Planes. These small planes have iron bodies and steel plane irons. The body of the plane is milled precisely so that the sole and sides of the plane are at ninety-degree angles. They don't have fences or depth stops.

Bullnose planes range in size from roughly three to four and a half inches; the larger shoulder planes range up to about eight inches in length.

Bullnose and shoulder planes are designed to finish rabbets, so their plane irons are wider than the plane bodies. They are also handy for all sorts of delicate trimming and shaving that larger planes cannot reach.

The blades in shoulder and bullnose planes are set, like those in a block plane, at a low angle, which allows them to be used to trim rabbets in end grain as well as to work with the grain.

That elegant plane at right is a plow plane; there's a simple rabbet plane at the rear, a bullnose at center, left, and a hefty shoulder plane in the foreground.

This iron rabbet plane is still manufactured today; its design has changed little in the last century. It requires more muscle power than a power tool such as a router, planer, or a dado bit on a table saw. But it's a lot quieter.

Different versions have different adjustment mechanisms. The simplest consist of a wooden wedge; others have adjusting screws or knobs. Some models have removable or adjustable noses to allow for enlarging the mouth of the plane; some shoulder planes have upper bodies that can be removed altogether, revealing what is essentially a chisel mounted in a frame.

Because of its size, the bullnose is useful for trimming stopped rabbets, in which the rabbet is not cut the entire length of the workpiece. The shoulder plane is used to cut rabbets, as well as to trim and square the "shoulders" (inside corners) of both tenons and rabbets.

THE MULTI-PLANE

The multi-plane is truly the muscle-driven equivalent of the router. Its handle is of wood, but that's where its resemblance to traditional hand planes ends. It is a highly machined, complex assemblage of adjustment screws, stops, fences, depth gauge, and interchangeable cutters, all of which enable it to plane grooves, rabbets, dadoes, sash moldings, reeds, concave and convex curves, and even stair nosing. A turn-of-the-century model was sold with more than *fifty* cutters supplied, and another forty-plus available as options.

Clearly, this is one plane that could – and still can – do a lot of different jobs. The multi-plane looks a bit like Henry Ford's answer to the antique plow plane. And those who elect to buy and use one today are more than a bit like people who collect other antiques, be they Model Ts or whatever. Multi-planes are expensive (the better part of $500 is a typical price for reproduction models).

The bullnose plane (top) is nickel-plated iron, about three and a half inches long; the shoulder plane (below) is about five inches, with a rosewood wedge. Handsome and efficient tools both, then and now.

The shoulder plane in use: It's held with its side flush to one edge of the rabbet, with the sole trimming the edge to a perfect perpendicular. The weight of the plane does much of the work, and helps to produce a neat, tight joint.

If the filletster plane (see photo-graph, page 92) is the ideal expression of the wooden planemaker's art, then this is the epitome of the metal plane. I do think Henry Ford would have been proud to have thought it up.

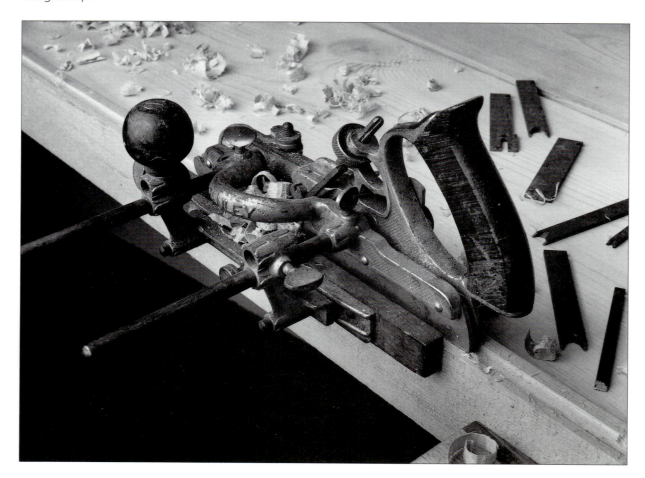

Several English companies continue to make multi-planes. I've included this tool here because, in a sense, it exemplifies the best of the old ways and the new. The body of the plane is flanked by an adjustable fence, but its chassis is iron, as is the fence. What gives the plane its flexibility is the variety of cutters, which are easily inserted into the body.

Combination Planes. This one is something of a crossbreed, being a near relation of both the metal-bodied plow plane and the multi-plane. The combination plane cuts rabbets and grooves with the grain, and its interchangeable cutters allow it to cut beads as well. But its primary distinction from the plow plane is that it has an additional cutter mounted near the toe.

Called the spur, this vertically mounted knife cuts the grain ahead of the plane cutter, which means that a combination plane can cut across (as well as with) the grain. The spur prevents the cutter from tearing out when crossplaning.

THE PORTABLE POWER PLANER

A power planer is to a jack plane as the portable circular saw is to a handsaw. Both the planer and the circular saw are powerful electric-powered tools; they do much the same work that the jack plane and handsaw do, or once did, but they do it more quickly, sometimes more efficiently and accurately, and always at a higher decibel level.

The power planer is a hand-held tool, but it operates like an upside-down stationary jointer (see *The Jointer*, page 165). There's a cutter-head with a pair of sharp knives that, like a plane iron, removes shavings of stock. The cutterhead is aligned with the rear portion of the tool's base; the front shoe of the plane adjusts to control the depth of cut.

Whatever kind of plane you are about to use, always take a moment before you put it to work to inspect the surface to be smoothed. If there are any nails, screws, or other metal elements to be seen, remove them first. Otherwise, you risk the long-drawn-out process of grinding and honing, which, when it's the result of carelessness, is a frustrating waste of time.

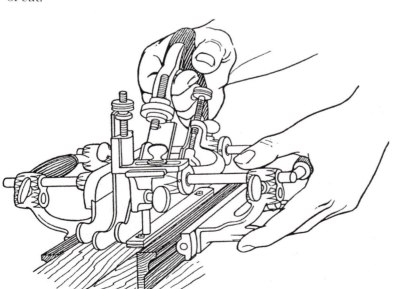

The multi-plane at work, from a 1916 instruction manual.

The compass plane is used to plane arcs, using its convex sole. By turning the knob on the metal version, the plane's base adjusts to different radii (some models will even assume concave shapes). The wooden plane might have been used for shaping wheel rims; either could have been used to shape curved furniture parts. Or, as in this case, for smoothing trim boards over a pair of arched French doors.

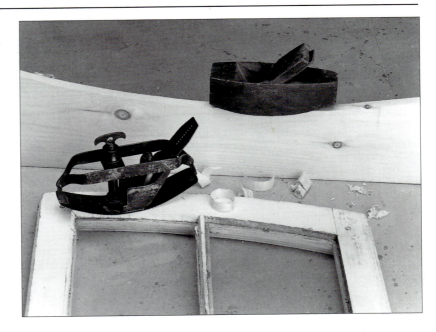

The portable power planer makes quick work of removing sawmarks after a board has been ripped. And it will bevel, chamfer, and perform a number of other finishing tasks.

The power planer cuts no more than a sixteenth of an inch at a pass. The depth of cut is adjusted on most models by a control knob mounted atop the front of the planer. Some power planers come equipped with an adjustable fence.

The size of the portable power planer is determined by the tool's maximum cutting width. Most models available on the market today plane a maximum width of between three and a quarter and six and a half inches.

Operating a power planer is similar to using a bench plane, but requires much less effort: You don't need to drive the plane, rather, you guide it along the path you wish planed. Clamp the workpiece securely and make sure your stance is balanced. Although little force will be required, use both hands to control the tool, with your left hand guiding the plane at the front, the right balancing the rear.

Before planing the length of a board, put some pressure at the front of the plane to ensure that the sole is sitting flush to the piece (rather than on an incline, with the toe lifted above the piece). Likewise, be sure the heel is parallel to the board at the end of the planing stroke, just as you would with a bench plane. This prevents dipping, the defect that occurs when more wood is planed from the ends than from the center of the stock. Check your work for flatness as you proceed, using a metal straightedge.

The power planer has many uses in a workshop, particularly a smaller workshop that doesn't have a full-sized jointer-planer or surface planer (see page 168). It will remove sawmarks, even off rough edges, and trim stock with ease. It's invaluable when fitting doors, either the full-sized or cabinet variety. It'll taper and surface, too.

A final word of warning is in order, however. Like the bigger jointer-planers, which are known for shaving off fingertips as well as stock, this machine has a wicked bite. Use it with care, planning, and respect.

TOOLS FROM THE TOOLBOX

Find safe but accessible places in your shop for these tools.

The Hammer. Hammers have countless jobs to do in the workshop. I find that for the sort of finish work more often encountered in a workshop a fairly light hammer (perhaps fourteen or sixteen ounces) with a smooth belled face (it's slightly convex) is good. A wooden mallet is handy, too, for driving chisels, fitting work-pieces, adjusting planes, and many other little tasks.

Chisels. A set of sturdy chisels will become invaluable to you over time. Good chisels are worth the added investment: They keep their edges and are safer to use (sharp tools require less pressure to drive and are less likely to break free when forced). On the other hand, top-of-the-line chisels are probably not required for the average Saturday-morning, let's-fix-the-broken-toy kind of workshop.

The Block Plane. For smoothing end grain, it's unsurpassed. For fitting and trim work, it fits right in a pocket. If you have only one plane, this is probably your best choice.

The block plane has an important place in the workshop, too; as do hammer, mallets, and, of course, chisels.

Chapter 7.

Cutting and Shaping Tools

In the previous chapter, we looked at length at planes, the shaping tool of choice in many instances for many years. Today, however, not a few of the jobs once done by muscle-powered planes have been assumed by the router and its amazing miscellany of bits. This versatile tool can be used to make moldings, shape joints, produce lettering on signs, and do a dozen other kinds of jobs. The tool is light, relatively inexpensive, and durable. With a purpose-made table, the router can also be turned into a quite affordable shaper, capable of much of the work handled by its freestanding equivalent (see *The Shaper*, page 171).

The router is at the heart of this chapter, but we will also talk about spokeshaves and files, traditional shaping tools that still have a place in any workshop, whether it's for detail work or finishing what another tool has started. And the chain saw, too, may have its uses, as may an axe or a hatchet.

The router has become perhaps the most essential shaping tool in most woodworking shops, and two are pictured here, a standard router (top) along with a plunge router. And there are spokeshaves (front, left), a small chain saw, a variety of files, an axe, a hatchet, and some sharpening tools. The various bits at center are used in the routers.

THE ROUTER

The router has, in recent years, become something of a must in the cabinetmaker's and even the finish carpenter's workshop. Its presence isn't due to the fact it does new things, performing tasks that other tools cannot.

In truth, a dado and a molding head mounted on a table or radial-arm saw will perform many of the same tasks, like cutting grooves and shaping molded edges. The router will cut mortises (more easily, faster, and, with the appropriate templates, more accurately than hand chisels) and dovetails (again, with an appropriate guide). And it will trim plastic-laminate edges for countertops, which almost nothing else will.

It is the router's versatility – the fact that it does *all* these jobs – as well as its light weight, reasonable cost, and portability, that have made it the tool of choice for many of them.

The router shares its name with a hand plane that predates it by a few centuries (see illustration, page 109). While today's power router accomplishes some of the tasks its ancestor used to (cutting grooves and rabbets), its lineage is closer to that of the electric drill.

Mounted on a round base, the motor of the router drives bits that protrude from the center of the base. It is most often operated with its

One explanation for the versatility of the router is the range of accessories available to adapt the tool to various tasks. Pictured here are a plunge router (left) and (moving clockwise) a router guide, an electronic router sitting atop a molding shaper, and a dovetail template. At center is an attachment that transforms the router into a plate joiner (see page 185). Those are bits and bushings at left.

base held horizontally, and flush to a workpiece. Its bits are mounted in a collet chuck, and the tool is held firmly with two hands grasping the pair of handles that flank the motor housing. The motor is preset to a position with respect to the base; where it is set determines the depth of cut.

As with most power tools, not all routers were created equal. There are inexpensive models and there are quite costly industrial-grade routers. Some weigh as little as three or four pounds, some more than twice that.

Speed is an important criterion in selecting a router. In the simplest possible terms, the better the router the faster it spins its bit. Maximum speeds range from fifteen to twenty-five thousand revolutions per minute or more. The advantage of greater speed is cleaner cuts: The high speed produces smoother surfaces, requiring a minimum of sanding. Some routers have electronic speed controls that adjust the speed as the router works, selecting the speed appropriate for the material and the size of router bit being used.

Power is another consideration. Some routers have as little as a one-half horsepower, some three horsepower or more. For most home craftsmen, however, one and a half horses are probably quite adequate. The less powerful machines may require more than one pass to produce a cleanly shaped groove or molding.

The ease with which bits can be changed and the depth set is another consideration in selecting a router. Chuck sizes vary, too: the collet chuck on the smallest models can accommodate bits with quarter-inch shanks, larger models half-inch diameter shanks. A more varied range of bits is available for routers with half-inch chucks.

Accessories. Guide fences are sold for use with most routers. Attached to the base of the router by guide rods, the adjustable fence enables you to make cuts parallel to an edge, to cut mortises and tenons, and even to cut grooves in the edge of a workpiece. Some have a Vernier scale and set screw set into the guide for precise adjustment; others can be used as a trammel to cut circles by fixing one point around which the router is turned.

Routers can also be affixed to the underside of a specially designed table. In this arrangement, the router is inverted, its cutters protruding through the tabletop. This transforms the router into a small-scale (and quite affordable) shaper. Workpieces are presented to the bit face down, with the edge pushed past the router bit. Quality router tables have blade guards, an adjustable fence, and miter gauge (with matching slot) that allows for end-grain and miter work. (See also *The Shaper,* page 171.)

Another accessory allows the router to be used as a biscuit joiner (see *The Plate Joiner,* page 185). A wide range of templates are sold, too, some of which make routing butt hinges a breeze; others are for dovetails or lettering or numbering. There are more options than there is space to describe; one adapter even allows the router to be used like a lathe. But you would do well to begin by using the tool for simple cuts, to get a feel for it and learn its idiosyncrasies. Then expand your repertoire as you desire.

Plunge Routers. Plunge routers are designed for making interior cuts: trying to drop a regular router into the middle of a piece of stock with its bit racing isn't at all a good idea. The plunge router brings precision and safety to the process.

The housing of the plunge router is mounted on a base with two posts that telescope, allowing the bit to be "plunged" into the workpiece from above. A depth stop is preset; then a locking lever is released, allowing the sliding carriage to be driven into the workpiece. When the operator releases the downward pressure on the router, springs return the carriage to the top of the stroke.

Plunge routers are especially useful for making stopped grooves or dadoes (in which the cut terminates before the end of the workpiece), mortises, and template-guide cutouts.

The traditional muscle-powered router, rarely seen today, is a member of the plane family. The cutting iron, mounted at center, could be easily changed for other shapes and sizes.

ROUTER BITS

This is a small array of router bits; there are dozens and dozens on the market. Note that some of these have pilot tips: They do not cut, but guide the router as it shapes the workpiece.

There are simply too many router bits to make anything like a complete list possible. Here are some of the most common and useful profiles. No doubt you'll recognize many of them in your own work, and in furniture and moldings around the house.

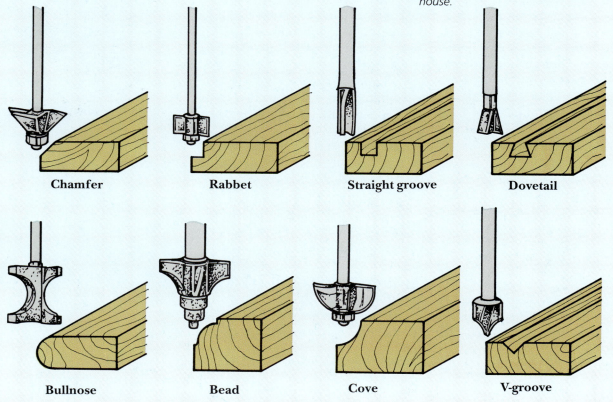

| Chamfer | Rabbet | Straight groove | Dovetail |

| Bullnose | Bead | Cove | V-groove |

An accessory available for most routers is a router table, which transforms a hand-held tool into a stationary one. The result is, essentially, a lighter weight version of the shaper.

"Choose the right tool for the job." Sounds obvious, doesn't it? Well, think about it this way: The right tool will not only save you time but also reduce your risk of injury. When using the wrong tool, you may find yourself forcing the tool (always a bad idea), or banging it, or otherwise treating it in a manner for which it was not intended. Broken tools, chipped blades, and out-of-control movements are among the greatest dangers in the workshop.

Router bits come in about as many shapes and sizes as there are edges to be shaped, quite apart from bits for cutting dadoes and rabbets, or for trimming laminate. Still others cut grooves, semicircular channels, mortises for hinges, dovetails, ogees, coves, chamfers, nosing, glue joints, and dozens of other profiles.

Router bits are made from high-grade steel, tungsten carbide, or a combination of both. The carbide bits, like carbide-tipped saws, are more expensive, but stay sharp much longer, especially when cutting materials more abrasive than wood, like plywood and particle board. Some carbide router bits have carbide tips that are brazed onto the steel, others are solid carbide.

Router bits are divided into two basic categories, *simple fluted bits* and *guided bits*.

Simple bits have one or two fluted cutting surfaces machined onto their length; the flutes extend to the tip of the bit. The double fluted bits cut more evenly, leaving a smoother finish than do the bits with one flute (which often leave a wavy cut line).

The guided bits have a ball-bearing guide at the tip that acts as a guide. Also called a pilot tip, it functions as a sort of mobile stop to ensure that the router's cutting edge shapes the wood to a uniform depth.

Shanks are a quarter inch to a half inch in diameter.

RUNNING THE ROUTER

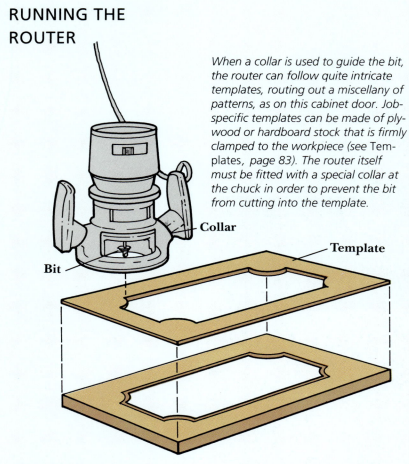

When a collar is used to guide the bit, the router can follow quite intricate templates, routing out a miscellany of patterns, as on this cabinet door. Job-specific templates can be made of plywood or hardboard stock that is firmly clamped to the workpiece (see Templates, page 83). The router itself must be fitted with a special collar at the chuck in order to prevent the bit from cutting into the template.

Collar

Template

Bit

Once you've grown accustomed to the router, the tool will fit naturally into your grasp. Initially, however, it may feel foreign indeed, quite unlike other tools you know and like. Wear ear protection, as well as safety glasses, since the tool tends to produce a considerable amount of noise.

Two-Hand the Tool. Use both hands when running your router, that's the first rule. Which means that you must fix your workpiece securely onto a bench or other surface.

Hold the router firmly until the motor reaches full speed. Keep the bit clear of the workpiece, as the rotation of the motor will make it want to spin

out of your grip if it's in contact with wood at startup.

Use the Rotation. When you look down at the top of the router, the motor turns in a clockwise direction. Use that to your advantage, moving from left to right on the edge facing you so that the rotation of the bit will draw the router into the cut. For routing the perimeter of a piece, work in a counterclockwise direction; when working on an interior cut, drive the machine clockwise.

Listen to the Tool. The motor will "talk" as you use the tool. With some practice, you'll learn to recognize the sound of a groan (when you are pushing too hard, it means don't

cut so much at a time) and the lonely squeal (when the blade spins at full speed with nothing to cut). There's a set of happier sounds in between, when the router is cutting its way at a measured, even pace.

Start with Straight Edge. When relying upon the pilot tip on a bit to guide your cut, make sure the workpiece has a straight or regular edge. If it doesn't, the shaped surface your router will make will reproduce any unevenness.

If you're cutting dadoes or grooves, a straight piece of scrap stock can be clamped to act as a guide.

Cutting End Grain. When shaping only the ends of a workpiece, start at either edge and meet in the middle. If you're doing all four sides of the piece, do the sides first and then the end grain. This will avoid tearing out stock at the corners.

Router Jigs, Guides, and Templates. The router is a remarkably versatile tool, and is made even more so when jigs or guides are used. Some are as simple as a piece of scrap clamped to the workpiece as a guideboard; commercially available jigs enable the router to make quick work of dovetails.

Follower guides (a bushing mounted on the base, through which the bit passes) are also very useful in many applications, to protect the templates while still guiding the cut precisely.

RASPS, FILES, AND SURFOAMS

The file card and brush at center is used to clean file teeth; that's a four-in-hand rasp next to it, along with several wood files. At top left is a surfoam, a square planing rasp, and some all-purpose files. At bottom are a couple of rifflers (left) and a triangular saw-sharpening file.

Files are easily taken for granted. They've been around for thousands of years, predating even the ancient Egyptian culture of the pharaohs and the pyramids. They're usually relegated to dusty drawers or toolbox trays, the dull tools of drudge work. After all, filing is no fun, and anybody can do it, right?

Actually, if you feel that way about files, thanks to some unimaginative industrial arts teacher, you probably haven't been properly introduced to these varied and extremely useful tools. If he didn't light the lamp of knowledge in this particular area of the shop, let's see if we can't offer a little illumination.

Files are shaping tools made of hardened steel that smooth wood or metal, removing burrs or rough spots. They can finish off or enlarge holes, and allow wood to be pared and shaved in places where planes and chisels just won't reach. Some metal files are used to sharpen other tools, including saw and other blades.

File "Cuts." Files have raised teeth on their surface that often look like crisscrossing rows of ridges. The teeth do the work of the file, removing small shavings from the workpiece. The "cut" of the teeth on a given file determines the classification to which that tool belongs.

Files with individually shaped triangular projections are called *rasps*, and are subdivided into wood rasp, cabinet rasp bastard, and cabinet rasp second cut, moving from roughest to smoothest. Files with their points cut in lines are graded coarse or bastard cut (twenty-six teeth per inch); second cut (thirty-six teeth per inch); or smooth (sixty teeth per inch). As a rule of thumb, the longer the file, the coarser are the teeth.

In the case of teeth that are cut in lines, they may be cut in straight lines that angle across the file in one direction or in two. Double-cut files are best suited to rough filing, single-cut for fine or finish filing and sharpening.

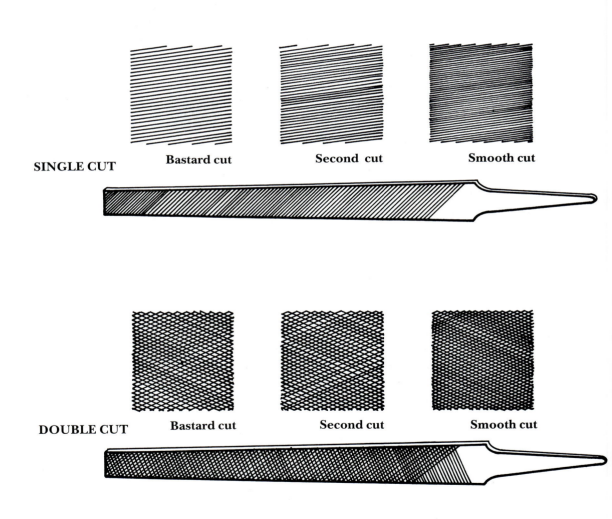

| | Bastard cut | Second cut | Smooth cut |
| SINGLE CUT | | | |

| | Bastard cut | Second cut | Smooth cut |
| DOUBLE CUT | | | |

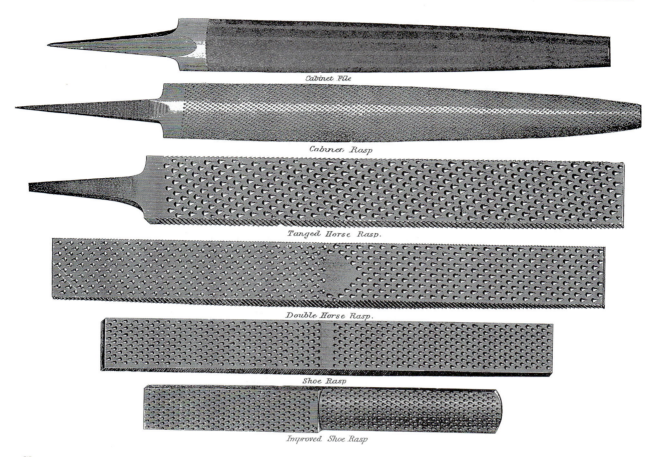

Cabinet File

Cabinet Rasp

Tanged Horse Rasp.

Double Horse Rasp.

Shoe Rasp

Improved Shoe Rasp

Shapes and Sizes. Files are sold in a multitude of shapes and sizes – more than *six hundred*, in fact. But if you want to invest in only one file, the half round wood file is probably the handiest file in a woodshop. It's flat on one side and rounded on the other, so it can round concave surfaces (with the half-round side) or smooth flat or convex areas (with the flat one). It's double-cut, and comes in a great variety of lengths, but a ten-inch half round is a versatile size. The cabinet file resembles the half-round wood file, though it's thinner and has finer teeth.

Next on the purchase list would be a mill file. The surface of a mill file is always single-cut. Mill files handle fine finishing and sharpening jobs; they'll do drawfiling (of a scraper, for example), smoothing (of wood or metal), and trueing of edges. They are tapered in width and thickness and belong in every workshop.

The general-purpose flat file is perhaps the most common file, flat on both sides, resembling the mill file. The flat file is sold in many lengths (the smallest will fit in your palm, the longest is half a yard long) and in different cuts. It's used primarily by machinists for the fast removal of metal, squaring holes, and making grooves. A hand file is a flat file with one "safe" edge (i.e., with no teeth).

There are round files, square files, and files that are triangular in section. The round rat-tail file is most useful in neatening up small

Rasps and files, as engraved in an English catalog dating from 1889. Sheffield steel then, as now, was of high quality and often used in the manufacture of tools such as files and chisels.

float (flow-t) n. *Toothed, filelike tools long used by planemakers in shaping wooden plane blocks. A float cuts faster than a file, more cleanly than a rasp, and has triangular teeth that run across the width of the tool. Now rare.*

FILING TECHNIQUES

The first time I saw my father cut a piece of stock with a handsaw, he made it look easy. When I tried it, I discovered it wasn't quite as simple as it appeared. Filing is the same way: It takes a little technique and some practice before the file fits naturally in your hand, and your stroke is smooth and regular.

Use a Handle. File handles are easily attached and detached (that way, you don't need one for every file, but one will serve several files of similar sizes). Insert the tang end (the pointed tongue) into the handle, and tap it in, using your benchtop or a wooden mallet; don't hammer the file into the handle. Using the handle is a good safety precaution: The tangs are surprisingly sharp.

Clamp the Workpiece First. Files are most efficient when wielded with two hands, one at the tip of the file, its handle in the other. Which means that the workpiece must be secured, perhaps in a vise or by bench dogs.

Find the Right File. Flat files are suited to smoothing flat surfaces and convex curves, curved ones for concave (inside) curves. Half-round files work best for large holes or curves, round files for arcs with smaller radii.

Filing Metal. For rough work, file in a straight line across the piece, keeping the file at roughly a thirty-degree angle to the length of the stock. File

When cross-filing (top), the handle should be toward your body as you work away from you, filing across the piece. This method of filing will cut away much material, and is useful for coarse shaping.

In draw-filing (bottom), the file is pushed along the length of the workpiece, with the file held perpendicular to it. Note, too, that the tang and handle must be in your right hand: The teeth are directional, and won't cut unless pushed in this fashion. Draw-filing is a finishing stroke, one usually done with a single-cut mill file.

away from you, varying the direction of your stroke (though not the angle) in order to be sure that your filing surface remains flat and true.

As with a handsaw, lift the file off the workpiece slightly on the return stroke. To drag it back across after a cut stroke won't file off any additional material and may dull the file.

More pressure should be applied for rough work, a light touch for less demanding filing.

For finishing the surface, draw a single-cut file along the length of the piece. This will remove the filing marks across the piece.

Filing Wood. For the rough shaping, use a rasp. It cuts rapidly, but leaves a coarse surface. Follow the rasp with a smoothing file.

*Not everyone needs a set of rifflers, but for occasional carving or smoothing tasks, they can be very handy. Rifflers have a flattened **S** profile, sometimes with the teeth of a rasp at one end and file teeth at the other.*

They are very useful for getting into small angles and tight corners on curved cuts and moldings. Many of the best rifflers are made in Italy. Maybe that explains the wonderful, complex rococo carving that characterizes some Italian furniture and architectural elements.

Wood files don't need to be broken in, but metal files do. Use them first on an old cast-iron pipe or other soft metal (brass or bronze will do, too). A few strokes over the entire surface of the file will make it a more efficient tool to use.

The name for this tool is just as odd as its appearance. It's a scorp, a kind of drawknife, only the blade has been bent into a circle. In fact, this tool is almost indispensable for hollowing out objects (wooden bowls, for example, or ladles, or small curved indentations in workpieces). Also called a wooden shave, the scorp usually has a hardwood handle and steel blade.

It's used one-handed, and, as with a drawknife, it's pulled toward its user. Various sizes are available, with blades between two and four inches in diameter.

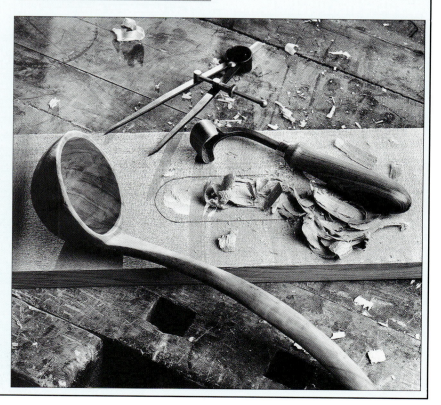

If a file becomes clogged with debris and you don't have a file brush at hand, try running the file over the end grain of a piece of hardwood. It should loosen the filings and return the file to usability.

openings, corners, or notches; these files are usually double-cut and tapered. The chain-saw file is also round, but not tapered.

Square files make neat, square corners in openings; they're essentially flat files. Triangular tapered files are indispensable for handsaw sharpening (see *Saw Sharpening,* page 122).

Rasps, too, are sold in varying profiles. The cabinet rasp and half-round wood rasp both have a flat side and a rounded side and are useful for the rapid removal of wooden stock. The equivalent of the metalworker's mill file is called a wood file: It, too, is single-cut, and is used for finishing wood surfaces. The flat wood rasp is a flat file, though it has the individually cut teeth characteristic of a rasp. Round wood rasps are sold in a variety of grades.

File Care. Treat your files respectfully. They may look indestructible, but they actually are quite brittle, and will snap in two if too much pressure is applied. Don't try to clean a file by striking it against your vise or any other hard object.

The areas between the file teeth tend to become clogged with debris that can render a tool close to useless. Clean your files regularly, using a file brush or file card. The file brush has two brushes, one on either side, one coarse and one fine. The file card is a clever design featuring wire picks on one side that will loosen the filings and a brush on the other for whisking them away. Whatever your cleaning tool, brush it in a direction parallel to the line of the file's teeth.

One old-timer's trick I favor after cleaning a metal file is to rub chalk into the voids between the teeth. This will help to prevent filings from accumulating there.

Given the surprising array of files on the market, what do you need in your workshop? Probably a half-round file at a minimum. And some mill files for sharpening. If you do finish work, a set of rasps may prove invaluable, too, probably a cabinet rasp and round rasp. But you needn't stop there, of course.

WORKSHOP SAFETY

You needn't use an antique padlock like this one, but locking up your tools, or even the workshop as a whole, from unwanted visitors (especially children) is an excellent precaution.

Safe workshop practices consist of more than wearing proper protective gear. Here are a few other guidelines:

Know Thy Tools. If you've just bought a new tool, especially a power tool, read the manual. As a matter of fact, even if you've had a tool for years, reading the literature that came with it will probably teach you something new about what the tool can do, or a better, safer way to do it.

Turn It Off Before Tuning It Up. When changing blades or adjusting a machine, unplug the tool. Always.

Clear Away the Clutter. Keeping too many tools and other objects on a benchtop makes your work more difficult – and makes tool operation there riskier. An accumulation of sawdust or offcuts on the floor is a stumble in the making.

No Smoking. Don't smoke in the workshop. Paints, solvents, and lots of other materials and supplies almost always found in a workshop are a potential fire hazard. Smoke outside, and, even there, don't stub your butt out in a pile of sawdust.

Store Your Tools Properly. Don't let tools accumulate underfoot as you move from one operation to the next. At cleanup time, put the tools back where they belong, in a tool cabinet, on a high shelf, or in other safe spots. Unplug them when you are finished.

Keep Your Tools Sharp. A dull tool requires added force (and increases the risk of injury). Maintain your tools carefully in other ways, too. Not only should cutting edges be sharp but they should be stored correctly to keep them that way, with their edges protected.

Keep It Grounded. Power tools should be properly grounded. Don't cut off the grounding prong on power cords, but plug them into matched receptacles or extension cords. Make sure plugs and power cords are in good order, with no bare conductors. Don't use the cord to lower the tool to the floor or to carry it around.

Never operate power tools on a wet or damp floor or in otherwise damp conditions. Dangerous electric shock can result. If you have a vintage power tool that isn't double-insulated, make double sure the tool is properly grounded.

Use the guards and other safety devices that came with your tools. Keep your working area well lit. Always use the right tool: Don't ask a minor league tool to do a major league job. And lift objects correctly (back straight, using legs for lifting), bending with your knees.

Surfoams. An alternative to the traditional rasps and files is the surfoam. The most common variety has a hollow aluminum body that looks a bit like a simplified block plane. Other types are longer (resembling a jack plane) or even long and cylindrical (like a large rat-tail file). Mounted to each are replaceable steel blades.

The teeth are formed by a stamping process that produces raised teeth and leaves the blade perforated (which prevents clogging by allowing shavings to pass through the blade). The raised and rasplike teeth make the surfoam useful in rough work in much the same way a rasp is. Blades are sold in fine, regular, and medium cuts.

Use the same technique as with a file, cutting on the forward stroke, angling the tool slightly to the workpiece. Surfoams can be used to shape or trim plastic, wood, fiberglass, wallboard, and soft metals such as aluminum, copper, and brass.

JOHNSTON PUBLIC LIBRARY
JOHNSTON, IOWA 50131

SPOKESHAVES

Most tools seem to develop in families. There are resemblances from one generation to the next, and cousins are recognizably cousins. But the spokeshave is something of an exception.

The spokeshave is a distant relation of the drawknife, I suppose, in that it has a knifelike blade that is worked along a length of stock. But most spokeshave users don't draw the tool toward themselves, like a drawknife; rather, they push the tool away from them. In truth, then, the spokeshave is more akin to a plane than to any other tool.

The spokeshave is used to smooth curves cut onto stock. It's at its best when cleaning up cuts made by a band saw or jigsaw. For generations of woodworkers, however, the spokeshave was a multipurpose tool used for shaping the seats, backs, and legs of chairs and in cabinetwork.

Virtually all spokeshaves manufactured today are made entirely of metal, but not many generations ago the tool consisted of a wooden body with a steel blade. Gradually, metal surfaces were introduced at the points at which the wooden lip tended to wear out, but today the norm is an all-metal tool. The handles that flank the cutting edge on metal models usually are shaped like wings.

The cutter in a spokeshave may be either straight or rounded (both convex and concave configurations are sold). It's fastened in a metal-

The metal spokeshaves in the foreground are virtually new; the wooden ones have been around a good long while. All are eminently usable tools, though the metal spokeshaves are easier to adjust and sharpen.

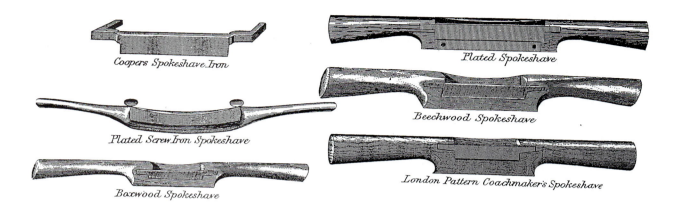

Coopers Spokeshave Iron

Plated Spokeshave

Plated Screw Iron Spokeshave

Beechwood Spokeshave

Boxwood Spokeshave

London Pattern Coachmaker's Spokeshave

bodied model with a thumbscrew; a pair of tension screws are used to adjust the setting. Nine or ten inches is a typical length for contemporary versions, though antique wooden-bodied spokeshaves are found both in smaller and in much larger sizes.

Antique wooden spokeshaves are frequently to be seen in shops and for sale from tool dealers. Their blades have a flat cutter with two perpendicular tongues (called "tangs"). The tapered tangs are set into the body of the tool. Unfortunately, since they are held in place by friction alone, setting a wooden spokeshave precisely is a bit tricky, requiring taps on the ends of the tangs or on the bottom of the blade to shift it this way and that. The blade may also require frequent resetting, as the tangs may no longer sit as tightly in their mortises as they once did. Buy one, if you wish, and admire its looks, but you may find you won't be able to rely on it for a great deal of shaving.

Wooden-handled spokeshaves, as manufactured and sold in England in the late nineteenth century.

The spokeshave is a two-handed tool. Some woodworkers find it works best on the pull stroke, as it is drawn firmly along the edge to be smoothed. You may be surprised at how quickly it comes to feel natural in your grasp.

121

SAW SHARPENING

A good handsaw, when properly treated, is a tool that can be passed with pride from one generation to the next. Essential to proper treatment is storing the saw correctly, in a place where the blade is protected and the atmosphere isn't too damp. An occasional wipe with a rag dampened with machine oil is good for the blade, too.

Over time, however, the best of handsaws, even those that are treated with proper care, get dull. The millions of collisions that the teeth experience in cutting wood both dull them and reduce their amount of

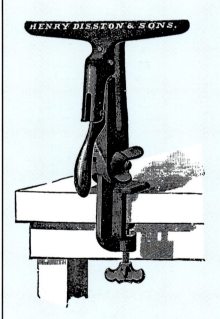

splay (called "set"). The saw will begin to cut more slowly (because the teeth are dull) and tend to bind (because the set has narrowed).

Fortunately, it doesn't take a magician to sharpen a handsaw. A little time, the proper tools, and a couple of simple techniques will restore that blade's cutting edge.

The Tools. You'll require a saw set for resetting the teeth, and a taper file or two. Both saw sets and taper files come in different sizes, so you'll need to determine the number of teeth per inch in the saw (or saws) you will be sharpening, and use a set and file that are appropriate to it.

Inspect the Saw. Remove any rust from the sawblade using fine sandpaper or a wire brush. Look closely at the teeth: Are they all the same height? If not, you will need to perform an operation called jointing. Simply clamp the saw in a vise, using wood blocks as a backboard to hold the spine of the saw rigid. Then file the teeth until they are of uniform height (see illustration, page 123). Use a double-cut, smooth metal file for the job, clamping it to a piece of scrap in order to keep it square to the sawblade.

Setting the Teeth. This step is necessary to make sure that the kerf is the proper width: Teeth that are out of alignment, regardless of their sharpness, will cut unevenly. The saw set makes this job a bit less painstaking, and ensures a more uniform set to the teeth.

The saw set resembles a pair of pliers, with a pair of long handles at one end, a small pair of jaws at the other, and a pivot in between. At the jaw end there is a rotating disk that, when turned, adjusts the travel of the tool, meaning that the plunger and anvil mounted on the jaws are closer together (or farther apart) when the handles of the tool are squeezed. When the set is then positioned against a tooth to be set, the tool will bend the tooth to the precise angle required for that size of saw.

Setting a saw can be done without a special tool but it's not easy. Each tooth needs to be bent from its midpoint, and all the teeth must be bent evenly; the bend must be no more than half the depth of the tooth; the set on each side must be identical. I'd recommend if you're going to go to the trouble of sharpening your own saws, that you invest in a saw set.

The tools for sharpening a saw in the workshop haven't changed all that much since this engraving of a Nash's New Patent Lever Saw Set (patented 1863) was published at the close of the Civil War. The saw vise – again, little changed over the years – appeared in this drawing in a 1909 catalog.

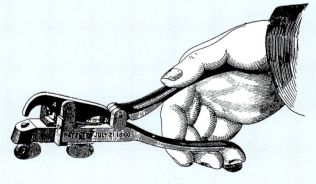

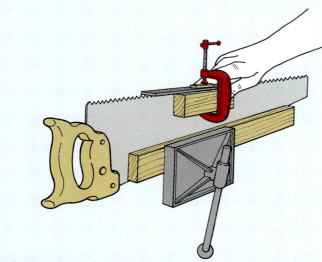

Jointing is the process of filing saw-teeth to consistent height.

To use one, you start by adjusting the saw set to conform with the number of teeth per inch on the saw, which may range from as few as four to as many as sixteen (saws with more teeth are probably best taken to a professional). Starting at one end of the saw, position the saw over the first tooth that is bent away from the tool's handles. Then squeeze the handles . . . and the tooth is set. Skip the next tooth (it's set in the opposite direction), and repeat the process, working down the length of the saw, setting every other tooth. Try to exert the same pressure on the grip to achieve a uniform setting. Then turn the saw around and do it all over again with the other teeth that are set to the opposite side.

Filing the Teeth. Taper files range in size according to the tooth sizes they are intended to sharpen. The smallest files will sharpen saws with fine or coarse teeth, but the larger files will sharpen the larger-toothed saws more efficiently. There is some argument as to whether single-cut or double-cut files are best (either will do), but for coarse (five to seven points or teeth per inch), a regular taper is suitable; for medium coarse (eight to ten tpi) use a slim taper; for medium fine (eleven to fourteen) an extra-slim taper; for

fifteen or more, a double extra-slim taper.

Whatever the size of the taper file, the shape is the same, as the file, in profile, is an equilateral triangle, meaning that each of its three angles is sixty degrees. This also means that the file will simultaneously file both the front of one tooth and the back of the one facing it, leaving them both shaped to the proper angle.

Clamp the saw, blade up, between two straight pieces of hardwood stock in a wood vise or purpose-made sharpening vise. The clamping arrangement should grip the sawblade close to the cutting edge, with the gullets (the troughs between the teeth) not more than a quarter of an inch from the jaws, to ensure that the blade is held rigid.

What's wrong with this picture? This can most charitably be described as a practice saw. It came with an old tool-box bought at an auction, and it's been sharpened so many times that its blade has narrowed (note the extra width at the heel of the saw). And, I'm afraid, the sharpener wasn't very skilled: The teeth are uneven and irregular, with more pitches than an out-of-tune piano. Though you can't tell it from this photograph, the previous owner of the saw apparently didn't own a saw set, either.

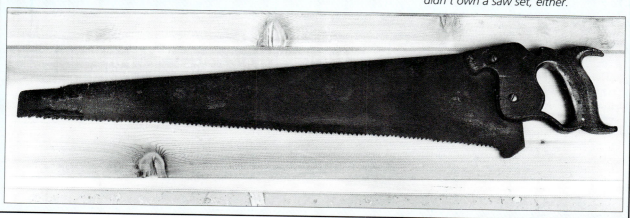

The goal in sharpening any saw, whether it's for ripping or cross-cutting, is to maintain (or restore) the original factory pitch of the teeth.

For a crosscut saw, position the file at about a seventy-five-degree angle to the length of the saw. Align it with the first tooth at the handle end of the saw that was ground away from you. Then tilt the end of the file down about fifteen degrees (in the direction of the tooth's set) and rotate it fifteen degrees, turning the bottom of the file away from the handle of the saw.

File across the gullet, lift the file clear, then repeat the procedure, filing until the face of the tool shines. Don't force the file, but gently smooth the tooth face. Two or three strokes should be enough, and try to file all the teeth the same number of strokes.

Work down the length of the saw, filing every other tooth.

For a ripsaw, the file is held horizontally at a ninety-degree angle to the length of the blade. Always, however, try to match the original angle of the teeth.

Then turn the saw around, and repeat the process for the teeth that are set to the opposite side of the blade.

If you had to joint the teeth (file their points), some will probably have flat tops. As you sharpen the saw, keep in mind that you only have to file *half* the flattened portion as you work down the saw the first time; when you make your second trip down, sharpening the teeth set in the opposite direction, the flattened point will automatically be sharpened.

Sharpening a Ripsaw. Sharpening a ripsaw is easier, because the teeth are ground perpendicular to the length of the saw. This time, position your taper file at a ninety-degree angle to the blade and rotate it roughly twenty-five degrees so that the angle of the file is parallel to the face of the tooth. (Remember, your aim in sharpening any saw, whether for crosscutting or ripping, is to restore the factory pitch of the teeth.)

The sharpening procedure is the same as for a crosscut saw: Make one stroke across the gul-

let (in the direction of the set of the tooth), lift the file clear of the teeth, return it to its original position, and stroke again. Repeat until the tooth shines, then move on, skipping a tooth, and do the one that follows. Again, work down the length of the blade, then turn it around, and do the other side. File each tooth the same number of times.

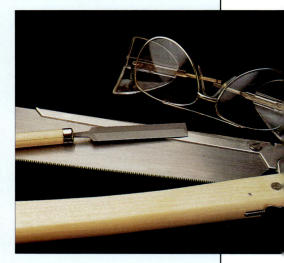

If you think sharpening a traditional handsaw sounds hard, then try sharpening a Japanese saw with its tiny teeth. Start by filing the points, working down first one side then the other at a ninety-degree angle to the saw's body. Then the bevel at the top of every tooth must be filed, holding the file at a sixty-degree angle to the saw body. While the bevel on the face of each tooth is cut, the back of the next tooth (which is set in the other direction) is also smoothed. One file stroke per tooth is it. The teeth are set after the filing is completed – using, believe it or not, a hammer with a face no wider than the teeth. Given the size and number of teeth, the whole process is kind of like a coordination test. But the saws are wonderful.

Pictured here is a small, finely cut file designed specifically for sharpening the dozuki, and a folding dozuki – one that, I'm glad to say, doesn't need sharpening just yet.

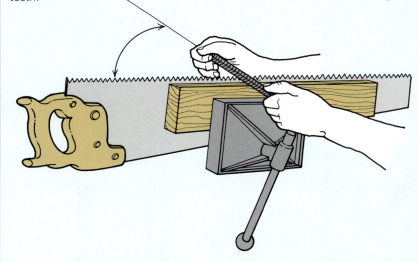

Working the Spokeshave. Fasten a piece of scrap firmly in a vise, with an edge upward. With the workpiece firmly clamped, you are free to use both hands to control the spokeshave, as with planes and the router.

The design of the spokeshave is such that there are two wings or arms, one on either side of the cutting edge. Wrap your fingers around these handles and position your thumbs behind the tool. In metal models, there are indentations cast to fit the pads of your thumbs. Once you've found a comfortable grip, push the tool along the edge of the stock. The hand position allows for your wrists to rock the tool toward you or away from you in order to control the cutter angle.

A bit of practice and you'll feel more at home with the motion. For rough shaping, the blade can be set to remove more stock than when doing finish work.

Sharpen a spokeshave in the same way as a plane iron, by grinding out large imperfections (if necessary) and then honing it on a sharpening stone (see *Some Sharpening Shortcuts*, page 164).

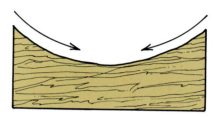

In using a spokeshave, you must take special care to work with the grain (otherwise the grain will probably tear out). This means that if you're cutting a convex (protruding) piece of wood, you'll probably need to work from the acme of the curve, shaving down one side, then returning to the top and shaving down the other. For a convex curve, you will likely need to work downhill again, but this time from the edges of the workpiece to the center.

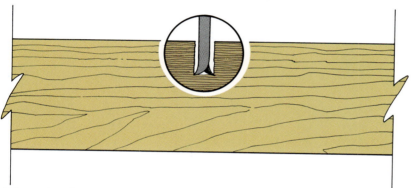

When a handsaw is at work, its blade cuts a groove called a kerf. In order to prevent the sides of the saw from jamming in the kerf as it cuts deeper into the wood, the teeth of the saw are "set." That means the teeth are alternately bent (set) beyond the plane of the blade itself, so the cut made by the teeth is wider than the body of the blade. See Saw Sharpening, page 122.

AXES AND HATCHETS

The tool we call an axe goes back into prehistory almost as far as the hammer. It, too, started out as a stone, but some clever Stone-Ager then lashed a handle to it. Next a slot was made in the handle and the head of the tool slid through it. Probably the next advance was a copper head.

This evolution didn't occur overnight, of course, but over the millennia a recognizably modern tool evolved, thanks in large part to the smiths of the Bronze Age. They were the ones who figured out that putting a hole in the metal head of the tool, rather than sliding a solid head through an orifice sliced into the wood or bone handle, would substantially increase the tool's usefulness and durability.

Hatchets new and old, along with a small-scale but easy-to-use axe. As with hammers, the metal-versus-ash-handle debate rages among hatchet and axe users, with yet another camp favoring fiberglass. Whatever kind you choose, use these tools with care and keep them far out of reach of those ill-prepared to treat them with respect.

An axe . . . *in the workshop?* . . . you ask? Maybe not in the workshop, actually, but the axe and its sister tools, the hatchet and the splitting maul, may have more than a few uses in preparing stock for use on the shop floor, or even keeping the place warm.

There are many kinds of axes, old-fashioned and new-fangled. The broad axe has Old World origins. Sometimes called a hewing axe, the sideways mounting of the head suits the squaring required in trimming a tree trunk into a beam.

The felling axe is, however, the most generally useful (and, very likely, the tool you picture in your mind when the word axe is uttered). It's regarded as an American innovation (the early settlers had a great many trees to chop down, a lot of which they turned into the wooden houses that dominate our landscape). The tool has a wedge-shaped head that aligns with its long handle, which may have a slight, graceful curve at the base. The heads on American axes tend to be thicker than European variations, but in America alone there have been many regional adaptations.

The axe's cutting edge is beveled and rounded. The blade thickens in a wedge shape: The edge cuts into the wood being struck, but the thickening of the head behind splits the cut open.

These days all of these tools are sold not only with the traditional hickory handles, but with fiberglass shafts. Heads vary in weight, typically from three to six pounds. The length of the handle varies with respect to the weight of the head, with the lightest axes having handles roughly two feet long and the heaviest heads three-footers.

There are hatchets and then there are hatchets, of course, but this is one traditional design. Called a Kent hatchet (after the English county of Kent), it has traditionally been used by carpenters for rough shaping and trimming.

Hatchets. Much as I admire the axe – its combination of grace and power has an atavistic appeal – the hatchet is probably more useful in the average workshop. It's a splitting and shaping tool, one proportionately smaller than the axe. The head is usually between one and two pounds, the handle fourteen to sixteen inches long. The head is steel, the handle hickory or ash.

A useful variation on the hunter's hatchet is the so-called half-hatchet, a tool with a hammer face on one end of the head and an axe head on the other. Unlike the traditional hatchet, its blade is not rounded but straight, which makes it handy for getting into corners for certain kinds of architectural work like trimming shingles and lath, as well as for splitting lumber for wedges and some rough shaping.

Mauls. Got a woodstove? A maul will make keeping it full of cordwood a breeze. It's safer and more efficient than an axe, with a dull blade (that's right) because the weight does the work, with the broad wedge shape doing most of the actual splitting of the wood.

THE CHAIN SAW

The forest primeval has seen few tools with the devastating utility – not to mention sheer volume – of the chain saw. If a strong man with a felling axe needs at least forty whacks to take down a tree, a chain saw can do it in a matter of moments with a great deal less effort.

Chain saws are sold in both electric and gasoline-powered models. In general, the electric models are smaller and less powerful (and, obviously, limited by the availability of electrical current). But they are somewhat quieter than their gas-powered equivalents, and are very efficient tools, particularly for more precise trimming and cleanup work.

The gasoline-powered models run the gamut from convenient around-the-yard tools to those that will cut down a tree big enough to crush your house if it fell on it.

Both electric and gas models share a basic design. The motor drives a chain that rotates around a steel guide called the bar. The saw is controlled from a pistol grip handle (for the right hand) with a trigger throttle control. The operator's left hand balances the saw while gripping a handle or bar across the top of the saw.

The chain remains still when the motor is at idle, and a centrifugal clutch disengages and engages depending upon the speed of the motor.

Gas chain saws are powered by two-stroke engines, meaning that the engine oil is mixed

If you heat your shop with cord-wood, a chain saw is indispensable. If you do any timber-framing, it'll also be invaluable. The model pictured here is compact (the bar is fourteen inches long) yet sturdy enough to do a good job of work.

with the gasoline. You need to get the mixture to the exact proportions specified by the saw's manufacturer, or you'll have difficulty keeping the saw running consistently and well.

The chain and bar must be kept properly oiled, too. There's a reservoir on the motor housing for chain oil, and it must be fed to the saw at frequent intervals, usually by means of a small button that pumps a few drops of oil onto the chain. Follow the instructions supplied with your saw.

The chain saw has come to be regarded as indispensable for a surprising variety of work. More than few "finishing" touches in log-cabin construction, for example, are done with chain saws cutting grooves or openings for windows and cabinets. Sculptors these days use chain saws, as do timber fra-

mers for certain kinds of rough shaping.

Be ever so careful with this tool. Don't cut upward with it, not ever, that's dangerous practice. Watch out for jams; they're hard on the tool and can put the sawyer in a predicament ("How am I going to get my twenty-pound tool loose from that two-ton tree?"). Never cut down trees with hanging branches, or that are braced against others.

Most important of all, don't imagine you're an expert too soon. Even pros who have felled a zillion trees are occasionally surprised by the fall of a tree.

TOOLS FROM THE TOOLBOX

In the workshop, your needs must dictate the number and range of saws you have, but the more exacting work typically done in a workshop argues for more rather than fewer handsaws.

No matter how many highly engineered power saws I collect, there will always be a place for handsaws in my workshop. Perhaps we don't need quite the same range that were required before electricity or even steam power became commonplace, but I'd recommend a minimum of a good crosscut handsaw, a hacksaw, a small backsaw (like a dovetail or a gentleman's saw, or perhaps the Japanese equivalent, a dozuki), and a coping saw. But there are arguments for a good many more, too. . . .

That's an all-purpose handsaw across the top of the photograph, with a Japanese dozuki immediately beneath it. There's a hacksaw and a coping saw on the left, a dovetail saw, and a plywood saw on the right.

The plywood saw is a recent and clever innovation. Its fine teeth are designed to cut plywood without tearing out the grain of the outside ply; it also has teeth on the toe that enable its user to cut into a sheet without making a starter hole.

129

PART IV.

CONTENTS

STAND-ALONE
TOOLS

Imagine for a moment that, in order to make a single ripsaw cut, you *don't* have to get out the Workmate, mount the portable table-saw to its top, rearrange a space around it, and *then* make the cut. Instead, you just turn on the stationary table saw and, straightaway, rip your workpiece.

That saving of time and trouble, that ease and convenience, constitute the greatest single advantage of a permanent workshop. The space allows for the introduction of some full-sized stationary tools. Instead of having to rely upon portable tools that have to be stowed away after use, the workshop offers the luxury of a stand-alone saw, perhaps, or maybe two. And a drill press, a sanding station, a grinder, or others of the numerous stationary tools.

In the two chapters that follow, we will consider the freestanding saws and the other stationary tools commonly found in home workshops. You probably won't need, have space for, or even want all of them; but each has important uses in the execution of certain kinds of work in the shop.

Even with high-quality, stationary power tools like this table saw, the key remains the same: Careful layout and setup procedures are essential.

Chapter 8.

Freestanding Saws

In the thoroughly equipped workshop, there are more tools than you could shake a furring strip at. You know the workshop I mean, the theoretical one in which the space is endless and there's a giant, industrial-grade table saw front and center. And a deep-throated band saw, a muscular radial-arm saw, and a more modest-sized bench grinder. And a planer, a shaper, and a drill press. Everything this side a candlestick maker, it seems.

Oh, it's hopeless, you say, I'll never fit all those/most of those/any of those in my space! Well, cheer up, I say, you don't have to. Most people don't need planers, or drill presses, or a shaper (hand-held planes, drills, and routers will suffice, after all). For a great many kinds of woodworking, the table saw is indispensable, but then some benchtop saws these days are remarkably good – and take up no more space when not in use than a medium-sized suitcase.

If woodworking isn't your thing, maybe your major need is a sturdy spot on which to set an engineer's vise. That just doesn't have to be hard.

All that said, however, this chapter is concerned with tools that usually stand alone though most of them can be found in small-sized varieties that rest on benchtops, sawhorses, or other temporary stands.

Which ones do you need? Which do you want? What do you have space for?

In deciding which stationary tools are essential to your shop, remember that more tools means fewer makereadies (that is, setup time to change blades or settings, or to fashion jigs). A purpose-made shaper saves the trouble of inserting the molding head into the table saw, the presence of a disk sander saves a blade change on the radial-arm saw, and so on.

On the other hand, a multipurpose tool like a Shopsmith or a SuperShop allows you to have a lathe, drill press, table saw (typically ten-inch), and disk sander (twelve-inch is common), and other attachments like a band saw, jigsaw, jointer, and belt sander – all in roughly the same number of square feet of floor space required by a bathtub. The downside is that every operation requires a changeover and, clever as such multipurpose tools are, the transformations do take time. More than a few woodworkers with limited space report the trade-off in setup time is worth it for the machine's versatility: there's no way they'd be able to fit the equivalent freestanding machines in the same space. It's your call.

The radial-arm saw is one of the most often used tools in my shop, since it makes accurate cutoff work quick and easy.

The Fatigue Factor. *Perhaps the single most common cause of accidents is fatigue: If your back begins to complain, if your legs stiffen, if you're stifling yawns, quit while you're ahead. Tomorrow, as they say, is another day . . . .*

For beginning woodworkers, however, I'd recommend starting with one basic stationary tool, either a table saw (my preference) or a radial-arm saw. A small investment in portable tools (a drill, portable circular saw, sanders, portable planer, and so on) will provide the support machines to undertake some basic projects.

The serious woodworker probably needs a band saw, table saw (and/or radial-arm saw, or both), a jointer/planer, perhaps a thickness planer, and a drill press. The sky's the limit, given space, money, and inclination. But don't be intimidated: I've seen top-grade work come out of virtual cubbyholes with the aid of a minimum of tools.

See how it goes: If you spend most of your time changing blades on your table saw, exchanging a basic blade for a molding head, maybe you need a shaper. If mortising seems to take forever, maybe a drill press and a mortising attachment are in order. Many a frustration at the slowness of an operation can be resolved with another tool.

THE TILTING ARBOR SAW

Its manufacturer called it a "saw bench" but this sturdy tool is a recognizable antecedent of today's tilting arbor saw.

For many woodworkers, the single most important workshop tool is the table saw. Though it is most often referred to by that name (and occasionally as a bench saw or contractor's saw), the more precise name is the tilting arbor saw. It's a large but deceptively simple tool, really just an upside-down electric handsaw, mounted to the underside of a steel tabletop. Its circular sawblade peers through a slot in the table. The arrangement makes for a tool that cuts quickly and accurately and, with easy blade changes, is quite versatile.

PROTECTIVE GEAR

There's nothing hard about wearing safety goggles or earplugs or a respirator when they are needed. The cost for such protective gear can be very small – for less than ten dollars, you can buy the most basic of safety glasses, earplugs, and a simple disposable mask. Consider such purchases as the equivalent of a small health insurance policy, money well spent.

If you are serious about the work you do in your workshop, and you have invested – or are about to invest – in an assortment of quality power tools and other shop equipment, it makes good sense to buy quality protective equipment as well.

Full-Face Shield. A full-face shield costs a bit more than safety goggles or glasses, but will give you maximum range of vision with essentially no blind spots. A shield is perfect for running a table saw or other stationary equipment where you work upright, feeding stock into a machine.

Hearing Protectors. If you use power tools, wear some sort of hearing protector. I understand the rationale that lots of people employ to avoid wearing one: "If the noise doesn't hurt, it really couldn't be very harmful, could it?" The answer is yes, it can and probably will cause hearing loss over time. Don't take the chance.

If you have an especially loud tool (a direct-drive table saw or a shaper, for example), consider buying protectors that resemble earmuffs. For most home workshops, plugs or foam pads mounted on a headband will do.

Lung Protection. For only a few cents, you can purchase a disposable fabric mask with elastic straps that hold it in place over your nose and mouth. For an occasional need, such masks are quite adequate, but if you frequently sand, strip, scrape, or paint, a more sophisticated variation of the same device would be in order.

Called respirators, they filter fumes and dust. Most have twin cartridges built into the chinpiece of the mask. The filters in the respirator will need to be changed occasionally, both because they get dirty (accumulating particulate matter over time, for example) and because different filters serve different needs.

Paper filters are best for dusty applications or when spray painting. Charcoal cartridges are suitable for working with chemicals or other tasks that involve fumes. When the paper becomes clogged (and breathing more difficult) or when you begin to smell the vapors, change the filters.

That's a face shield with the blue brow protector; it offers maximum range of vision when you're running stationary machines in the shop. The safety glasses are a less expensive but practical option. The earmuff hearing protector generally eliminates more sound than the earplug varieties. The two-cartridge respirator is a top-of-the-line model that may be used when spray painting as well as for dust protection.

Blade Depth. *The blade should be set at a height only an eighth to a quarter-inch greater than the thickness of the stock to be cut. A taller setting increases the risk of kickback.*

A good combination square is machined to very precise tolerances, producing a highly accurate tool of machine-shop quality. It can be used for many makeready tasks in the workshop, among them the initial setup of table saws to be sure that the blade is running at precisely correct angles.

The saw gets its name from the shaft on which the blade spins (the *arbor*). That axle can be tilted with respect to the horizontal tabletop (for cutting at angles) and raised or lowered to adjust the blade's cutting depth.

(For word mavens who like technical terms, the tilting arbor saw is distinguished from the motor-on-arbor saws, like the hand-held circular saw and some benchtop table saws in which the arbor and the armature of the motor are one and the same. The tilting arbor saw, with its pulley and belt drive, usually allows more of the sawblade to be used. And, in general, it's much quieter than the direct-drive motor-on-arbor saw.)

The saw will make crosscuts (across the grain). Thanks to a pushing device called a miter gauge, it can cut stock at angles perpendicular to the tabletop; with the arbor tilted, the table saw can also cut compound angles. Using a rip fence, wood can be ripped (that is, cut with the grain) and rebated. It will re-saw, too (often a two-step ripping operation in which thick stock is sawn to a thinner dimension by sending it through the saw once on one edge, then flipping it over and ripping the other edge; for further discussion of this and other techniques, see *Toolbox* , pages 76–79). Table saws will also take dado and molding heads for making rabbets, grooves, and shaped moldings (see *Specialty Table-Saw Blades* , page 138).

Most table saws are freestanding, though benchtop models are economical, both in terms of initial investment and space required for

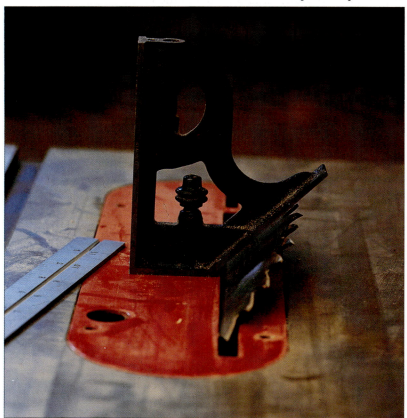

use. Otherwise, the two key variables that distinguish one table saw from another are *blade size* and *table size*.

Blade Size. Ten inches in diameter is probably the most common table saw size, though smaller and larger diameters are also available. A ten-inch blade will cut stock up to about three and a quarter inches deep, while a twelve-inch blade will saw through stock that is more than four inches thick.

Table Size. For miscellaneous cutting and ripping, the size of the table-top is less important than the presence of additional props (wings or roller tables) to support the stock as it approaches and passes beyond the blade. However, if cutting sheets of plywood or other large panels is in your future, be sure that the rip fence can be set at widths of up to two feet. The surface area in front of and beyond the blade will help stabilize the workpieces, both for safety and accuracy. Less than ten inches of support in front of the blade is insufficient for other than simple cutoff work.

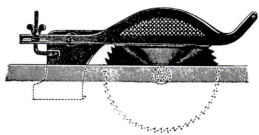

Make sure you use the blade guard, splitter, and antikickback fingers on your table saw. They've come a long way from the days of this one, manufactured in Germany at the turn of the century.

Don't forget your pusher, either, whenever your fingers will come any closer than five inches from the blade.

THE BAND SAW

Some cabinetmakers of distinction assert that the band saw is the single most important stationary tool in the workshop, more valuable even than the table saw. I, for one, haven't yet unplugged my table saw and offered it at a tag sale; but I have to agree that the band saw is a very useful piece of equipment.

Unlike the table saw, the band saw is well suited to freehand cutting. That's one reason it makes cutting curves seem easy, whether for chair seats, arched trim, or rounded tabletops. Nothing makes compound cutting easier than a band saw. (Compound cuts are the sort required for making curved furniture legs, for example, in which a square piece of stock is cut on one side, the offcuts reattached, and then the adjacent side is cut.) The band saw's depth of cut is unequaled. Among other things, that means that if you are doing repetitive saw work, the band saw will save time, allowing you to cut through several pieces of wood in a stack to make identical parts.

A band saw is ideal for cutting lumber of considerable thickness. And for re-sawing (thinning) wide stock. And for cutting curves, too. A furniture-maker friend of mine says that for shaping chair seats, aprons, or for any cut that isn't strictly rectilinear, the band saw is indispensable.

As its name suggests, this tool relies upon a blade that is shaped like a ribbon. The blade is a closed steel loop that circles two wheels, one above the other. The lower wheel is driven by a motor, usually by means of pulleys or gears.

I should note here that there are smaller, benchtop band saws with three wheels. The third wheel is located at the rear of the saw, so the blade follows a triangular path rather than an up-and-down one. This

When deciding upon a table saw, be sure to check the specs. A blade speed of at least 5,500 revolutions per minute is necessary for efficient use of high-speed specialty blades like dadoes and molding heads. Don't buy a table saw with less than one horsepower, and two is preferable for the heavy demand of a serious woodshop. I also recommend spending the extra few dollars to get one with a ten-inch blade.

SPECIALTY TABLE-SAW BLADES

Two other types of blades can be mounted on the table saw for specialty work, the dado and the molding cutter. Both require special setups and, in most cases, additional equipment. A larger table insert will be necessary to give the wider cutting surfaces of these blades adequate clearance where they break the plane of the tabletop.

You'll also need to protect both the blades and your fence by attaching a fence shield to the fence. A shop-made fence shield is easily made of scrap stock (see drawing, facing page).

Dado Blades. The dado cuts rectangular recesses in wood. There are two types of dadoes. The less expensive (and somewhat less precise) variety is called an adjustable or "wobble" dado. It is essentially a heavy-duty sawblade with a hub mechanism that allows it to be adjusted so that it spins at angles slightly less than perpendicular to the arbor. The resulting wobble of the sawblade produces a cut that is wider than the saw kerf.

When using a molding head, especially one with a deep-cut profile, don't be in too much of a hurry. Often the best result is achieved by making the cut in two or even three passes, with the saw set at increasing heights with each pass. That way, the molding head makes lighter cuts on each pass. No one pass should cut more than three eighths of an inch on softwoods and at most a quarter inch when working with hardwood.

The molding head (left), together with several of the blade profiles it will accommodate, make quick work of simple moldings. The dado blade being mounted onto the arbor of the saw is a dado set, the one at right a wobble dado. Both will cut rabbets and grooves with speed and accuracy.

For more accurate work, a dado set or dado head is used. It consists of two outer circular blades, called grooving saws, sandwiching inner blades (the chippers). The outer blades cut the sides of the groove or rabbet while the chippers clear

Making a slip-on fence shield is a very simple proposition. Rip a piece the width of your rip fence, then two more to match its height (plus the thickness of the top piece, of course). Then screw the three together. Finally, cut out an arched area to match the path of the dado or molding head.

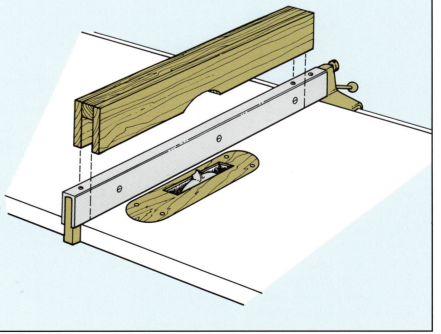

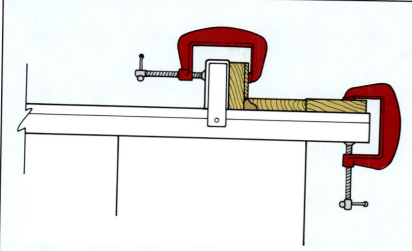

When making moldings, stops above the molding head and outside the workpiece, as well as a fence shield, will help ensure that the moldings you make are regular.

the center. Typically, the grooving saws are an eighth of an inch thick; chippers are usually sold in sixteenth, eighth, and quarter-inch thicknesses. A dado set will usually come with two grooving saws and several chippers. For fine adjustments of the width of a dado cut, shim washers can be inserted between the blades.

Dado sets are sold in diameters of six and eight inches. For most purposes, a six-inch set is quite adequate (and a lot cheaper).

Both the wobble dado and dado head are mounted on the arbor like a standard circular sawblade. When mounting a dado head, stagger the chippers; the teeth on adjacent blades shouldn't bind. Don't forget the alternate table insert (the plate that covers the mouth in the tabletop through which the sawblade protrudes) and to protect the fence with the fence shield.

To run the dado head, allow the saw to reach full speed. Once it does, present the workpiece gently: The saw will require more time to cut a groove or rabbet because the sheer amount of waste being

removed is greater than on a simple rip or crosscut. Use a push stick and, as always, wear your safety glasses or goggles.

The Molding Cutter. This device cuts profiles in wooden stock, profiles that can vary from very simple to quite complex. The device consists of a steel cutterhead that is fas-

tened like any other circular saw would be to the saw arbor of your table saw or radial-arm saw. The cutterhead in most molding cutters holds three identical blades with contoured profiles; set screws hold the blades in place. Some models use as few as one or two, but blade chatter is more likely with fewer blades, which make for a less well-balanced head.

Among the many commercially made molding profiles for molding heads are coves, beads, flutes, quarter rounds, and many more. You can also grind and hone your own to match existing shapes in restoration work.

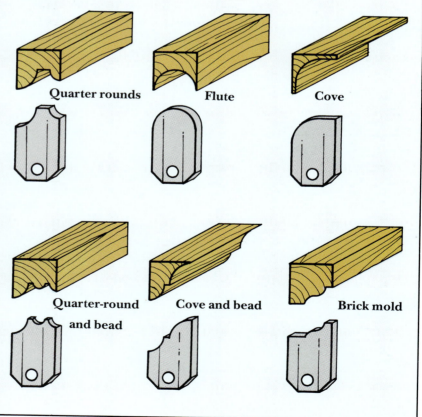

Quarter rounds **Flute** **Cove**

Quarter-round and bead **Cove and bead** **Brick mold**

MAKING A TAPERING JIG

In the woodshop, making identical elements is often one of the biggest challenges: Balusters, stretchers, or staves for a given job must be exactly the same. Freehand work just isn't the answer in such situations.

When it comes to making tapered cuts on a radial-arm or table saw, a tapering jig is the solution. It's very useful for repeated, identical cuts: The jig will ensure that they are uniform, cut to the correct angle.

You can buy a ready-made tapering jig, but why go to the expense? In about twenty minutes, with the purchase of one hinge and a small, curved sliding lid support and a scrap piece of one-by-four stock, you can fabricate your own.

Begin by ripping a three-foot piece of one-by-four in half (make sure it's straight and clear). Cut the two lengths to thirty inches each. Now, glue and screw a three-inch block of

The tapering jig makes straight, accurate angle cuts safer and easier. Make sure when you use it to reset the blade height to the thickness of the stock plus a quarter inch or less. And use the blade guard, too (the one on this saw was removed for the photograph to reveal the blade and kerf).

the same stock atop the ends of each of the arms, as the thirty-inch-long pieces are called. A third block will be glued to the outside edge of the left arm; it will act as a stop.

After the glue has dried, attach a double-strap hinge to the

built-up ends. The curved lid support is then attached to the top face of the arms. A useful, though not essential addition, is a handle. I used a Shaker-style peg, set into a half-inch hole in the end.

This jig can be set to guide cuts of up to fifteen degrees

means that the throat on a relatively small saw is much deeper than it would be for a similar-sized three-wheel model.

The extra depth is helpful for scrollwork on large workpieces. There is a cost, however, as the sheer cutting power is decreased, and cutting wood at or near the saw's stated capacity may strain the saw, producing more smoke and screech than cutting. If you want an all-purpose saw, buy a two-wheeler; if you want a sturdier jigsaw for scrolling around panels, a three-wheeler may be the answer for you.

The blade itself is housed in a metal case, visible only where the cutting work is done, in the area immediately above the worktable. Two sets of blade guides keep the blade aligned. One set is fixed below the tabletop, and the other is adjustable to varying heights above the table. The tension of the wheel is set by an adjustment located on the upper wheel housing. Another adjustment controls the tracking of the blade, which should travel at the center of the wheels.

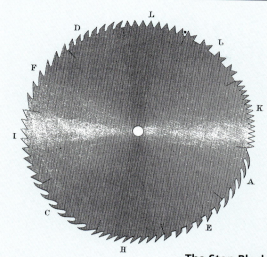

For those who don't have the luxury of a full-time workshop but still harbor woodworking aspirations, the benchtop table saw may make attaining some of them plausible. In about two minutes flat, you can get it out of the closet, set it up on your deck or driveway, and voilà! the instant workshop comes to life.

What's wrong with this picture? Look at the sawteeth: There are ten, count 'em, ten different kinds. This engraving is from an 1889 English tool catalog.

(if you need to cut larger angles, you may wish to make a tapering jig with *shorter* legs). Whatever the size, set the jig to the angle you desire, position the right arm flush to the ripping fence, and set the fence so that the workpiece, its side flush to the left arm and end butted to the stop, is aligned with the blade for a cut of the appropriate width.

The Stop Block. *This is an easy one: When you need to make stopped dadoes or other cuts that terminate short of the edge of a workpiece, clamp a stop block to your fence.*

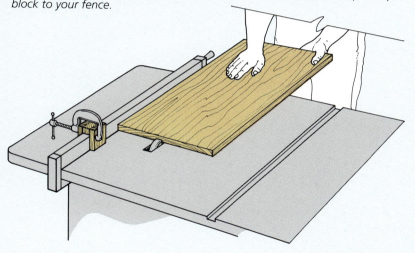

The blade travels in one direction at a great rate, typically two to three thousand feet per minute.

Band saws vary greatly. Large ones have been used to saw gigantic redwood trees into lumber; several very popular models these days fit on benchtops. The size of the tool is identified by the depth of the saw's throat, namely the clearance between the blade and the vertical housing at the rear of the tool (which is, in turn, determined by the diameter of the wheels on which the saw turns). Common home workshop sizes include ten-, twelve-, fourteen-, sixteen-, and eighteen-inch sizes, but in industry band saws with throats of up to forty-eight inches are common. The capacity of the tool is identified by the depth of the cut the tool will make. A twelve-inch band saw is adequate for most home workshop jobs, typically cutting up to a six-inch capacity. Cabinetmakers would do well to opt for a larger one, perhaps one with a sixteen- or twenty-inch throat.

The blades for band saws come in a variety of sizes and types. Each

The introduction of cases and guards has made today's band saw much safer to use, but the other basic elements have changed relatively little from this 1899 model.

is identified by the number of points (teeth) per inch, the gauge (thickness) of the blade, and its width. Most band-saw blades are between an eighth of an inch and a half inch wide, though larger blades are to be found in bigger machines. The spacing and configuration of the teeth vary depending upon the purpose to which the blade is to be put (see *Band-Saw Blades,* page 144).

The table on a band saw is typically small (a foot square, plus or minus), but don't be deceived: The saw can and will cut long pieces of stock, and when positioning the tool in your workshop, you should allow for considerable space on either side. The table should have a removable and adjustable fence to act as a guide, as well as an adjustable miter fence. The table itself should tilt; if the model you are considering has a fixed table, look a little further and find one that can be tilted. Some models are sold with a convenient variation, namely, that the housing, with the band-saw blade and pulleys within, tilts with respect to the table, rather than vice versa. This has the distinct advantage of leaving the operator with the familiar, horizontal worktable on which to present the work.

The workpiece is presented to the blade firmly braced against the miter gauge, whether the cut is a precise perpendicular or a miter cut. Push the gauge with one hand, and balance the stock with the other.

Most band saws have an adjustable table that can be set at an angle to bevel (as in this photograph) or to make chamfer cuts.

BAND-SAW BLADES

The narrower the blade, the tighter the curve that can be cut with it. An eighth-inch-wide blade will cut a radius of about a quarter inch; a quarter-inch blade will cut a three-quarter-inch hole; a three-eighths blade a one-inch radius; and a half-inch blade nothing tighter than a one-and-a-quarter-inch arc.

As with saber and other saw-blades, more, smaller teeth are suited to cutting metal (in the range of twenty-four teeth per inch) while fewer, larger teeth are used to cut wood. A coarse-toothed band-saw blade with, say, six teeth per inch is best suited to rough-cutting thick lumber, while finer teeth produce a smoother cut.

Band-saw blades also have varying kinds of teeth. Some have cutting teeth set to either side, like those on a handsaw, but with unset teeth called rakers interspersed; others have wavy-set teeth, on which the teeth are set sequentially at a greater (then lesser) distance from the thickness of the band, producing the wavy appearance. Blades with wavy-set teeth are best suited to cutting metal, while blades that have raker teeth, which clear the waste efficiently from the kerf, are best for wood and coarse metals.

Toothless blades are used to cut ceramics, plastics, and for very smooth cuts in other materials. The cutting edge on toothless blades consists of a surface that has tungsten carbide chips bonded to the teeth.

The profile of the teeth varies, too. Skip-tooth blades have deep gullets and are a good choice for general woodwork. For very smooth cutting (which is done at a slower pace), a regular or standard tooth is best. For high-speed cutting (which leaves a coarser cut), hook- or saber-toothed blades are appropriate.

If you have a small band saw, however, you may find that the usual standards don't quite apply. Many smaller saws do their best work using a narrower blade (one, say, a quarter inch wide) rather than a half-inch

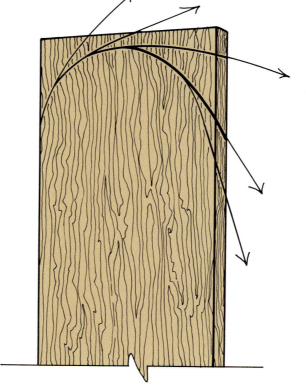

When using your band saw to make convex curved cuts, you'll find it's often easiest to make a series of cuts that go off along lines tangential to the final curve you wish to saw. When the blade begins to bind, run off the edge of the board in the waste stock. Then start again and repeat the process.

or three-quarter-inch band-saw blade. Buy bimetal blades (their teeth are cut from a strip of cobalt steel that is electron-welded to a spring steel blank before the teeth are cut). They're stronger and last longer.

For the weekend band-sawyer using a small-scale band saw, I'd suggest a bimetal, hook-tooth, six-teeth-per-inch blade for all-purpose work.

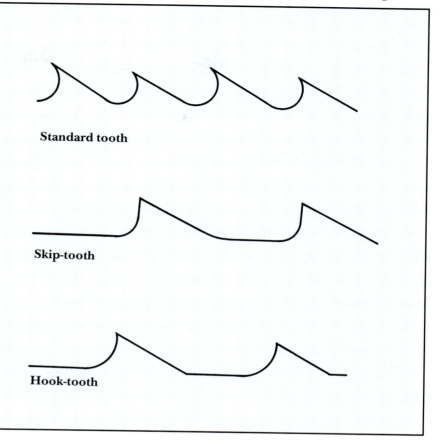

Standard tooth

Skip-tooth

Hook-tooth

The three main types of band-saw blades are the standard or regular blade, which makes smooth cuts but cuts rather slowly; the skip-tooth, an all-purpose blade that works at medium speed; and the fastest of the three, the hook-tooth.

THE JIGSAW

The jigsaw resembles the band saw in that the workpiece is presented to the blade atop a small table (nine inches by seventeen is about average; some brands have larger tables). Curved workpieces can be done on both the jigsaw and band saw, but that's where the resemblance ends.

Also called the power scroll saw, the jigsaw differs in several significant ways from the band saw. For one, the blade is not continuous, but rather is short and straight, cutting in a reciprocating (up-and-down) motion. More important, the jigsaw cuts more slowly than a band saw and with very much less power; it's used to cut quite intricate shapes. Most models have variable speed controls.

As with the band saw, the depth of the throat determines the flexibility of the tool; sixteen inches is a practical size, though models with smaller and larger throats are sold. A depth of cut of an inch and half is common, but one- and two-inch maximums are found on smaller and larger models.

A variety of jigsaw blades are available, with the teeth per inch ranging from as few as seven to twenty-five or more. Most are *jeweler's blades*, which are five inches long, between one-twentieth of an inch and a quarter inch wide. Others are blades designed for use on a saber saw.

BAND-SAW SAFETY

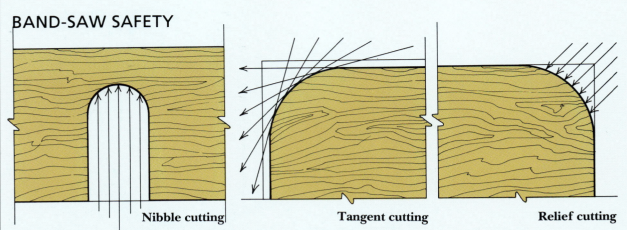

Nibble cutting **Tangent cutting** **Relief cutting**

This is a powerful cutting tool and must be used with proper respect and care.

The Saw Table. Keep it clear of debris, moving waste scraps away from the workpiece. Set the upper saw guide so that it will just clear the workpiece by an eighth to a quarter of an inch. If it stands well above the work, the saw is less likely to make a neat, perpendicular cut; and more blade is left exposed, a potential hazard to the sawyer. Install the blades and make any adjustments with the saw unplugged.

The Blade. If it makes a clicking sound as it saws, turn off the saw immediately. The click probably means that the blade is cracked and may be about to break. Wait for the saw to come to a stop, then replace the blade.

Use blades that are big enough to do the job you are requiring of them. Using small blades for large stock is asking for a broken blade, a dangerous and wasteful practice. Check the tension and tracking of the blade: It should be taut (take care not to overtighten it) and should travel at the center of the wheels.

Don't Go Too Fast . . . Wait for the saw to reach full speed before bringing the workpiece in contact with the blade. Don't feed the stock too fast into the band-saw blade. If you do, the blade will chatter, cutting unevenly. (Don't go too slowly, either, or the blade will tend to burn the workpiece.) There's essentially no risk of kickback, however, as the motion of the blade tends to drive the workpiece against the worktable.

. . . and Don't Push Too Hard. Push too hard, and you'll probably displace the blade to one side or the other, producing an irregular cut. Too much pressure or too much speed will also dull the blade rapidly.

Cutting Curves. Not all curves are cut with the same technique on a band saw. Three different approaches can be applied, depending upon the radii of the curves and whether the cut is inside or outside.

A technique called nibble cutting is used to cut inside radii. A series of cuts are made within the path of the cut, removing much of the waste. Then the band saw can more easily make the arched cut.

For outside curves with large radii, the cutting path can simply be presented to the band saw, and it will cut its way around the curve. For tighter curves, however, making a series of tangent cuts will make the job easier and the result cleaner. Another option is to make a series of cuts perpendicular to the tangents; that approach is called relief cutting.

Protect Yourself. Wear safety glasses or goggles. Oh, yes, there's one last thing: As with any saw, keep your fingers away from the blade when the saw is running. At least six inches away, in fact. And when the sawing produces loose scrap pieces, don't be tempted to use your fingers to remove them. Have a stick or small piece of scrap at hand (a piece the size of a desk ruler is about right) to push the unwanted pieces out of the way.

The jigsaw will cut curves and complex shapes with ease. It's forte is lightweight work, as its thin, fragile blades will break if worked too hard.

Jeweler's blades are fastened at top and bottom in clamps, with the teeth facing forward and pointing down. Saber-saw blades are installed in the lower chuck only, with the point of the blade directed upward.

On most saws, the blade can be turned, so work can be presented to it from the front or the side of the saw. Different blades are designed for different tasks, but one or another will cut just about any wood, metal, or plastic. Some tiny ones are sold, as small as one one-hundredth of an inch thick and only about two one-hundredths wide. They are perfect for delicate marquetry work.

The blade used for a given task must be suited to the material to be cut: Finer-toothed blades are appropriate for metal and hardwoods, coarser blades for softwoods.

The speed at which the saw cycles is another consideration. Slower speeds are best suited to cutting metal, faster ones for softwood. It may seem odd at first, but cutting plastic is done at slower speeds (too much blade speed will actually melt the plastic, allowing it to weld together again after the blade passes through). Hardwood will also heat up if the speed is too fast. Speeds of up to about seven hundred and fifty strokes per minute are regarded as slow, while fifteen hundred or more strokes per minute is fast. Not all models come with variable

The narrower the blade, the tighter the curve that can be cut with a jigsaw. However, since narrower blades also break more easily, use a wider blade for shallower curves. A blade of almost any weight could be used for replicating these Victorian balusters.

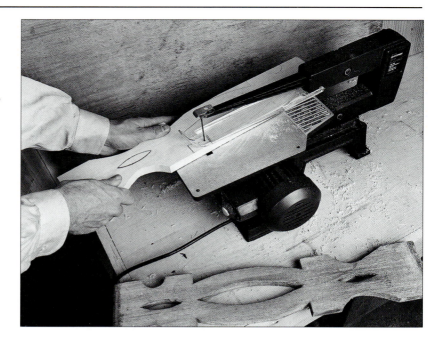

speed controls; on some, as on certain drill presses, the drive belt is shifted from one set of pulleys to another.

The jigsaw also has a holddown device which acts very much like the adjustable foot on a sewing machine, holding the work down (without it, the up-and-down motion of the saw tends to lift the workpiece). The worktable on most models tilts up to forty-five degrees for bevel cuts. Most models have stands available, and some are sold with vacuum attachments and with sawdust blowers to keep the cutting area free of debris.

Cutting Curves with the Jigsaw. This is the jigsaw's forte. Even so, a little thinking ahead will enable the saw to do the best possible job. For complex cuts full of twists and turns, drill turning holes at the tightest corners to enable the blade to make the turn without straining (and possibly breaking) the blade. This will also ensure a more regular cut.

Use the holddown, and feed the stock at a measured pace. The jigsaw doesn't race through wood like a circular saw: Take special care to keep the blade from bending or twisting.

Internal Cuts. These are cuts in which the opening being sawn is entirely within the perimeter of the workpiece. You'll need to cut a hole through the waste area inside the piece, and fit the jigsaw blade through it (after first disconnecting the blade from the upper chuck). An easier method is to use a saber-saw blade. Drill the starter hole first, then lower the piece over the blade.

The tension placed on a jigsaw blade is important to its function. If it's too tight, the blade will break frequently. If it's too loose, you may find that your cuts wander out of square. Experiment on scrap stock to be certain the tension is right for the job at hand.

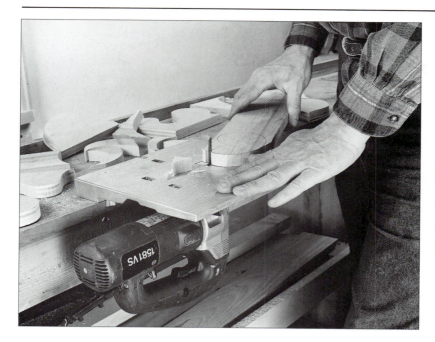

A space-conserving and money-saving option for the small workshop is an adapter table for your saber saw. Many manufacturers of hand-held saber saws sell a table that clamps directly to a bench or other work surface. The saber saw is then mounted, upside down, to the underside of the table, with the blade protruding up through it. The arrangement leaves you with both hands free for guiding the workpiece, producing more accurate work than if you were holding the saber saw in one hand, the workpiece in the other.

THE RADIAL-ARM SAW

There are always ongoing debates within a universe of people who are committed to their work. One such argument among woodworkers pits the radial-armers against the table sawyers.

One side holds that the table saw is the perfect workshop centerpiece. The design is ingenious and it's easy to use and maintain. The table saw rips and crosscuts, and happily divides large sheets of stock into smaller panels. They say the radial-arm saw is difficult to adjust and, unless everything is perfectly aligned, makes cuts that are less than true.

The radial-arm saw contingent argue that their favored tool is much more versatile than the table saw. It's unsurpassed at accurate, easy cut-off work (no doubt that's the reason it's sometimes referred to as a cut-off saw). They say it can sand and plane and, like the table saw, rip long boards at a single pass.

So which is right for your shop? If you can't make up your mind (and you have enough space), maybe you need both.

The radial-arm saw is, in essence, a right-side-up portable circular saw mounted on an adjustable arm (or overarm) that slides the suspended blade over a fixed cutting surface. Blade and motor are connected to the overhead arm by a yoke, which is adjustable along both horizontal and vertical planes, enabling it to swing in any direction. Adjustment is crucial: Follow the instructions in your manual to the letter.

The radial-arm sawblade can be tilted for cutting angles by releasing the bevel lock (usually at the front of the motor housing) and reading the desired angle off a protractor gauge. It will also swivel right and left for mitering, and the blade and motor housing can be turned a full

When setting up your radial-arm saw, cover the table surface with a thin sheet of plywood. Since the blade actually cuts through the plane of the tabletop, the plywood will protect the surface below and is easily (and inexpensively) replaced.

The radial-arm saw calls for careful setup – and attentive use, as it's a powerful and potentially dangerous saw.

ninety degrees to right or left, meaning that the saw can be used to rip boards with the miter clamp releasing the yoke. (For some operations, like ripping, the saw is fixed in place and the stock pushed through the blade.) The motor and blade can also be raised or lowered (via a crank, either on the overhead arm or beneath the cutting surface). The saw will lock into any of these paths for precise work.

Radial-arm saws are identified by the size of the blade for which they are designed. Like many table saws, most radial-arm saws use ten-inch blades. Typically, they cut stock up to three inches thick and will cross-cut pieces more than a foot wide. Radial-arm saws will also take molding and dado heads for cutting molding profiles and rabbets (see page 138).

The fixed worktable over which the radial-arm saw is suspended has a fence at the rear for holding work firmly in place. On some models there are two fences (one set behind the other for ripping work), while others have a single fence but two or more positions at which to locate it.

An ideal position in a workshop for the radial-arm is against a long wall, more or less centered, with extension tables on either side of the saw. The fence should extend along the flanking tables, too.

Blade guards are essential: above and below and, when ripping, with adjustable antikickback fingers in place. Ripping is tricky and, if not done properly, can be dangerous on a radial-arm saw. If you use a molding or dado head, a shaper guard should also be in place. A brake, too, should be in functioning order. Preferably it's automatic

SLIDING CIRCULAR SAWS

This is something of a catchall term, but one I find convenient to describe several different saws that are of related design. The classic Delta sawbuck belongs here, as do the new breed of chop boxes called sliding or "pull-through" miter saws.

The hinged blade assembly on a sliding saw swings down like a paper cutter. What distinguishes it from the miter saw from which it evolved is that a pair of rods also allows it to be drawn toward the operator. This sliding action means you can cut wider stock than with a stand miter saw (some models will cut twelve-inch widths). Most models also tilt and turn, allowing miter and bevel cuts. Saws of the sawbuck school don't swing down, but do slide, tilt, and turn.

These tools are more versatile than the basic miter saw we discussed in *Toolbox*; on the other hand, they don't offer all the options of a radial-arm saw. But for those woodworkers who do a minimum of ripping and don't need to make moldings or do sanding jobs on the cut-off saw, a sliding circular saw may be an economical and portable option. These saws can be stored and moved easily and require a minimum of alignment.

This sliding circular saw was designed for the work-site, with a folding frame and a sturdy, yet lightweight sawtable. But a sawbuck like this one, especially when attached to an extension table, can do cutoff work in the shop as well.

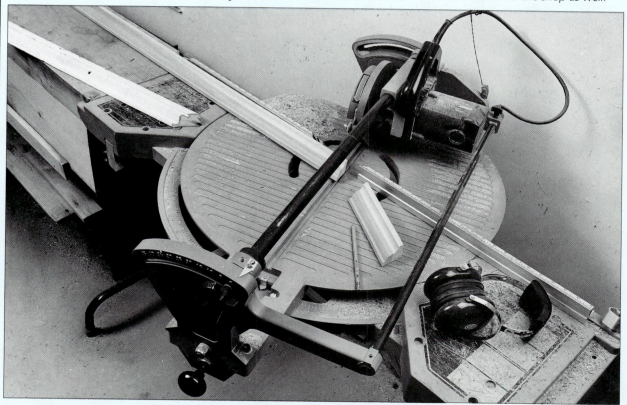

(bringing the blade to a halt the moment the power stops), but at a minimum your saw should have a manual brake that can be engaged when a button is depressed.

Options. The radial-arm saw can also be equipped with optional blades and accessories so that it can function as a drum or disk sander, router, or drill press. Even planer and jointer heads are available for some

SAW
SAFETY

Rules regarding saw safety are many – but there is, of course, very good reason for that. These tools can make carelessness dangerous indeed. So take these guidelines seriously.

Unplug the tool whenever a blade is being changed, repairs are to be made, or the guards are removed.

Always use the guards. Adjust the guards – whether they are shields, splitters, or antikickback fingers to suit the setup.

Don't make even minor adjustments while the saw is running. Turn it off, tune your machine, then start it again. When you have the guards off for blade changes or any other reason, unplug the saw.

Never use a dull sawblade. If the blade tends to pinch or bind or burns the wood, it's dull and should be sharpened or replaced.

Feed the stock *into* the teeth of the spinning blade. If you try to cut in reverse (working from the rear of a table saw, for example, when trying to make a stopped groove), the stock is likely to be turned into a dangerous missile.

Screwdrivers, pliers, sockets, and wrenches (allen, adjustable, and combination) all have many essential tasks in the workshop. Not the least of them is in the setup and adjustment of the stationary saws and other tools.

Keep your fingers in the clear at all times, never closer than four or five inches from any blade.

Wear your safety glasses, goggles, or face shield. If the saw is loud, protect your ears, too.

models. Check your manual or with the manufacturer of your saw to determine what options are available.

Keep in mind that every change from one operation to another (say, from sawing to sanding and back again) requires setup time. The more serious you are about your workshop and the projects you do, the more likely you are to want to acquire specialized tools. Then it's a matter of moving from one station to another, rather than retooling a machine as you shift tasks.

Radial-Arm Saw Safety. Take special care when you use a radial-arm saw. The nature of its design – the sawblade itself moves – makes it trickier than, say, a table or band saw.

Never position your hand in the path of the saw. The tremendous power of this saw can tend to jerk the blade forward when it encounters variations in the wood. The same goes for the area behind the blade, too.

Perhaps it should go without saying but . . . *don't* remove the guards. And always wear safety goggles, since the saw has been known to throw out loose stock at an amazing rate. Ear protection is crucial, too, since, according to the Occupational Health and Safety Administration (OSHA), the biggest radial-arm saws are the loudest tools in the woodworker's shop.

Blade Direction. *Make sure that the sawblade you mount in any circular saw is set to spin in the proper direction. If it isn't, little cutting will get done – and you may be putting yourself as operator in jeopardy.*

Most tools have arrows indicating the direction of spin, but, in general, radial-arm saws spin in such a way that the teeth at the top of the blade turn in the direction of the operator; table-saw blades spin the same way, toward you. On the other hand, a portable circular-saw blade spins so that the bottom of the blade spins away from the operator.

Note that the direction of spin has a significant impact on the workpiece. Tearout occurs on the side from which the teeth emerge, so on radial-arm and table saws the good side should be up; on portable circular saws the finished side should be down.

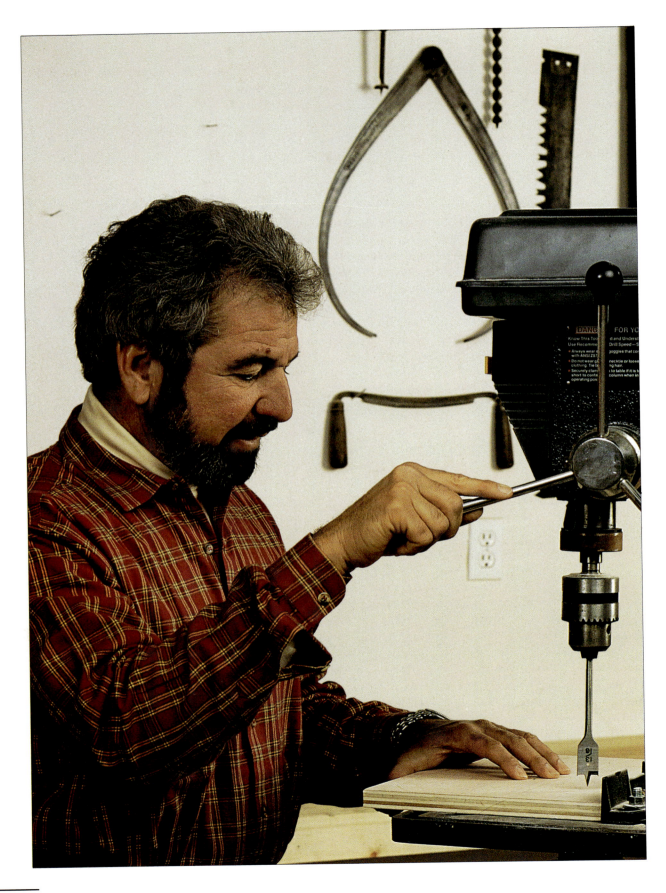

Chapter 9.

Stationary Tools

The table, radial-arm, and band saws are at the heart of many workshops, but once the work begins to get a bit more sophisticated, other powerful stationary tools may begin to seem essential, too. The drill press is easy to use, and instantly makes even the novice capable of drilling holes neat and square to a workpiece. The grinder can mean the difference between sharp and dull tools, a major convenience and an important safety factor. The jointer, surface planer, and shaper all have time-saving roles to play should you get really involved in cabinet or other woodworking labors.

So if you're serious about your workshop, read on.

The drill press makes cutting regular and perfectly aligned holes very easy indeed. And it's a tool that takes a matter of minutes to learn to use.

THE DRILL PRESS

The drill press is a fixed-in-place version of the simple hand drill with a worktable beneath. A hole at the center of the table allows the drill bit to pass cleanly through the workpiece. A drill press can be purchased as a benchtop tool or as a freestanding floor model. For most home workshops, a benchtop model will perform all jobs asked of it at a somewhat lesser cost.

The drill press has significant advantages over the hand-held drill, the principal one being accuracy. Its design means that it will drill at precise angles to the workpiece (usually ninety degrees); and it will drill holes of identical size and depth and position as many times as you wish.

As with a band saw and jigsaw, the flexibility of the tool is determined by the size of the throat, the distance between the supporting column at the rear and the axis on which the spindle of the drill turns. A throat of seven and a half inches is common; such drill presses are referred to as fifteen-inch models because they will cut to the center of a fifteen-inch workpiece.

The depth of cut is determined by the length of the bit, of course, but also by the length of the column. Benchtop models are, obviously, shorter than freestanding presses. Both benchtop and freestanding models have heavy cast-iron bases that can be bolted in place. The worktable slides up (or down) along the column; in the case of the free

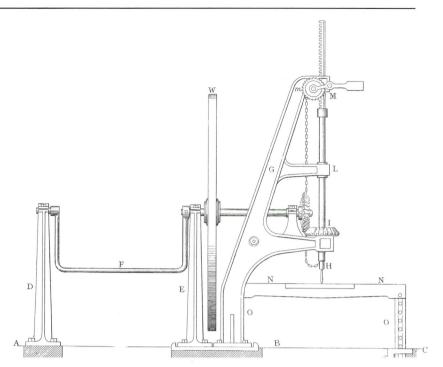

I have to admit, this doesn't much resemble any drill press I've seen in use of late. But then not many tools designed, as this one was, in 1834 have remained unchanged in the intervening century and a half.

standing models, the travel is much greater. Some models are designed so that the worktable can be tilted for drilling angled holes.

Bench drills, as bench-mounted models are often called, are powered by electric motors mounted behind their columns. The motor spins the drill itself, driving it via a system of belts and pulleys or gear wheels, depending upon the model.

At the lower end of the spindle is the chuck, into which the bits are inserted and tightened, just as they are in a hand drill. The spindle itself slides in and out of the head of the drill press in a cylinder called the quill; a hand-powered lever mechanism drives the drill down as it spins; a spring pushes it back up when pressure on the lever is released. Half-inch chucks are usual on home workshop presses, but five-eighths-inch and three-quarter-inch chucks are found on the largest tools.

The throw of the drill is adjustable, depending upon where the depth stop is set. When countersinking screws, for example, setting the depth stop makes the work faster and more accurate.

Horsepower ratings vary depending upon the size of the drill, ranging from as little as one-sixth horsepower to two horsepower or more on the largest presses. However, it is the variability of the speed at which the drill is driven that determines the versatility of a particular drill press. As with other cutting tools, slower speeds are suited to cutting metals, higher ones to wood. Exceptions are large-diameter drill bits or attachments like a circle-and-hole cutter, which should be used at slower speeds.

Attachments. There's a remarkable range of drills available to cut circular holes, including spade, brad point, twist, extension, and

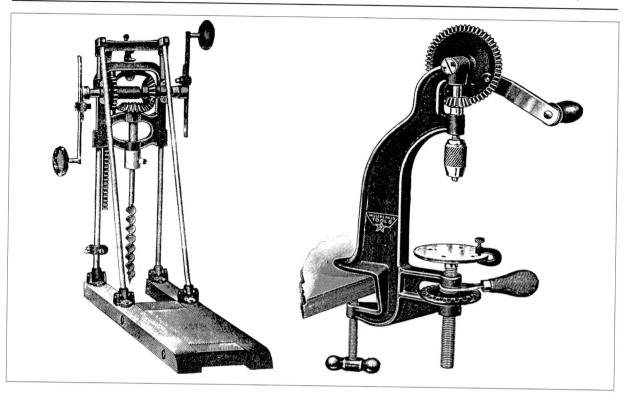

Forstner drills. And there are plug cutters, too. Router bits can also be fitted to a drill press, although the rotation speed of most drill presses isn't fast enough to make good, clean router cuts. Rotary rasps, dovetail groovers, and even a mortising attachment can be used (see *Making a Mortise and Tenon Joint*, page 192).

Two muscle-powered ancestors of the drill press, the boring machine (left) and a tool then known as a "bench drill press."

A drum sander bit can be a very useful attachment for your drill press, making it ideal for sanding the inside curves of arcs and other irregularly shaped pieces. You will need to fabricate a very simple jig, namely, a tabletop (it can be made of three-quarter-inch plywood) with a hole cut in it slightly larger than the diameter of the sander drum. Then the sander bit is set into it.

OPERATING A DRILL PRESS

The controls vary from one drill press to the next, but there are a number of elements that remain largely the same.

Read and follow the instructions provided by the manufacturer of your drill press. The drill should be unplugged while you are setting it up for use.

Set the Speed. The speed on most drill presses is adjusted by moving the drive belt from one pulley to another. In general, the smaller the pulley on the chuck axis, the faster it spins. A rule of thumb, as with any cutting operation, is that slower speeds are better for drilling metal, faster speeds for wood. Again, consult your manual for the manufacturer's recommendations.

Fit the Bit. Open the chuck, slide in the bit, snug the chuck by hand around the bit's shaft, then tighten the chuck's three jaws with the key. Make sure to remove the chuck . . . if you don't, it'll become a dangerous projectile when you turn on the drill. When drilling large holes, drill a smaller, pilot hole first.

Adjust the Table. Some models have a crank that adjusts the table height, others move freely once the clamping lever has been released. Set the table to the desired height for the operation you are to perform.

Gauging the Depth. If you are simply drilling a hole in a piece of stock, you may not need to adjust the depth gauge, the threaded rod that controls the distance the spindle travels. However, if you are concerned with a stopped hole of a fixed depth, lower the bit to the desired height, and adjust the pair of knurled nuts on the depth gauge to the proper stopping point. One of them should stop the spindle; the other locks the first nut in place.

Secure the Workpiece. Before operating your drill press, be sure that the workpiece to be drilled is fixed in place. The rotation of the drill bit may try to spin the wood or metal workpiece, so it must be clamped to the worktable, braced against the supporting column at the rear of the machine, or otherwise secured. *Never* operate the tool without firmly anchoring the workpiece.

Drilling. Once the drill press setup has been completed, putting it to work is easy. Make sure the drill is spinning at full speed, then present the bit to the workpiece, lowering the bit by swinging the rotating lever. Once you've finished drilling the hole, release the pressure on the lever and its spring-loaded return mechanism will return it to its original position.

A circle-and-hole cutter allows good-sized holes to be cut quite easily – and the investment in one bit allows you to cut a great variety of sizes.

Make sure the workpiece is clamped firmly in place and remember to slow down the speed of the drill when using a circle-and-hole cutter. (Using this bit on a hand drill, by the way, is a very tricky proposition. If you have the option, use the drill press instead.)

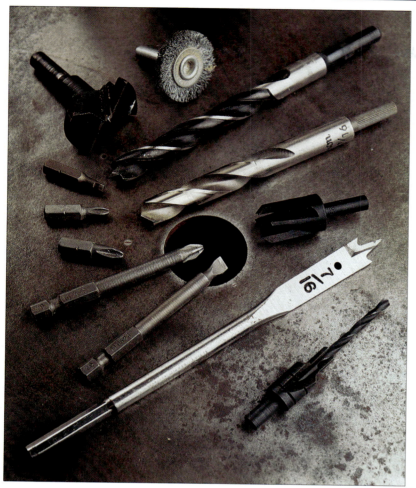

There's a Forstner bit (left, rear) and (moving clockwise) a small wire-brush wheel, a brad-point bit, a twist drill, a plug cutter, a seven-sixteenths spade bit, a countersink set, and a range of drivers. All can be used in either hand drills or drill presses; the most accurate and controlled cuts, however, are produced with the press.

THE BENCH GRINDER

The bench grinder is to the workshop as the trainer is to the team. It doesn't run out on the field when a tool goes down, of course, but if it weren't for the grinder in my shop, there would be a lot more dull tools (and probably more injuries).

The bench grinder isn't very expensive, is roughly the size of the box in which a pair of work boots arrive from the shoe store, and requires only to be secured firmly to a workbench or other mount. It'll grind smooth the rough cutting edge on wood and cold chisels, plane irons, drill bits, scissors, and knives; it'll repair screwdrivers and punches, and can be used for smoothing welded joints or other imperfections, and even grinding off rivets. With a buffer wheel or wire wheel, it also cleans and polishes many different tools and objects.

The bench grinder has two grinding wheels, one on either side of the motor housing. Most of each wheel is covered by a guard, but roughly a ninety-degree arc of each wheel's perimeter is exposed at the front of the grinder. An eye shield is mounted above the opening in the guard; below is a tool rest.

The bench grinder is relatively inexpensive – yet invaluable in the workshop. This model has a well for cooling oil at front, and two grinding wheels, with matching lights, guards, and tool rests.

Most home workshops will never need a high-powered, heavy-duty grinder. One powered by a one-quarter to one-half horsepower motor is probably adequate, with half-inch or inch-wide wheels of five or six inches in diameter. Larger grinders, with more powerful motors and wheels eight inches or more in diameter are also available. Typically, the speed at which the wheels rotate is between 3,000 and 3,600 revolutions per minute.

Grinding Wheels. A wide variety of wheels is available. They are man-made stones of grit bonded together at high temperatures. The abrasive varies depending upon the use to which the grinder is to be put. Vitrified aluminum oxide wheels are best suited for grinding steel; silicon carbide (white quartz sand) is best for cast iron, as well as brass, aluminum, or copper and other nonferrous materials.

The abrasive particles, or grit, do the work of the grinding wheel. They act like countless minute knives that cut away tiny pieces of the metal being ground. As the individual particles of grit become dull, they break off, exposing new, sharp particles that continue the work.

The usual arrangement is to mount one wheel that is coarser than the other, typically, wheels in the midrange, say one medium-coarse, one medium-fine. Coarse stones are used for rough shaping or for removing deep nicks in a blade. Finer gritstones suit sharpening or honing tasks.

Since grinding wheels are easily broken or cracked, set up your grinder in a quiet corner of your shop where it's less likely to get banged or whacked by incoming materials or workpieces in motion.

Take the precaution of checking the wheels, as well, by doing a wheel test periodically. Tap the wheel with a rubber-faced mallet or a wooden screwdriver handle. Listen for a ringing sound when you strike it about midway between its outside edge and the mounting hole at center. A ring means that the wheel is sound; a dull thud means you must replace it. Do not use the wheel if it's cracked, because it might shatter.

Remember, too, that as handy as a bench grinder is, it isn't the whole story as far as sharpening is concerned. Final honing is always best done by hand, probably on a naturally occurring stone like Arkansas (see *Some Sharpening Shortcuts*, page 164).

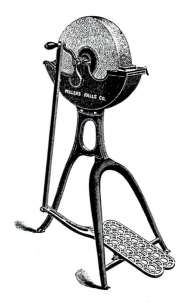

SHARPENING A SPADE BIT

Spade bits, it seems, are always encountering nails, at least in the kinds of rough drilling chores that renovation work involves. But they are among the easiest of cutting tools to sharpen.

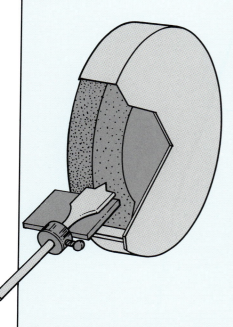

Set the tool rest on your bench grinder eight degrees down from horizontal (that is to say, eight degrees past three o'clock, when looking at the end of the grinding wheel).

Position the bit with one of its shoulders flush to the wheel. *Before* starting the grinder, tighten a stop collar on the shaft of the drill about a sixty-fourth of an inch from the edge of the tool rest. Now, start the machine and grind the edge until the stop collar prevents further grinding; turn the bit over, line up the cutting lip on the opposite shoulder, and repeat. The stop collar will assure that the bit is ground symmetrically.

To sharpen the tip or "spur," swing the bit diagonally to the wheel, and align the cutting edge parallel to the surface of the wheel. Go to the other diagonal to grind the other side.

Grindstones are flat circular stones, often made of sandstone. Usually suspended from a spindle mounted in a frame, the stone was turned, usually by means of a crank, treadle, or, as in this case, a combination of both. In most cases, the lower portion of the wheel was set into a water trough. Grindstones have certainly been in use since the Renaissance, and possibly were first employed by the Romans. But, sad to say, they don't do the job anywhere near as well as a bench grinder.

BASIC GRINDING 101

I've never seen the guy so angry: His wife used a favorite chisel to open a paint can and my friend Dominick took it personally. The big nick in the edge of that chisel was, well, just about criminal in his eyes.

Ordinarily, a chisel or plane iron needs little more than an occasional honing on a water- or oilstone – unless, of course, it's been abused. A nick or other significant imperfection in its edge as the result of an encounter with a nail (or a paint can) or another tool will mean a more difficult sharpening job. The bench grinder is the tool of choice for such tasks.

One advantage the grinding wheel has is speed: It's quicker than using a coarse whetstone. Another is its shape: The tiny arc the wheel grinds into the tool is a hollow-grind, which means that the tool is likely to retain its sharpness for many honings.

To return a tool to usability, three steps are required to sharpen a chisel or a plane iron.

1. Square the Cutting Edge. Set the tool rest so that its top surface points directly along the radius of the wheel. The front edge of the rest should be approximately an eighth of an inch from the wheel. Put on your eye protection, start the machine, and, when it's up to speed, gently but firmly slide the chisel back and forth across the wheel.

2. Grind the Bevel. Matching the original angle ground onto the edge is essential (note that the angle varies from tool to tool). One way to transfer the angle from the tool to the grinder is by using a bevel gauge to set the tool rest to the right angle. Another option is to use a grinding attachment that is set at the proper angle.

Now, with goggles on and your machine at full speed, move the blade back and forth across the wheel. Do it *gently*. And don't forget to bathe the tip of the tool in a water or oil bath. A blade that has been allowed to get blue hot loses its "temper," namely, the hardness or resiliency of its manufacture. In practice, the loss of temper means the tools will not hold a sharp edge, dulling quickly with minimal use. So dip the blade frequently in a water or machine oil bath while grinding.

3. Hone the Tool. Now that the shape of the tool has been restored, hone it on a oil- or waterstone (see *Some Sharpening Shortcuts*, page 164, and *Keeping Your Chisels Sharp* in *Bob Vila's Toolbox*, page 112).

Squaring a Driver Edge. A chipped or rough-edged screwdriver is easily sharpened on a bench grinder. The steps are the reverse of those for a chisel.

Hold the bevel of the chisel to the wheel, and slide it from side to side as the wheel revolves. Be sure to cool the blade frequently so as not to rob it of its temper.

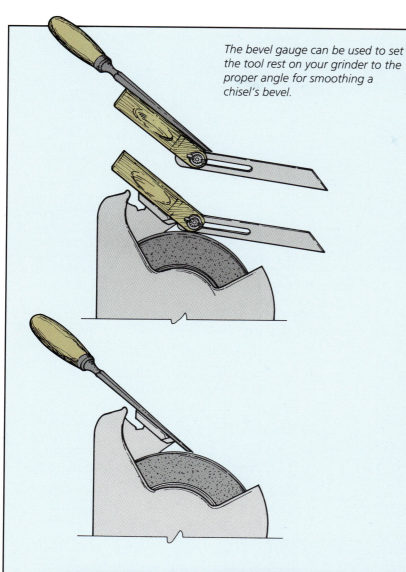

The bevel gauge can be used to set the tool rest on your grinder to the proper angle for smoothing a chisel's bevel.

Start by grinding the broad, flat edges of the driver tip, holding the shaft of the driver so that it is tangential to the blade. This grinds a slight convex curve into the tool (again, a "hollow grind"). After hollow grinding, reset the tool rest so that the shaft of the tool points at the center of the wheel. Grind the tip square, gently but firmly sliding the tip back and forth across the flat edge of the wheel.

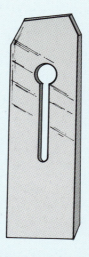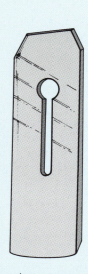

When grinding plane irons, most should be sharpened flat, square to the face of the iron. For a plane that is to be used for rough smoothing, however, a slightly rounded blade will be less likely to dig in at the corners, gouging the workpiece.

The bench grinder can be used to sharpen dulled or broken screwdrivers. Make sure you hold the shaft aligned with the radius of the wheel; otherwise, the tip will not be ground square.

THE THREE Gs OF GRINDING

In talking grinding, there are three key words that will help you get what you want.

Grit. Wheels consist of bonded abrasives, particles called "grit."

Grain Size. The "grain size" of that grit identifies whether the wheel is coarse, medium, fine, or some gradation in between. The larger the grain, the coarser the wheel.

Grade. The hardness of the bond between the grains of grit determines the hardness of the wheel. Hard wheels are used for grinding soft materials, and soft wheels for harder materials.

SOME SHARPENING SHORTCUTS

I've said it before, and I'm a little tired of saying it, not to mention hearing it. But, still, the old saw bears repeating: Sharp tools are safer tools. So here are a couple of hints for keeping your cutting tools sharp.

Use a Honing Guide. No, in truth, if you have a steady hand you don't have to have one. But a honing guide assures that the bevel on your chisel or plane iron is maintained at a constant angle to the stone – and saves you the time and trouble of worrying about the pitch with every stroke. Set it once, and hone to your heart's content.

Invest in a Natural Stone. The man-made stones are less expensive, but the natural stones have some significant advantages. Natural stone is better for honing a fine edge, because of the density of its stone and the fineness of the grit. (Ironically, man-made stones are actually harder, but I guess that's just one of life's little surprises.) Arkansas stones (that's right, abrasive stones mined in the home state of our forty-second president) are the favorite of many in the honing and sharpening crowd. An Arkansas or any other natural stone won't make you a honing expert, but it won't hurt either.

A Refresher Course in Sharpening. Position the chisel, plane iron, or other edge so that the bevel is flat to the stone. Use both hands to steady the chisel (even if it's mounted in a honing guide), and slide it backwards and forwards on the surface of the stone. Be careful to maintain the proper angle to the stone at all times. Vary the area you cover as you hone, perhaps even zigzagging slightly, in order to prevent uneven wear on the surface of the stone.

There's still no substitute for a good sharpening stone and an able pair of hands when it comes to honing a chisel.

THE JOINTER

The very name speaks to the nature of this tool. If you aspire to be a joiner, a person who specializes in fastening pieces of wood in tight, precisely shaped joints, then the jointer probably has a place in your shop. If your workshop will be used to work metal or do miscellaneous fix-it jobs, then this imposing power tool would probably be a waste of space and money.

Often called the jointer/planer, it's used to plane the edges, faces, and ends of boards or panels. In fact, the jointer essentially is a powered, stationary version of a bench plane, but is faster, more flexible, and very accurate when properly set up. Jointers can be used to bevel and taper stock, and some models will also cut rabbets and tenons. In

Perform the whetting process first on a medium surface; then, repeat on a fine surface.

Making a Microbevel. The sharpest of chisels actually has two bevels, the second one cut at the tip of the blade at an angle about five degrees steeper than the first. Just a few strokes on the finest stone are required at a pitch just lightly steeper than the initial sharpening.

Flattening the Burr. The sharpening of the bevel (and the microbevel) will produce a burr, a tiny ridge that extends out from the tip at the back of the chisel. You can feel it with your thumb, stroking along the length of the back of the blade (be sure to stroke *away* from the handle).

To remove the burr, turn the chisel onto its back (bevel side up) and hold it flush to the surface of the fine stone. Rub the blade in a circular motion on the stone's surface; be careful to keep the chisel's back flat on the stone.

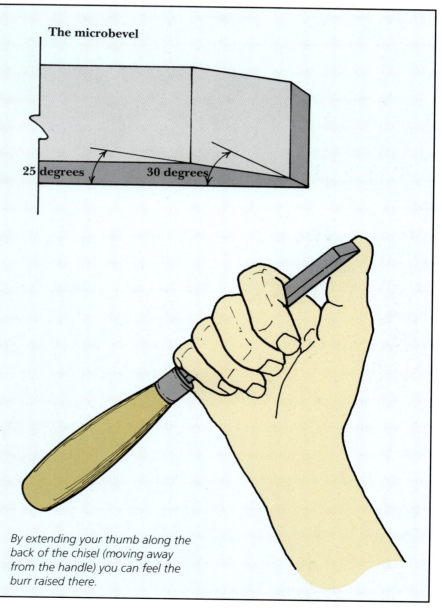

The microbevel

25 degrees   30 degrees

By extending your thumb along the back of the chisel (moving away from the handle) you can feel the burr raised there.

The jointer squares edges precisely and quickly. But use it with care: When edge-planing pieces less than six inches wide, use push blocks like those pictured in the foreground.

shops with limited space, a quality jointer can do the job of the surface planer, too.

The jointer consists of a worktable through which the revolving blade (called the cutterhead) of the tool protrudes. A motor, via pulleys and a belt, drives the cutterhead from below. The cutterhead has two or three knives attached to it with set screws. The width of the knives determines the size of the jointer. Four- and six-inch sizes are usual in home workshops, though machines up to twenty-four inches are to be found in industry. Midsize planers have power ratings in the three-quarters to two horsepower range.

The design of the jointer's worktable distinguishes this machine from others in the workshop. Rather than having a single, level tabletop like a table saw or band saw, the jointer table has two separate work surfaces, one on each side of the cutterhead. The left-hand surface is called the outfeed table or bed, the right the infeed table.

In setting up the jointer/planer, the blade height is adjusted so that its highest point is precisely the same as the outfeed table to the left. The offset between the infeed table and the top of the blade determines the depth of the cut the jointer will make, typically between a thirty-second and an eighth of an inch. Cutting more than an eighth of an inch is likely to produce kickback, especially if the wood has knots.

For end or edge cuts, limit the cut to a sixteenth of an inch.

An adjustable fence rests at the back of the table. A blade guard covers the cutterhead but shifts aside as the workpiece is passed over it.

The worktable on a jointer needn't be large, but keep in mind when deciding which model to buy that the larger it is, the more stable will be the workpiece being shaped.

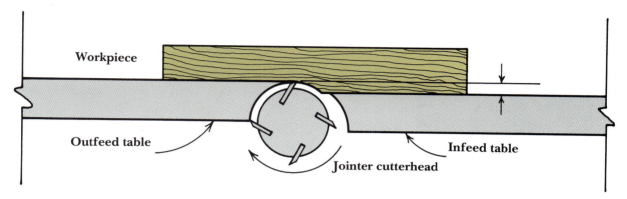

Using the Jointer. Whatever the cut you are making, apply pressure against the piece in three directions: one, down onto the table; two, against the fence; and three, right to left, in the direction of the cut.

The rate at which the workpiece is fed to the cutter is critical. Too much pressure increases the risk of kickback, as well as producing uneven cuts. Working at too slow a rate may result in burn marks on the wood.

To edge-plane a piece (the operation is sometimes called jointing), the stock is fed through on its edge, with one of the faces of the piece held flush to the fence. Use a pusher unless the stock is six inches or wider. Again, don't try to remove more than an eighth of an inch from the stock at a pass.

Inspect the edge after the first pass: If the grain has chipped, you were probably planing against the grain. Reverse the board and feed it again. When the fence is set at an angle other than ninety degrees for beveling edges, the operation is much the same as jointing.

To surface the face of a workpiece, feed it through with an edge flush to the fence, the face flat to the worktable. Use push blocks or a push stick, keeping your hands clear of the cutterhead at all times. Inspect the piece after planing. Again, if the grain has chipped, you were probably planing against the grain. Reverse the piece and plane again.

To plane end grain, present the workpiece as you would for jointing an edge. However, when planing end grain, lift the piece straight off the table after you've planed no more than two inches. Then reverse the piece, front to back, and plane the full end grain. This procedure will avoid chipping the end grain.

Some jointers will also cut rabbets. Those models have an adjustable ledge at the front of the infeed table. It is set to the appropriate height, and the fence is moved forward so that the exposed cutterhead is the width of the rabbet to be cut.

The depth of cut the jointer makes is the difference between the height of the infeed and outfeed tables.

Jointer Safety. This is a powerful tool, one that has seriously injured many experienced woodworkers. Respect the raw power of these blades by using push blocks or a push stick, especially when shaving pieces shorter than eighteen inches, to propel the workpiece across the cutterhead. Push blocks or shoes are positioned on top of the workpiece to hold it firmly atop the blade, and the push stick drives from the rear.

Don't try to machine workpieces twelve inches or less; it's just too dangerous. Plan ahead and try, if possible, to surface stock as longer, wider pieces. Then rip or cut them to the desired sizes.

Don't stand behind the machine or in the line of the cut but to one side or the other of the cutterhead. Hold the stock tight to the fence. Don't remove the guard.

Again, don't try to plane more than an eighth of an inch from a workpiece in a single pass. If more stock needs to be removed, do it in two or more passes.

THE THICKNESS PLANER

The thickness planer at work, smoothing a wide pine board. The crank on the right adjusts the depth of the cut; the machine powers the wood past the cutter at its own pace.

The planer is a tool for woodworkers who require large quantities of planed stock and who elect to buy it rough cut. A couple of trips through a planer and smooth, surface-planed stock emerges, often at a fraction of the cost of the milled boards sold at your neighborhood lumberyard. This tool is also known as a surface planer.

(Note, however, that in order to plane rough-cut stock successfully, the board must have one true face. If neither face is true, a jointer/planer can be used to smooth one face, then the other side can be planed parallel to the first on the thickness planer.)

The freestanding planer is a near relation of the jointer/planer. It, too, cuts with a cutterhead, but the planer smooths the face of much wider stock. Benchtop models will plane twelve-inch-wide stock, but some freestanding models will plane pieces with widths of thirty-six inches or more. The size of the machine is determined by the thickness of the stock it will plane. Most twelve-inch planers will plane stock up to six inches thick; eighteen-inch planers take nine-inch-thick stock. Planers of these sizes typically have between one and a half and three horsepower.

The cutting is done from above rather than from below. The workpiece is presented to the machine by hand, with one face against the feed bed. A pair of rollers, one at the front and one at the machine's rear, then power the stock through the machine at a constant rate. Between the rollers is a cutterhead with several knives affixed. The knives do the actual planing, assisted by a pair of bars that rest on the stock as it travels through the planer.

The first bar is called a chip breaker, and it helps prevent the grain from tearing out. The second, called the pressure bar, keeps the stock

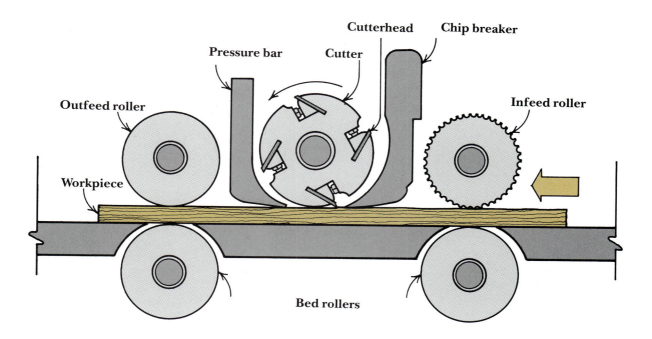

flush to the feed bed. The design of the machine – with the cutterhead contained entirely within the housing of the machine – means that, unlike the jointer/planer, with which this machine shares many design elements, the surface planer is relatively safe to use.

Surfacing the Surface. The planer must be set to suit the stock to be planed. The feed bed is adjusted to the proper height, so that no more than about a sixteenth of an inch is planed in any one pass. Most machines have a feed control wheel that adjusts the speed at which the stock glides past the cutterhead.

When setting up the planer, be sure to measure the thickness of the stock at the corners and at the piece's midpoint. Set the planer to surface the stock at one sixteenth less than the maximum thickness.

If the stock tapers, lead with the thinnest end. As you feed the stock in, stand to one side. Support the stock so its weight doesn't lever its top surface into the cutterhead. Once the planer has planed about half the length of the piece, go to the other side of the machine and support it there. Or, better yet, have a helper stationed to receive it as it emerges.

When planing thin stock, use a carrier board to deliver the workpiece at a height adequate for the cutters to reach its surface.

Some surface planers can also be used to cut moldings. In place of the standard cutters, molding knives are mounted on the cutterhead. Planer/molders, however, tend to be a good deal more expensive than surface planers.

Again, keep in mind that if you're planing to surface rough-cut stock (boards that haven't been planed smooth, but have the toothy surface left by the big blades at the mill), you must be sure they have one true surface (or make one true with a jointer) before surface planing.

If you're planing thin stock (wood less than three-eighths of an inch thick), you will need to use a carrier board. A piece of three-quarter-inch plywood will do; make it the width of the planer and slightly longer than the stock to be trimmed. Compensate for the added three-quarters of an inch when setting the height, and feed the carrier board and the workpiece together. Be sure to set the carrier board aside for future use.

Most planers won't take stock less than twelve inches long (the distance between the rollers). If you need to plane shorter pieces, follow up the shorter one with a piece of scrap of the same thickness that's twelve inches or longer. It'll push the short one through.

Today's portable models certainly have advantages over this early nineteenth-century planer. On the other hand, those early thickness planers revolutionized woodworking, house building, and just about every other trade that used wood as a raw material. These powerful machines made smoothly planed wood a commercial product, rather than the end result of a laborious handwork process.

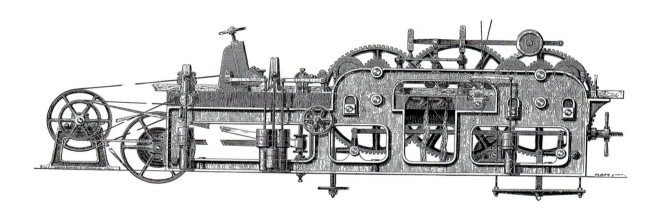

THE SHAPER

For those woodworkers for whom a molded edge, a contoured decorative curve, is the difference between a proper job and an unfinished appearance, the shaper can be an invaluable tool. A shaper not only cuts ornamental edges on straight stock for drawer fronts, picture frames, and panels, but also edges curved stock.

Not everyone needs a shaper, since a variety of other tools can perform shaping tasks, including the router, a wide variety of hand planes, and molding heads mounted on table or radial-arm saws. However, the higher speed of the shaper produces smoother cuts than a molding head and the shaper takes less setup time than adapting other power tools.

The shaper consists of a worktable with a fence at the rear. Protruding vertically through the tabletop is the motor-driven shaft, or spindle, onto which blades are fastened. The workpiece is presented to the

The shaper makes molded edges (like those on this cherry drawer front) as easy as a series of simple passes past the cutterhead.

The Small-Piece Syndrome. *Plan ahead in order to avoid the need to use table saws, jointers, and shapers on small pieces of stock (shorter than, say, a foot in length) or, in the case of the jointer, thinner than a half inch). The smaller the piece, the closer your fingers are to the blades.*

spinning blade, which cuts the stock to match the shape of the blade. Freehand work is done with the fence removed.

The shaper is, in a sense, an upside-down router that is permanently set into a frame. The shaper cutters produce results very similar to the router's. For certain kinds of work, however, the stationary nature of the shaper is preferred; for others, the portability of the router is a distinct advantage (see *The Router,* page 107).

The spindle on most workshop shapers is a half inch in diameter. The spindle's height is adjustable, as is the fence. The cutter is slid over the threaded spindle and fastened with a washer and two nuts. Shaper cutters are not interchangeable with router bits, which are mounted on shafts and gripped by a collet chuck. Like the guide or pilot tip on router bits, a collar can be placed over the cutter on a shaper. This establishes a limit on the amount of stock removed.

There are two basic configurations for cutters. One is a solid piece of steel, usually with three cutting surfaces or wings that extend out from the center of the cutter. The other type is an assembled cutter, which consists of pairs of separate, straight cutters that are fastened to a head that, in turn, is bolted to the spindle. They are more difficult to adjust than the solid cutters.

Shapers are sold with motors between a half and a full horsepower, or even more in some cases. You'll want a spindle speed in the range of about ten thousand revolutions per minute. A shaper that is reversible adds convenience: At the flick of switch, the rotation of the cutter can be reversed, allowing the workpiece to be fed from either side of the machine.

For shaping end grain, a sliding fence, similar to the bevel gauge on a table saw, is used to push the end of the workpiece into the cutterhead. The gauge slides within a groove cast into the tabletop.

For curved or irregularly shaped pieces, special jigs can be made to guide the cut. Another option for ovals or unusual curved shapes uses a collar around the shaper. This serves as a bearing surface, usually against the upper edge of the workpiece. It should have a minimum of a quarter inch of contact with the top edge of the stock.

With the fence removed, a pin (or pair of pins) is set into the tabletop to help start the irregular cut. The workpiece is pushed against the pin before any portion of it is brought into contact with the cutters. Turn the piece gently into the cutters, with the piece still firmly against the pin to protect against kickback. Once the cutters are cutting freely, you can work away from the pin (if you wish); a second pin is often helpful for completing the cut when the workpiece is drawn away from the cutters.

Using the Shaper. Because some or all of a shaper's cutters are exposed, this tool poses a great potential danger to fingers and hands carelessly placed too close to the speeding blades. Put the shaper to work with all due care, keeping whatever guards the machine has in place and using pushers and holddowns. Most shapers have a ring guard atop the spindle that suspends a guard in front of the spinning cutter.

In order to shape the side edge of a straight piece of stock, the workpiece is presented to the cutters with the rotation of the blade driving into the end grain of the workpiece, tending to push it into the fence. Typically, that means that the cutter will spin counterclockwise, when looked at from above, so the stock will come from the right. Straight workpieces are held flush to the fence, ensuring the stability of the piece and that the shape is cut straight.

Freestanding and benchtop shapers are sold. The benchtop models are considerably less expensive, they require a great deal less space, *and* they perform the same basic tasks. However, freestanding models have more power and larger tables that make it easier to keep the work stable.

SHAPER SAFETY

When the shaper is not used with proper care, it can be a very dangerous tool. Respect the power of its rapidly revolving cutter, taking especial care not only to keep your fingers and hands a safe distance from it, but also to present workpieces to it properly.

Setup. Make sure the knives and cutters are fastened correctly. Before starting the motor, position a piece of scrap adjacent to the cutters, checking to see that the shaper will cut the profile you want. If you are using a cutter with a guide collar on top, make sure that some stock (preferably a quarter inch or more) will remain at the level of the collar to guide the workpiece.

Shaping Stock. Present the work so that the rotation of the blade is spinning into the wood; if you were foolish enough to do the reverse, the shaper might well jerk the piece out of your hands, send it for a dangerous ride across the room, and, worse yet, pull your hands into the cutter in the process.

Stand out of the path of the piece; standing behind it puts you at risk in the event of kickback.

Use pushers, holddowns, and the ring guard.

Instead of shaping small pieces of stock, shape a longer, more easily (and more safely) managed workpiece. Cut it to the length or shape you want *after* you have finished shaping its edge.

Don't try to shape badly warped or heavily knotted stock.

Don't get greedy and make extremely deep cuts. Make two passes or more instead of one, removing a portion of the waste at a time. Don't attempt to remove more than a quarter of an inch at a pass.

HAND-HELD POWER TOOLS

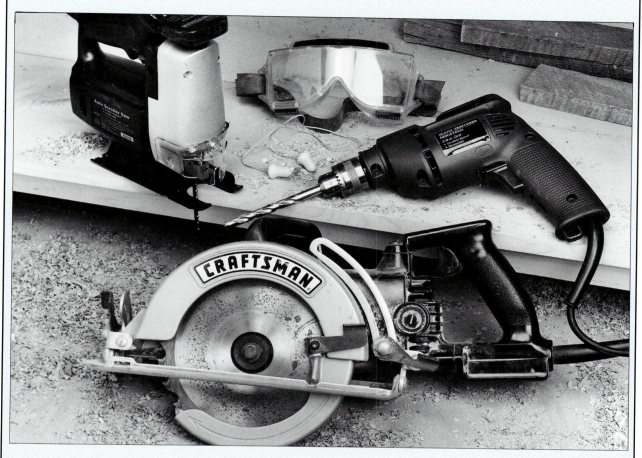

Drill. The electric drill is an indispensable tool, together with a range of drill bits. A high-quality, three-eighths-inch drill that has variable speed control and is reversible will very quickly pay for itself in labor saved.

Portable Circular Saw. Even if your workshop has a radial-arm saw, a table saw, and a band saw – and especially if it doesn't – a portable circular saw will earn its keep. A sturdy seven-and-a-quarter-inch portable saw is a must in almost every workshop or tool chest.

Saber Saw. A saber saw is handy, too, even in the presence of a stationary jigsaw. It'll make plunge cuts, and can go lots of places to a workpiece (rather than having the workpiece brought to it).

Old reliables like the hand-held circular saw, drill, and saber saw have almost as many uses in the workshop as at the work-site.

PART V.

CONTENTS

FASTENING AND FINISHING TOOLS

The parts have been marked and measured. With small tools or large, they have been cut and shaped. Now it's time to fit and fasten them together, in ways that suit the demands to which the products of your workshop are to be put.

Thus, in Chapter 10, we will talk of joints and clamps and glues. Next comes another painstaking process, the finishing of the work. The tools for sanding and then for painting or applying other finishes are our subject in Chapter 11. Last, but hardly least, comes the time to put the tools away: Our business in Chapter 12 is proper storage of tools for reasons of safety, security, and ease of access.

The finish work can enhance – or obscure – all the hard work that came before. Invest the time required . . . it will be worth it.

Chapter 10.

Fastening Tools

Nails are the right answer to lots of fastening questions. Certainly, when building a wood-frame house, nails are generally the most efficient and economic fastener. Wood screws and bolts of various kinds have a multitude of uses, too, in and around the house.

Yet in the workshop, especially when the emphasis is on furniture or cabinet work, simple fasteners like the nail and screw often aren't sophisticated enough. Nor are glues or adhesives sufficient. More often, joints shaped from an object's integral parts, such as dovetail or mortise-and-tenon joints, distinguish the well-made finished product from inferior work. Such joints are also the reason why, for generations, people who made objects from wood were known as joiners: The joints were all-important.

In this chapter, the time has come to assemble the pieces that have been laid out, cut, and shaped with the tools discussed earlier. This means talking about shaped joints and other options as well, some of which utilize tools like the jointer, the "biscuit" or plate joiner, and jigs like the one for doweling. There will be lots of talk about clamps, too, as we did little more than introduce them in *Toolbox;* in this book, we'll describe some new ones (including the lever cam clamp and corner clamps, for example) and really put them to use.

Clamps, glues, air-powered tools, the plate joiner, and the dovetail jig all have advantages in certain applications over simple nails and screws.

THE DOWELING JIG

A convenient method of joining boards is a dowel joint. Especially useful when two or more boards are being joined (butted) on the same plane (as for a tabletop, for example), dowel joints are strong and relatively easy to align, drill, and glue.

A purpose-made tool called a doweling jig will guide a drill in making perpendicular holes in the edge, end, or face of a board. With a good jig, the challenge of layout and proper alignment is met with ease.

A variety of doweling jigs are produced by tool manufacturers; you also can accomplish the same result by using a piece of wood with nails or sharp metal pins positioned in its end. Since the hole centers must be located exactly, and the holes should be cut precisely at a ninety-degree angle to the edge of the stock, homemade doweling jigs may not produce the accurate result you desire.

WOOD JOINTS

The language of the joiner is filled with words that we know well from ordinary usage but here have new and distinct meanings: Lap, edge, butt, and finger joints are technical terms to woodworkers. Joinery jargon gets still more complicated when you add in some other kinds of joints, like mortise-and-tenon, tongue-and-groove, dovetail, dowel, dado, spline, and rabbet. Not to mention such combination joints as cross laps, dado rabbets, dovetail laps, and keyed miters.

Yet this is, to say the least, a rather incomplete list of wood joints. With the introduction of the biscuit or plate joiner, any number of these joints are strengthened or varied thanks to the presence of the little, football-shaped wafers (see *The Plate Joiner,* page 185).

Don't be intimidated by all these possibilities. Try thinking of them as an embarrassment of riches. Pretty soon you will find that it's fun to figure out which will work best for a given project or a particular application.

If you are just making your first foray into the land of the joiners, you'd probably do best to start with a simple joint like a dado or a rabbet. (If you've ever made anything, you've almost certainly made a butt joint already.) A picture frame typically uses a miter joint, so perhaps you've done that, or would like to try.

So here they are, the basic kinds of wood joints, in something approaching simplest-to-hardest order.

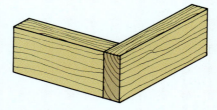

Butt Joint. When you join two squared-off pieces of wood, you've made a butt joint, whether the workpieces are joined edge to edge, face to face, edge to face, or at a corner. A butt joint is the simplest to make, requiring little shaping beyond cuts made to trim the workpiece to size. As with all joints, however, the surfaces to be joined must fit together tightly; if they don't, a block plane may be used to smooth the end grain. Glues, nails, screws, dowels, and other fasteners may be used to secure a butt joint.

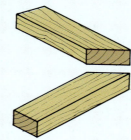

Miter Joint. As you know from the miter box and the miter gauge on your table saw, a miter cut is basically an angle cut (though if you consult your dictionary, you'll get told something like, "A miter is an oblique surface shaped on a piece of wood or other material so as to butt against an oblique surface on another piece to be joined with it.").

To put it another way, a miter joint is a butt joint that connects the angled ends of two pieces of stock. The classic example is a picture frame, with its four butt joints, one at each corner, with the ends of all the pieces cut at a forty-five-degree angle, typically in a miter box.

The miter joint has two signal advantages over a butt-corner joint: First, no end grain shows, making for a more regular and attractive joint; second, the surface for gluing is increased. Miter joints may also be fastened with nails, screws, dowels, or other mechanical fasteners.

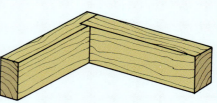

Rabbet Joint. A rabbet (or rebate, as it is also known) is a lip or channel cut from the edge of a workpiece. A typical rabbet joint is one in which a second piece is joined to the first by setting its end grain into the rabbet. Rabbet joints are frequently used to recess cabinet backs into the sides, or to reduce the amount of end grain visible at a corner.

The rabbet joint is much stronger than a simple butt joint, and is easily made either with two table or radial-arm saw cuts (one into the face, the second into the edge or end grain) or with one pass through a saw equipped with a dado head (see *Specialty Table-Saw Blades,* page 138). A router or any one of several traditional hand planes, including a plow plane, will also cut a rabbet. Glue and nails or screws are frequently used to fasten rabbet joints.

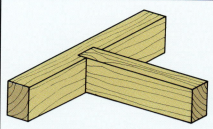

Dado Joint. When a channel or groove is cut in a piece away from the edge, it's called a dado; when a second piece set snugly into it is joined to the first with nails, glue, or other fasteners, a dado or groove joint is formed. Some cabinet-makers differentiate between groove and dado joints, insisting that grooves are cut with the grain, dadoes across. Whatever you want to call them, grooves or dadoes are cut easily with a dado head on a radial-arm or table saw.

The dado joint is perfect for setting bookshelves into uprights, and can be fastened with glue and other fasteners.

Lap Joint. A lap joint is formed when two pieces have recesses cut into them, one recess in the top surface of one piece, the second in the lower surface of the other. The waste material removed is usually half the thickness of the stock, so that when the shaped areas lap, the top and bottom of the joint are flush.

Lap joints are used to join ends (half-laps) or mitered corners (miter half-lap). Dovetail-shaped laps are sometimes used to join the ends of pieces to the midsection of others (dovetail half-laps).

Lap joints can be cut with dado heads, as well as with standard circular sawblades on radial-arm or table saws. Gluing is usual, though other fasteners, including dowels or wooden pins, are also common with lap joints.

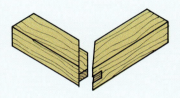

Spline Joint. A spline is a thin strip, usually of wood, that fits snugly into grooves on surfaces to be joined. Miter, edge-to-edge butt, and other joints may incorporate splines. Once the surfaces to be joined have been cut to fit, a table saw can be used to cut matching kerfs.

The spline itself adds rigidity to the joint, and also increases the gluing area. As most splines are thin, they are usually made of hardwood or plywood.

Tongue-and-Groove Joint. Flooring, bead-board, and a variety of other milled, off-the-shelf stock are sold with ready-made tongues and grooves on opposite edges. The edges can also be shaped with table or radial-arm saws; in the past, matching hand planes did the job (see *Molding Planes,* page 92).

For finish work, nails are driven through the tongues of the boards, and the groove of the next piece is slid over them ("blind-nailing"). For rougher work, as with certain kinds of novelty siding and subroof or sheathing boards, the stock is face-nailed. Glue is used only infrequently, as one of the chief advantages of a tongue-and-groove joint is that it allows for expansion and contraction caused by changes in temperature and moisture content.

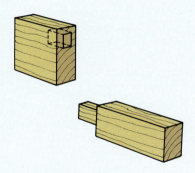

Mortise-and-Tenon Joint. The mortise is the hole or slot (or mouth) into which a projecting tenon (or tongue) is inserted. Most often, the mortise and tenon are both rectilinear in shape, but round tenons and matching mortises are to be found. The mortise-and-tenon joint is harder to shape than other, simpler joints (both pieces require considerable shaping), but the result is also a great deal stronger. (See *Making a Mortise-and-Tenon Joint,* page 192.)

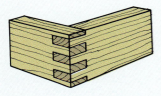

Finger Joint. Also known as a drawer or box joint, this one is most often seen in drawer joinery. Interlocking rectangular "fingers" are cut into the end grain of drawer sides and ends.

Though precise cutting of the fingers is essential, finger joints require only relatively simple ninety-degree cuts that can be made by hand or using a router, radial-arm, or table saw.

Finger joints, like dovetail joints, are sometimes used as a decoration, adding a contrasting touch as well as strength to the joined pieces.

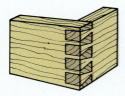

Dovetail Joint. Occasionally, there's a bit of poetry even in the workshop. As early as the sixteenth century, this joint was identified by its resemblance to bird anatomy. A thesaurus of the period termed the joint "A swallowe tayle or dooue tayle in carpenters workes, which is a fastning of two piece of timber or bourdes together that they can not away."

The dovetail is one of the strongest of all wood joints. It's also one of the most challenging to make, requiring careful layout and the investment of considerable cutting and fitting time. Its shape is a reversed wedge, cut into the end grain of one piece, that fits into a corresponding mortise on a second workpiece. Dovetails are traditionally used to join drawer sides and ends and, in the past, for many kinds of casework furniture.

The good news is that there are some jigs on the market (though they're hardly inexpensive) that make layout and cutting dovetails a snap. The jig is generally used along with a router with a dovetail bit.

A commercially available doweling jig and drill guide may be a good investment. The adjustable fences allow for presetting them to the width of the stock being used in order that each hole will be located precisely from one piece to the next.

Doweling jigs that act as drill guides have metal bushings or sleeves into which the drill bits are inserted. The bushing holds the bit in the correct position, both at the center of the workpiece and square to the edge being drilled. Most doweling jigs come with several different sleeves for different-sized drill bits. The diameter of the dowel to be used should be roughly half the thickness of the stock being joined.

Another handy tool in the drilling process is a bit depth gauge, essentially a collar with a set screw that is attached to the bit itself to ensure that the holes drilled are of uniform depth.

The doweling jig sets up as quickly as a clamp, and guides the drill bit straight and true into the workpiece. Be sure to allow a little extra depth in the hole for the glue that is driven deeply into it by the dowel.

Set the depth carefully. It should be roughly one-sixteenth of an inch deeper than half the length of the dowel you are to use, which leaves adequate space for glue but will also keep the dowel centered on the joint for maximum strength. Drill the holes at four- to six-inch intervals along edge joints; don't set one closer than one inch from the end grain. For end-grain joints, you may drill holes at one-inch intervals, but no closer than half an inch from the edge of the stock.

Alignment is everything: Make sure your dowel holes match up, not only by setting the dowel gauge to cut at the center of the boards being joined, but also to match across the joint. Draw a line across the face of the boards to be butt-jointed, holding the edges flush and aligned. Then transfer the line to the edges, using a square.

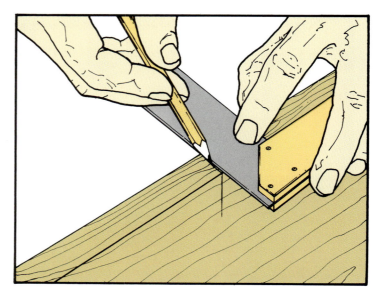

It seems like every time I open a catalog, there's a new device for putting glue exactly where you want it. The roller (center, rear) is great for butt joints, but that's just the start. There are also (moving clockwise) tips for biscuit gluing, accordion injectors, inexpensive glue brushes, high-pressure injectors, glue spreaders (some are long and flat, others shaped like postcards with a toothed edge). And there are the glues, some made from animal hides, others of synthetics (including the epoxy in the applicator on the right). And I can't pretend to you that this list includes this week's latest innovation.

Inserting the Dowel. Once the holes are drilled, test them for size: the dowel should be snug, but not so tight that you can't insert it with your fingers. If it fits, then pour a little glue into each hole, and apply a thin film along the length of the wood edges to be joined. Insert the dowels in one of the pieces to be joined, but only partway, perhaps a quarter of their length (this will make fitting the mated piece easier). Fit the second piece, and tap the assembly together. Clamp the joint securely and wipe off any excess glue.

Dowel rods of the sort sold at hardware stores and lumberyards won't do as good a job as those that have glue channels in them. Once a piece of plain dowel is inserted into the matching holes, the glue is displaced, and the pieces are likely to pull apart with a minimum of use. That's why dowels with spiral or fluted glue slots are stronger.

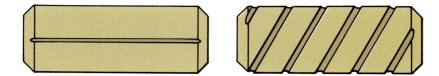

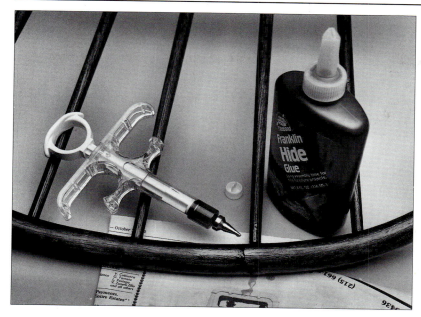

Fixing this old Windsor chair was tricky: The oak hoop-back wasn't quite broken in two, just cracked. The tip on this high-pressure injector makes the repair possible, forcing glue deep into the crevice.

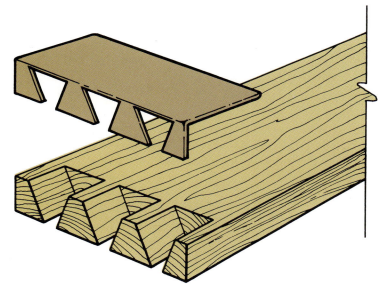

A shop-made dovetail template fashioned from sheet metal can be positioned over the end grain of one piece and over the face of the other piece of stock to be joined perpendicular to the first. The cuts are then made: In one piece, the area left exposed between the tails of the template is eliminated; in the other, the area hidden beneath is cut out.

There are, of course, a wide variety of factory-made dovetail jigs (for varying price tags, ranging upward to several hundred dollars). But making your own template and trusting to your skills with a dovetail saw is another option.

THE PLATE JOINER

The world of woodworking got along quite nicely, thank you very much, without the plate joiner. Yet making furniture and cabinetry hasn't been quite the same since this clever device arrived. Sure, there are the orthodox woodworkers who refuse to budge from their old habits, but there are lots of others who have found that even traditional joints are made stronger and better with the addition of a few little wafers inserted just so.

The plate joiner, also known as a biscuit joiner, is relatively new to the home workshop. For the amateur woodworker, it is a double blessing:

The plate or biscuit joiner is really just a portable circular saw disguised as a specialty tool. However, the design of its peculiar costume enables it to make precisely shaped and located cuts in workpieces for the insertion of the "biscuits," which are then glued in place.

The layout and shaping of a biscuit joint require only a matter of minutes to master. By using the football-shaped "biscuits" to reinforce a butt, miter, or edge joint, you can add considerable strength and durability.

The biscuit joiner is, in essence, a specialized saw. Most models have a four-inch circular sawblade mounted horizontally. When at rest, the blade is withdrawn into the base of the joiner, with a sliding fence in front of it. When in use, the fence is held flush to the edge to be joined, and, with the blade spinning at full speed, the saw is plunged into the piece.

The blade cuts a rounded kerf of a size determined by a depth adjustment. A corresponding groove is then cut into the piece to be joined to the first. A few drops of glue are applied to each groove, and the beech biscuit is inserted.

Don't glue first, then look for clamps . . . the plate tends to swell almost immediately. Get ready first, do a dry run on the joint, then apply the glue. The glue causes the biscuit to swell, which helps to strengthen the joint. The joint is then clamped tightly until the glue has set thoroughly.

Like a doweled or splined joint, the biscuit joint is invisible after assembly, and produces a tight, strong bond.

Plate joiners are sold as distinct tools by many manufacturers. Conversion attachments are also sold for some routers, angle grinders, and drill presses that allow those tools to do plate-joiner duty as well as their usual tasks. Benchtop stands are available for most standard biscuit joiners; they allow a series of workpieces to be presented to the joiner, rather than requiring each piece to be secured individually.

A biscuit butt joint is quite like a doweled joint, only simpler still. A line is drawn across the joint; the joiner cuts the slots for the biscuits to be glued and inserted; and then the pieces are clamped.

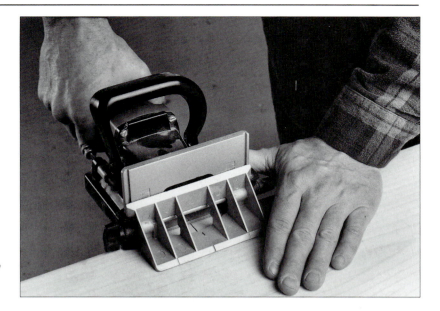

Use the handle on your plate joiner for carrying – not for wielding the tool. Hold the tool with one hand on the rear housing, with the other holding the fence firmly in position.

The biscuit joiner is well suited to joining plywood. It's handy for face frames on cabinets (the fixed horizontal and vertical elements that frame the doors and drawers). Miter joints, too, are greatly strengthened by the presence of biscuits.

How many biscuits should you use? Place them at roughly six-inch intervals. On thick stock, insert two, top and bottom, at similar intervals. Stay two inches or more from the end grain when working on an edge; when gluing end grain, place the biscuits at three-inch intervals.

Safety Suggestions. Clamp the workpiece or fix it in position securely with a bench hook or other stop. Don't try to balance both machine and workpiece. Don't force the machine: It's powerful enough to cut rapidly, but you'll get neater, more regular work at a more measured pace. Let the saw whir to a stop before you put it down, too.

With a specially designed base, the plate joiner can be adapted for stationary use. That allows the wood to be presented to the tool, enhancing safety and accuracy.

CLAMPS

In *Toolbox*, we talked of clamps, specifically hand-screw, bar, spring, strap, pipe, and C-clamps. They remain the basic tools on which any workshop relies, used to hold assemblies in position while glue cures or while nails or screws are put in place.

Clamps are immensely helpful – even essential – in performing certain tasks. Yet they aren't foolproof. Clamps can be tightened too tightly, exerting so much force as to mar or even break elements being assembled. And some clamps are just right for some jobs, but ill suited to others. Plan ahead and select your clamps carefully.

When acquiring clamps, you might also consider some of these possibilities, as well as the more traditional ones mentioned earlier.

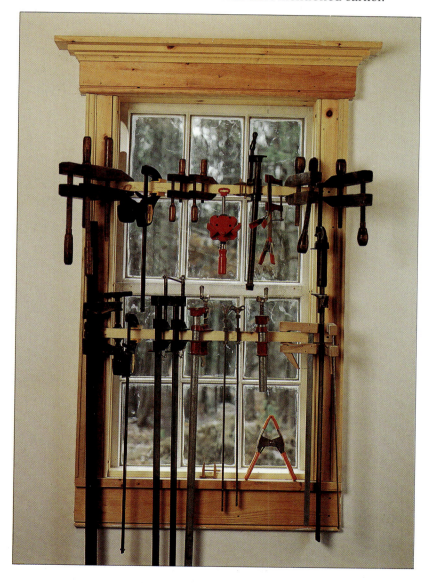

There's no such thing as too many clamps in a workshop, and here's quite a range, including hand-screw, bar, pipe, trigger, spring, and others.

Wooden bar or door clamp

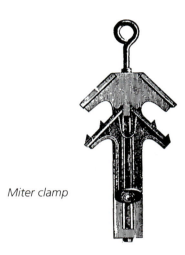

Miter clamp

Frame Clamps. As the name suggests, picture frames are the usual use for these clamps. Yet other clamping and gluing work that involves fastening mitered corners is also performed with frame clamps – tasks like making windows and cabinet doors.

The frame clamp consists of four brackets that are positioned at the corners of the frame or other object to be clamped. These brackets or corner blocks hold the adjacent pieces of the frame perpendicular to one another and are then tightened. The tightening mechanism varies: It may be a cord or web with a lever and ratchet device like that on a strap clamp. Or it may consist of a more elaborate steel mechanism of threaded rods and nuts.

A miter clamp makes repairing a corner joint a simple matter. In this model, the jaws of the clamp are drawn together with a screw drive, producing a neat, tight corner.

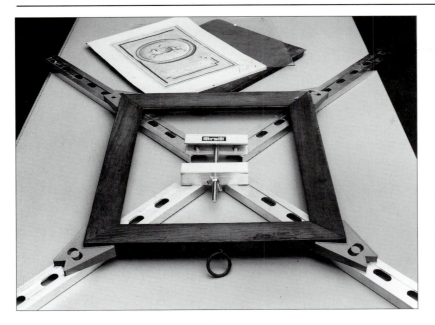

Clamping mitered corners exactly square isn't easy – unless, of course, you have a frame clamp designed specifically for such tasks. If you have cut the corners of your picture frame accurately, this frame clamp will make the gluing process very much easier than trying to do the job with a miscellany of other clamps.

Corner Clamps. Miter clamps, as corner clamps are also known, allow you to glue a single miter joint (rather than four, as with a frame clamp). The corner clamp has a fixed right-angle fence that will hold pieces on the inside of the corner. On the outside are adjustable screw-driven "feet" that are tightened to hold each piece in place.

Lever Cam Clamps. These have wooden jaws with cork faces. They are gentle but surprisingly strong, relying upon a cam action to tighten the sliding lower jaw to the fixed upper jaw. Lever cam clamps are suitable for veneer work and general light-duty gluing, as their frequent use by makers of musical instruments suggests (as a result, they are also known as instrument-maker's clamps). Their light weight and cork clamping surfaces make them suitable for quite delicate work. They're sold in a range of sizes, with maximum jaw openings that range from just under eight inches to as much as thirty-one inches.

Grip-Drive Clamps. Also called quick-grip bar clamps, these feature a relatively new design and are very easy to use. A trigger lever releases the bar so that the mouth of the clamp can be slid open or closed; the handle is squeezed to tighten the clamp. Removable pads on the jaws protect the workpiece being clamped.

Trigger clamps come in a variety of sizes, ranging from six-inch to thirty-six-inch jaw openings. They're very handy all-purpose clamps: With their padded jaws in place, they can do delicate work; without the pads, their grip is solid and direct.

Clamping Techniques. With most kinds of clamps, the same rudiments apply. Starting by setting up your work on a flat, level surface. And always do a dry run first, *without* glue.

Go gently as you clamp: Make sure the workpieces are square (if you're using more than one clamp, tighten them alternately). Use

Whatever variety of clamp you're using, always do a dry run before applying glue to your workpieces. That way, you can be confident of the lineup and that the clamps are the proper size and design for the job, and ensure that you won't waste time scraping off prematurely applied glue.

MAKING A MORTISE-AND-TENON JOINT

The preferred style of joint for furniture and cabinetwork is the mortise-and-tenon joint. It's strong, durable, and little affected by the expansion or contraction of wooden members as a result of temperature and humidity changes. When shaped properly, a mortise-and-tenon joint can even be a decorative element in the finished appearance of a piece.

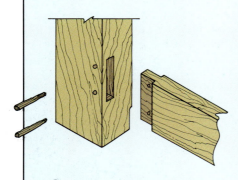

In some instances, the tenon or tongue extends all the way through the piece in which the mortise is cut; that's a through mortise-and-tenon joint. In others, the tenon stops short, extending only partway through the piece to which it is joined; that's a stub joint.

In still other cases, the joint is drawn together by "drawboring," in which the predrilled holes in the tenon are set roughly a sixteenth of an inch deeper than the mortise pinholes. By using a sharpened pin, you draw the joint together when you drive the pin. The result is a very strong joint indeed. (Note, however, that the hole drilled in the mortised piece shouldn't pass all the way through to the far side.)

Making a mortise-and-tenon joint may be a daunting prospect to the novice woodworker, but with the proper tools, shaping the parts is a quite straightforward process.

Laying Out the Joint. As any experienced cabinetmaker will tell you, proper layout is just as important as the cutting and shaping to follow. A perfectly shaped tenon that's the wrong size or shape is no accomplishment at all.

The tenon should be between one third and one half of the thickness of the stock from which it is made.

Set your mortise gauge to the chosen tenon thickness, positioning the points so that it will score a pair of lines that distance apart. Then set the block on the gauge so that the lines will be drawn equidistant from the sides of the stock. Mark off the shoulder lines, too, where the stock is to be trimmed above and below the tongue. (See *Marking, Cutting, and Mortise Gauges*, page 73.)

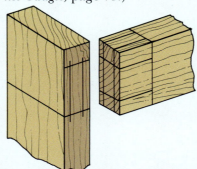

Good, clean marking is important in laying out a mortise-and-tenon joint. Use your mortising gauge, if you have one, or a try square to scribe the cut lines on both the mortise and the tenon. The more precise your marks are, the more accurate your cutting is likely to be.

Cutting the Tenon. Your backsaw can do the job. A shaper or router can be used, too, as can a dado head on a table or radial-arm saw.

In each case, set the blade height separately for the shoulder and face cuts. On the table saw, position the fence so that the distance from the opposite side of the blade to the fence matches the desired length of the tenon.

Cutting the Mortise. The mortise depth should be roughly three times the thickness of the tenon. It can be cut in several ways, among them the traditional approach of using sturdy mortising chisels and a mallet to chisel out the hole by hand. Another option is to use a Forstner or auger bit on your drill or drill brace to start the mortise, then clean and square it with a chisel. You can also use a router; a plunge router is especially useful for mortising.

A much easier method is to use a mortising attachment on your drill press. The device consists of a yoke that clamps the attachment just above the chuck onto the quill (the main stationary shaft of the drill press, within which the spindle turns). At the bottom, the yoke is fitted with a hollow, square-cornered chisel, within which a bit turns. Different sizes of chisels are sold, with matching bits.

When using the mortise attachment, the drill press is operated in much the same way as when it performs ordinary drilling tasks. The spinning bit will do most of the cutting, but the chisel squares off the corners

With the workpiece firmly clamped and the cut lines marked off with a mortise gauge, a fine-toothed tenon or other backsaw is used to cut the tenon.

Mortise attachments can transform a standard drill press into a mortising machine in a matter of minutes. They're very handy for cabinet door and other joining work where mortise-and-tenon joints are desirable.

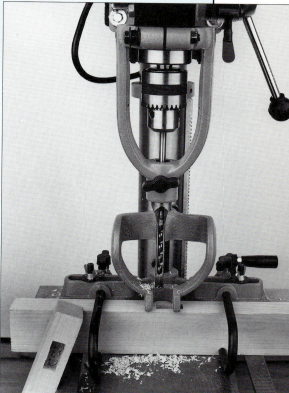

around the hole, producing the shouldered mortise hole.

Make sure the workpiece is properly secured to the table, perhaps with a clamp or a fence or both. In cutting accurate mortises, it is essential that the sides of the chisel be square to the stock. Don't force the drill: Let it establish a rate of cutting that doesn't cause the bit to bind in the wood.

Fastening the Joint. Glue is often used to connect the mortise-and-tenon joint, as are dowels driven through the joint. A combination of both is the strongest.

Before applying the glue, clamp the joint together dry to be sure the fit is just right. Drill out the holes for the pins or dowels, disassemble, and apply the glue. Clamp the pieces together, and insert the dowels, leaving them protruding from both sides of the joint. Scrape off any visible excess glue from the surface of the wood being joined.

After the glue has set, remove the clamps and cut off the dowels, using a sharp chisel or a flush saw.

Quick-grip clamps are perfect for many light clamping jobs. They are by far the easiest clamps to adjust: Operating them is merely a matter of squeezing the handle to tighten the jaws or pulling the trigger to release them. The removable pads on the jaws also won't mar the gluing surfaces. The downside is that the clamps aren't tremendously strong, and won't drive together resistant joints as the trusty bar clamp will.

leather or hardboard pads to protect your work from metal clamping surfaces. Don't tighten too much.

Apply the glue to both surfaces to be glued. Enough glue should be used to coat the joint area thoroughly. When the joint is clamped, a little glue should be squeezed out (if none appears, there probably isn't enough glue for a strong bond). Too much glue doesn't make the joint stronger, but it does add the time required to clean up the mess. Wipe off excess glue immediately. Use a paint scraper to get most of it, and follow with a damp cloth. After the glue dries, a hand scraper is the best choice for removing the dried residue.

Clamp Care. Most clamps are sturdy, utilitarian tools, and a minimum of care is necessary to keep them functioning at their best. When not in use, clamps should be stored, preferably on a rack away from dampness. To prevent rust, rub them occasionally with a rag dampened with machine oil.

THE COMPRESSOR

The compressor is a machine that compresses the gases in the air around us to pressures greater than that of the normal atmosphere.

Most of us first made the acquaintance of a compressor when our bicycle tires needed pumping up, and the basic mechanism hasn't changed all that much.

The compressor consists of a motorized pump; a tank for storing the compressed air; an on/off control (governor) that tells the pump when to start and stop in order to keep the pressure within preset limits; and a regulator to control the pressure at which the air escapes the tank to suit the needs of the tires (or the tools) being serviced. There's a metal frame on which all the rest of the parts are mounted, perhaps a handle and, in some cases, wheels. And various pipes, gauges, nozzles, cords, and other hardware.

The big difference between the service station compressor of your training-wheel days and the present is the portability and widespread use of compressors for many different kinds of workshop (and work-site) tasks. You would have to be a descendant of Rip Van Winkle not to know about nail guns. And spray-paint attachments, sanders, and a dozen other kinds of attachments.

Not every workshop needs a compressor, but a busy shop can be made more efficient with the addition of compressed air. An air line with a plain nozzle on the end is handy for blowing sawdust out of a workpiece or any number of other tasks. Not to mention the efficiency of some of the pneumatic tools.

Called a door or panel clamp, this tool was, and still is, used to hold the frames and panels of doors and paneling in place, usually in order to assemble (or, as in this case, repair) mortise-and-tenon joints. Bar and pipe clamps will do the job, too, of course, but these purpose-made tools are very efficient and easy to use.

Probably the greatest advantage of air-powered sanders, drills, and other tools is their light weight. That makes them easier to use (and less tiring to hold), especially when you are performing repetitive production tasks. They are also compact and don't heat up (there's no armature and motor inside). Since they have fewer moving parts, pneumatic tools require less maintenance and are less likely to break down.

The sales talk for compressors involves a confusing array of technical terms. The key ones both concern the output of the compressor. It's measured in how many standard cubic feet per minute of air (scfm) are delivered at how many pounds per square inch (psi).

Various machines require differing volumes (scfm) at different pressures (psi). Before buying a compressor, you must identify the tools you plan to use, and match the compressor's output to the pressure requirements of the tools. Most tools required three or four scfm at ninety psi, though sanders typically demand more volume.

Another consideration in selecting a compressor is portability. Many compact models can be carried (with some effort) by one person to a work-site, an essential requirement if you plan to put the compressor to use in framing your new workshop. On the other hand, if it is to be set in place in your workshop for good, buy a stationary compressor. Two-stage models (in which the air is compressed twice with

Compressors are very power-sensitive. Do not use undersized or long (more than twenty-five-foot) extension cords to power them. If you do, the resultant voltage drop can cause the motor to overheat (shortening its life expectancy) or fail to start properly (producing no compressed air). Note, too, that some compressors also require two hundred and twenty volts service.

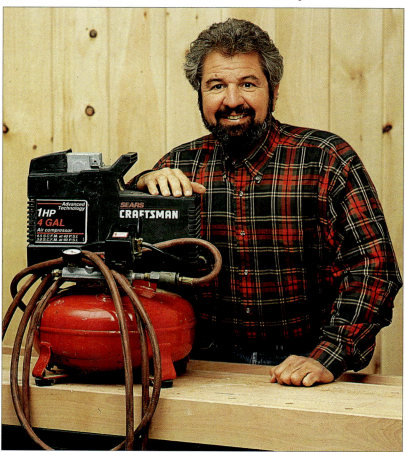

Compressors are large and small, and come in a variety of shapes. This "pancake" design is just one of the many convenient portable varieties.

an intermediate stage in between for cooling) produce higher pressures more efficiently and, typically, last longer. The trade-off is in expense and weight.

Check the oil at least weekly; change it frequently (check the manual for the manufacturer's recommendations). Use the weight oil prescribed. Empty the air tank frequently, then open the drain tap at the bottom of the tank. This will allow any water that has condensed to drain off before any of the machine's components corrode.

Accessories. The list is long and increases every year as more and more uses are found for compressed air, and the price of components becomes more affordable. The random-orbit sander will be discussed later (see page 207), and it is available in a air-powered model. There are the ubiquitous construction nail guns seen at work-sites almost everywhere. At the local tire shop, you've seen the impact wrenches that handle lug nuts as if they were M&M's.

And that's only the beginning. As well as random-orbit sanders, there are straight-line and orbital sanders. There are drills, some with variable speeds and reversibility. All sorts of pneumatic grinders are sold, including die, pencil, and vertical grinders; there are angle cutters, too. Carving hammers and ratchets are joined by laminate trimmers and saws, including jig, circular, panel, even reciprocating saws. Spray equipment for finishing can also be run off compressors.

An equally wide range of nail guns are sold for specific purposes (no one gun accommodates more than one kind of nails). Roofing, framing, finishing, and brad nailers, as well as crown staplers are on the market. Sand blasters, power washers, and even drain cleaners are also available.

At rear are two nail guns, a coil-fed siding nailer (left), and a stick nailer for framing. Up front are a sander, impact wrench, and finish nailer. All are pneumatic tools, powered by compressed air delivered by an air line.

Chapter 11.

Finishing Tools and Techniques

Having assembled our projects, we need to finish them: Enter such tools as the furniture scraper, finishing sander, belt sander, and disk sander.

These tools run the gamut from the rough and ready to the pure and simple. The belt sander is on the rugged side, ready to smooth the roughest surfaces in a single session. The hand scraper, in contrast, is a tool for perfectionists, smoothing at a pace that only the patient and painstaking among us can truly appreciate.

Once the surface is smoothed, the paint or other finish can then be applied, using brushes or other implements. The remarkable range of brushes and finishes is discussed here, as is the process of taking off the paint, using heat guns and plates.

That's a belt sander (bottom, left), with palm and random-orbit sanders above it (left and center, respectively). The heat gun (right, middle step) is used for stripping, the hand scrapers up top (center) for precise smoothing. The paint and varnish brushes, of course, are almost as varied as the paint and sealer options with which they are used.

THE SCRAPER

This is a tool for minimalists, for those who admire simplicity of form and function beyond all else. That's because the hand scraper consists of little more than a piece of high-quality steel in the shape of a playing card, only slightly larger, typically two and a half by five inches, and about a thirty-second of an inch thick. (Let it be noted here, though, that while most scrapers are rectangular, there are curved ones, too.) In earlier centuries, the hand scraper was made from broken sawblades. The broken blades were of quality steel that otherwise was of no use.

Even today, the hand scraper is quite a bargain, costing only about five dollars.

The cabinet scraper is a hand scraper mounted in a frame that resembles a spokeshave. A pair of set screws holds the blade in position, and a thumbscrew allows for fine adjustments of the scraper blade.

Scrapers are a good deal more intriguing and useful than they may at first appear. One of the edges is "sharpened" in order that the tool can smooth wood, usually hardwood. It won't lift the grain of the wood and, while it performs something of the same function as sandpaper, its waste products are small shavings rather than dust. A scraper will remove as much material as medium-grade abrasive paper without introducing the countless little scratches that sandpaper leaves behind.

The black two-handled tool at center is a cabinet scraper, a spokeshave-like frame that ensures that the scraper within is presented to the surface at the proper angle. The tool that resembles a screwdriver is a burnisher, as is the boxlike tool above it. The flat, shiny metal tools are all hand scrapers, including the "whale" or gooseneck-shaped molding scraper.

If you are intrigued by the scraper but have never tried one, I'd recommend it. I'd also suggest you experiment with it first on scrap stock. Lessons are almost always better learned at harmless play than at serious work.

Another advantage is that the scraper's shavings are easily brushed off, while the sanding dust can clog the grain of the wood. There is simply no newfangled machine that can do as good a job at producing a smooth finish on a wood surface. The scraper will also allow you to work in areas much smaller than those you could smooth even with a block plane, and without encroaching upon adjacent portions of the wood.

The cutting edge on the scraper is actually a tiny burr, a small projecting lip at the edge of the tool. Almost imperceptible to the human eye, the burr (or hook, as it is also called) makes the scraper a very efficient smoothing tool. The sharpening process, during which the burr is rolled over to form the edge, is trickier even than using the tool once it's been sharpened.

Sharpening the Scraper. When your scraper produces dust rather than shavings, it needs to be sharpened. In keeping with the simplicity of this tool, this task probably won't require a file or even a sharpening stone. Most of the time, a rounded piece of steel is all you'll need. The back of a gouge will do, though a tool made for the purpose, called a burnisher, costs about fifteen dollars. We'll get to the burnisher step in a minute, but there are other stops first.

A scraper with a badly dulled or pitted edge needs to be filed. The long edge of the scraper is drawfiled, meaning the scraper is clamped in a vise and a single-cut mill file is drawn along the edge.

In this and other steps, a key consideration is straightness: You want the edge straight and perfectly perpendicular to the face of the scraper. The scraper is ready for the next step when the corner at which the face and the edge meet (called an *arris*) feels sharp to the touch.

After drawfiling the scraper to even its edge (see page 116), hone the faces and edges (in that order) on a sharpening stone. Hone first on a medium, then on a fine stone.

Next, you shape the burr, drawing the burnisher back and forth across the face of the scraper. The burnisher should be pressed hard against the scraper's corner, at a slight angle, so that its end is just off the scraper's face.

One pass per edge with the burnisher, at about an eighty-five-degree angle to the scraper's face, is all that is needed to finish the sharpening job.

Now, hone the scraper on a sharpening stone. Use a medium stone first, honing first the face, then the edge of the scraper. Repeat with a fine stone. Again, your goal is a perfectly perpendicular edge that is perceptibly sharp to your fingertips.

Now comes the clever part (and it's here you will return when your scraper isn't truly dull, but just needs tuning up).

Begin by holding the scraper flat on your benchtop or other work surface. The burnisher is then held at about a five-degree angle to the scraper (just off horizontal). Run it back and forth along the arris. This will produce a burr parallel to the face. If you don't hear a noticeable click as you drive the burnisher off the edge of the scraper, you're not applying enough pressure. Now, having raised the burr, you must turn it over. To do so, you draw the burnisher once along the edge of the scraper, holding the scraper at about an eighty-five-degree angle to the scraper. Larger burrs can be turned by two or more passes, but start with one pass. The fine hook of steel you've shaped will do the actual work.

Note that if you do both sides of a working edge of a scraper, you can then scrape with both sides. Or even both sides of both long edges of a scraper, producing four hooks.

Scraping the Surface. Actually putting the scraper to use is about as far removed from machine work as you can get. It's just your hands, the workpiece, and your scraper.

The scraper is gripped with the first two or three fingers of each hand at the front of the tool, with the thumbs behind. Angle the top of the scraper away from you (at roughly seventy-five or eighty degrees to the workpiece). Gently push the scraper, scraping along the surface of the wood, applying enough pressure to the rear of the scraper so that the bottom edge forms a slight curve. That means the corners of the scraper will lift slightly off the wood and the center will make contact with the surface to be smoothed.

The pressure you exert with your thumbs determines the sharpness of the curve, which in turn determines the nature of the cut. More

The end result of the sharpening process of a hand and cabinet scraper (see facing page): a hook burnished at the arris to do the actual scraping.

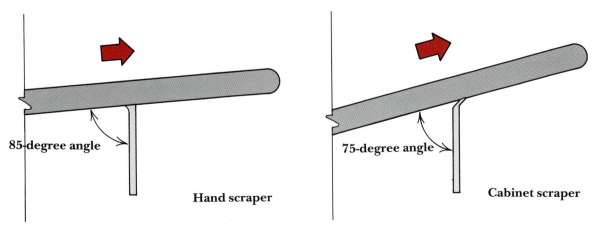

85-degree angle

Hand scraper

75-degree angle

Cabinet scraper

bending means that less of the scraper scrapes the surface (good for highly localized scraping, as is necessary to remove a specific imperfection in the wood); a nearly flat application is preferable for an overall scraping job.

As with smoothing flat stock with a bench plane, work first diagonally across the workpiece. For smoothing surfaces, work in long strokes across the wood, introducing as little curvature into the scraper as possible. Put pressure on the scraper only after it's in motion; lift the scraper from the surface as you reach the end of each stroke. For the final smoothing, work with the grain. Scrapers also remove excess glue with ease.

Scrapers can be used to smooth localized imperfections like knots. Keep in mind, however, that too much intensive scraping in a small area may make that area stand out from the surrounding wood. One good rule of thumb to apply: For every two or three scrapes you make to fix the localized problem, scrape a long stroke on either side. For every three or four local scrapes, scrape strokes that are two scraper widths away. And so on.

When the scraper begins to dull, burnish the edge. Do both burnishing steps, forming the burr first by burnishing the face, then turning the burr by burnishing the edge.

The Cabinet Scraper. This tool resembles a spokeshave (see page 120) but is actually a hand scraper in disguise. It has an iron body into which a hand scraper is affixed, using thumbscrews. Once the scraper blade is set in place, this two-handed tool makes scraping easy.

Sharpening the scraper blade used in a cabinet scraper is a slightly different process from putting an edge onto a hand scraper. The cabinet scraper's edge is first filed to a forty-five-degree bevel (a bastard mill file will do the job nicely). This raises a burr on the backside, which can be polished off with a few strokes on a sharpening stone, holding the back of the scraper flat to the stone. A couple of strokes across the bevel are next, to polish it.

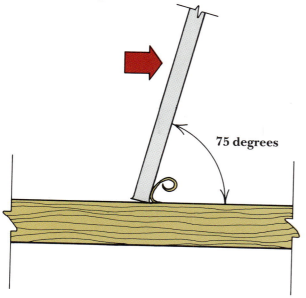

75 degrees

This schematic drawing suggests how the hand scraper actually works, as the burr scrapes tiny shavings from the surface of the workpiece.

SURFACE PREPARATION, PART 1

Before we get to the sanders, let's talk about the surface of the object you are making. How smooth is it? Are the heads of the nails or screws flush or, better yet, recessed below the surface to be finished? How about saw, planer, or other machining marks to be seen? Are there chisel, knife, or other tooling signs?

The belt sander can solve some of these problems, the finish sander almost none of them. So now is the time to correct or camouflage these flaws in your work. There are a number of techniques and materials available to help you do so. Address these problems as follows:

Nail Holes. Unless the nail heads are intended to be decorative, you'll probably want to rely upon finishing nails that are driven below the surface of the wood with a nail set. This leaves a small round hole to be filled with wood putty. Apply it with a narrow putty knife. If you plan to sand the surface, allow a small amount of excess putty to stand slightly proud of the surface; the sander will smooth it flush.

Screwheads. Screws are functional indeed but, you've got to admit, their heads just aren't pretty. It is best to countersink them into the work, and to fill the resulting hole with a plug. The plug is glued in place and, once the glue has set, the top of the plug is removed with a sharp chisel or a flush saw.

Filling Cracks. Use wood putty, working your putty knife across the crack rather than with it. This angle of approach helps drive the putty deeper into the crack and make a better bond. Unless you will be sanding the entire surface, scrape off any excess putty before it dries.

Stains and Other Marks. Erase any pencil marks. If there's any glue on the surface, make a mental note to yourself to do a better job next time of wiping it off at the moment it squeezes out of the clamped joint. A belt sander will take off glue that has already dried, but a scraper or chisel may be required to remove it from hard-to-reach spots. Stains can be bleached using commercially available products made specifically for bleaching wood. Most on the market today involve two solutions applied in sequence. Follow the manufacturer's instructions.

Now, it's on to the sanding process. The belt sander (see below) will take off most machining marks and will cut down adjacent surfaces that are not quite flush to smooth, even surfaces. Follow with the finish sander.

Now for the burnisher. With the scraper bevel down on the workbench, smooth the back of its edge with a few strokes parallel to the face of the scraper. Then secure the scraper in a vise and burnish the bevel. Start at the angle of the bevel; gradually, lessen the angle (bringing the burnisher gradually toward the horizontal). The last stroke should be just short of horizontal, perhaps fifteen degrees. Insert the blade into the scraper and go to work.

THE BELT SANDER

The belt sander always seems to be in a hurry. When fitted with a coarse paper, it will sand away dense layers of paint and smooth rough surfaces at a surprisingly fast rate. Like any tough tool, however, it must be handled with appropriate care. The risks it poses are less to the user than to the workpiece, as it can quickly sand away large areas, particularly if left stationary in one area.

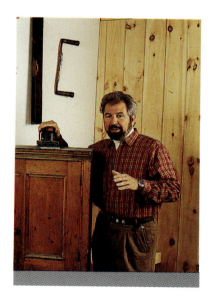

The belt sander is a rough-and-ready tool, the orbital sander (right) more delicate. Whichever you use, a respirator is an excellent precaution.

The belt sander has two cylindrical drums around which a closed loop of abrasive paper travels continuously. One drum is driven by an electric motor, the other is spring-loaded to maintain tension on the belt. The belt sander is best equipped to smooth flat surfaces and the edges of workpieces cut along the grain. Most models on the market today have built-in dust collectors, an especially handy feature in a tool that generates as much dust as this one can. Variable speed features are also useful, especially when you wish to do finer work.

Belt sanders are sold as portable and as benchtop models. The former is hand-held, and presented to the work; a benchtop machine is fixed in place and workpieces are brought to its sanding surface. Both are valuable tools, but you will need to consider the nature of the work you want to do with a belt sander before deciding upon one or the other. If both seem necessary, sanding stands and fences can be purchased to convert some portable belt sanders into stationary models. Another option is a combination belt and disk sander (see page 210).

Stationary Belt Sander. This tool is mounted on a tabletop. If you have an appropriate space, fix it to the surface; if not, some models come with stands that allow the tool to be quickly set in place (and just as quickly removed).

The top, horizontal surface of the benchtop belt sander is used. If the workpiece is shorter than the top of the belt, a fence is set over one drum to function as a stop, allowing the workpiece to rest in a stationary position as the belt spins beneath it. Work the piece from side to side so that the belt will wear evenly.

For smoothing end grain, the tool can be repositioned so that the working surface is vertical.

The most common belt size on home workshop stationary belt sanders is four inches wide by three feet long. Larger machines take six-inch by forty-eight-inch belts or even larger ones.

Whatever sort of sander you're using, remember the rule, Keep it moving. In the case of a stationary sander, I mean the workpiece; with hand-held sanders, I mean the tool. The point is that a sander that remains at work in the same exact spot on a workpiece is likely to produce an uneven surface, even burning or otherwise permanently marring the work.

Portable Belt Sander. The basic elements are the same: a belt, two drums, a motor, and a switch. While the stationary belt sander is designed to be fixed in place in the workshop, the portable belt sander can be taken just about anywhere an extension cord can reach.

Rather than having the workpiece presented to it, the portable belt sander is generally presented to the surface to be sanded. This may be a board clamped to a benchtop, or the benchtop itself. Or surfaces in situ, such as architectural elements still in place.

One task in the cabinetmaker's shop for which the belt sander is the right tool is removing glue lines and making joints flush on facers (the front-facing vertical and horizontal elements that frame doors and drawers). Final smoothing is then done with a finish sander.

The portable belt sander is a two-handed tool, so the workpiece must be securely located. When the machine is turned on, the belt should not be in contact with the work.

Once the machine has reached its full speed, it is lowered gently onto the workpiece; touch down with the rear of the belt first. Unless you are trying to remove material from the surface rapidly, the weight of the machine will probably provide all the force required, so pressing down on the sander isn't usually necessary.

Sand with the grain. For leveling an uneven surface, you may sand diagonally across the grain, but a follow-up step will then be required, using fine paper parallel with the grain. This will remove the scratches produced by the diagonal sanding.

When operating a stationary belt sander, feed the wood against the rotation of the belt. This increases sanding efficiency, and prevents the sander from pulling the board from your grasp and launching it across the workshop. With small workpieces, you may opt to use a push stick, too, to protect your pushing hand from the abrasive belt.

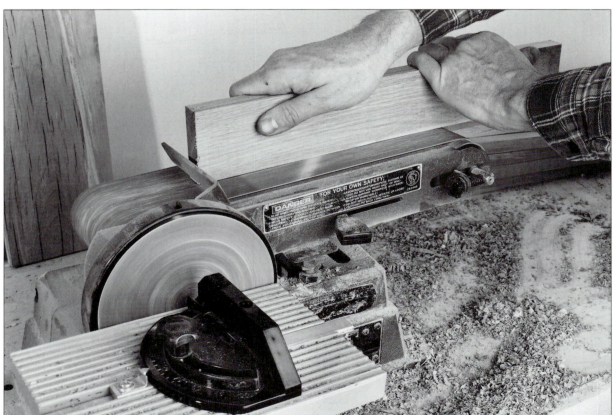

FINISHING SANDERS

Names like orbital sander, pad sander, and oscillating sheet sander are used to identify finishing sanders. In *Toolbox*, you'll find a finishing sander, too, the palm-grip sander, which is a reasonably priced, easy-to-use, efficient tool. Technically speaking, it's an orbital sander, meaning that it sands in a rotating pattern.

Some finish sanders function in a different fashion, sanding in a straight-line mode, backwards and forwards, much like hand sanding. Some finishing sanders move from straight-line to orbital sanding and back again at the flick of a switch. Do you need to be able to do both? The consensus among the pros is that straight-line sanding is less likely to leave little whirls of cross-grain scratches, so for the final pass, it's preferred to orbital movements (though if little pressure is applied to an orbital sander using fine paper, the scratches will be minimal).

There are a great range of sizes for such finishing sanders, generally identified by the portion of a standard sheet of sandpaper they require: one-half, one-third, one-quarter, one-fifth, or even one-sixth of a sheet.

Most of these sanders are held in one hand, are driven by an electric motor, and have the proper sized sheet of sandpaper mounted in twin jaws that hold the paper tight to a rubber pad at the base of the unit. (Some have an added handle up front for two-handed work.) All these tools are capable of doing a perfectly acceptable job, though some are faster or slower than others, or easier or harder to use. Some offer only one speed, others two, still others a variable-speed adjustment.

But I've come to favor a different species of finish sander, a clever variation on the familiar orbital sander. The basic design of this sander has been around for years in auto body shops, but is just coming into general use in the woodshop. Called a random-orbit sander, this sophisticated tool is now affordable for just about anybody who is ready to invest in a basic finish sanding machine.

The sandpaper used in a random-orbit sander is shaped like a disk, but it is the action of the machine that makes it truly different from its predecessors. The sander's motor spins a shaft on which a counterweight is mounted. The combination of the weight, the spinning shaft, and an offset thrust bearing produces a random, varying motion. To put it less technically, it spins and wiggles, never the same way twice, and does a nice, neat job, producing little or no scratching across the grain. Another advantage of the random-orbit sander is that a great deal of material can be removed without scratching the finish.

The varying motion also tends to clean the sandpaper, meaning that it lasts longer. Purpose-made sandpaper disks are required; they are sold with backing that is pressure-sensitive (adhesive) or has hook and loop (Velcro) fastenings. The latter can be removed from the sander and reused over and over again.

The random-orbit sander is a flexible alternative to some other finish sanders: It has the cutting power to do rough finishing, as well as the later finishing and smoothing.

Whatever sort of finishing sander you use, the last step in the sanding process should be to hand sand your workpiece. Do it strictly with the grain, in order to remove any sanding marks against the grain that could mar the work.

Random-orbit sanders are sold in single-speed and variable-speed models.

Most models come with a dustbag attachment (it's an inexpensive option from some manufacturers). This, too, reduces the frequency with which the dust clogs the paper on the machine, and results in a cleaner work area. I recommend it.

In addition to models powered by electric motors, random-orbit sanders that run on air power are also available. You need a compressor and an air hose to power this variety, but if your workshop is so equipped, this is a quieter and lighter-weight alternative.

Some of the motor-powered random-orbit sanders are in-line models, with the motor mounted vertically (they resemble rounded-off palm sanders). Right-angled models look a bit like a saber saw, in that the motor and its housing are perpendicular to the driveshaft. Right-angled models are more expensive, but since they have more powerful motors and allow for a firmer, two-handed grip, they are also more versatile machines.

Using a Finishing Sander. To use the sander, switch it on and let it come to full speed. Then set it on the surface to be sanded. Move it in the direction of the grain, exerting gentle pressure on the tool. (Remember, the tools described here are to be used to put a finish surface on a workpiece, not to give it a basic shape, so don't put too much pressure on them; for rougher sanding, see *The Belt Sander,* page 204.) Keep the base of the sander flush to the surface being sanded at all times, to avoid creating undulations in the surface.

THE DISK SANDER

Sanding disks are prefabricated disks of abrasive paper. They can be mounted on a variety of tools, including the radial-arm saw, bench grinder, and electric drill. The tools I have in mind here are designed to function as sanders only, whether they are hand-held portable models or stationary models fixed on a stand or benchtop. Most sanding disks, however, are used in a similar way regardless of the tool to which they are attached.

A steel or aluminum backing plate supports the abrasive sanding disk. A motor drives the disk in a circular motion; a screw and washer at the center are recessed so as not to protrude into the work area of the sanding surface.

In the case of the benchtop disk sander, an adjustable worktable is fixed in front of the disk and is used to hold the workpiece during sanding. The worktable can be tilted for end cuts, and often has a slot in which a miter gauge slides for aligning miter-cut workpieces. Disk diameters typically range from as small as four inches up to eight inches, though disk sanders with capacities as great as twelve inches are common in commercial applications.

SELECTING SANDPAPER

Sandpaper isn't made of sand, of course, but of fine grains of the natural mineral garnet, or of synthetics like silicone carbide, aluminum oxide, or alumina-zirconia (zirconium). The ground-up materials are sifted though graded screens. The smallest particles are used in making the finest papers, the coarsest grains for coarse "coated abrasives," as sandpaper is technically known today. The size of the grit is identified by a number.

The fine, medium, and coarse papers (there are, by the way, more precise gradations within these three main subdivisions) are used for different kinds of tasks. The standard grades of papers are these:

Extrafine. This grade of sandpaper is used between coats of paint or varnish. Grits of 240, 320, 400 are termed very fine, while extra- or superfine sheets with grits of up to 600 are available for polishing jobs.

Fine. Fine abrasive papers have a grit in the range of 120 to 220. For most home workshops, fine will suffice for final sanding before the work is finished.

Medium. Some final shaping can be done with medium, which has a grit range of 60 to 100. General sanding work is often best done with medium-grade sandpaper.

Coarse. Rough shaping is the strong suit of coarse paper, as is the removal of previous finishes. The grits are typically in the 40 to 50 range.

Extracoarse. This stuff is really rough, usable for removing paint and varnish that you think might never come

Sandpapers come in sheets, belts, and disks, and in a great many grades for all uses, from fine to medium to coarse.

off. The sanding of old floors, too, sometimes requires the abrasiveness of extracoarse sandpaper. Don't even think about using it on any but the toughest jobs.

The circular motion of the stationary disk sander makes it most suitable for smoothing end grain, or straight and miter cuts, as well as curved edges (if used with the grain, it will scratch the wood). The wood should contact the disk on a stationary sander on its downward path, so that the motion of the disk holds the stock to the worktable. Several light passes are preferable to one hard cut.

In the case of a portable sander, the workpiece is fixed in a vise or secured by bench dogs, and the sander brought to it. Also called an

When using a stationary disk sander, use the miter gauge. It helps stabilize the piece, and ensures that the end grain is sanded at the desired angle to the grain.

offset disk sander (because the disk spins on an axis perpendicular to the sander's housing), this tool is best suited to face sanding. The tool should be held at a slight angle to the workpiece with approximately a third of the disk in contact with the surface to be smoothed. Keep the sander moving in order to avoid gouging the surface; don't apply too much pressure, as this can make the sander burn or dig into the stock.

Combination Belt and Disk Sander. Stationary disk sanders are often sold as a combination tool with a belt sander. The belt sander is well suited to sanding with the grain, the disk sander to end grain, and the combination tool can be an economical (and space-saving) alternative to buying two separate sanders, offering the functions of two tools in the space of one. (See also *The Belt Sander*, page 204.)

Another inexpensive option is to transform your table saw into a disk sander. For less than thirty dollars, you can purchase a disk and sandpaper and, as quickly as you can change blades, you have a disk sander.

SURFACE PREPARATION, PART 2

Your project is sanded and ready for finishing. So now it's time to pop open the paint or varnish can, grab a brush or rag, and get it done, right?

Not so fast. The investment of a few minutes of careful preparation now can make a big difference in the quality of the final product.

Remove Any Dust and Dirt. The piece must be thoroughly cleaned of any sanding dust or workshop dirt and debris. Use your shop vacuum for the first pass, but then try the old cabinetmaker's trick: Use a tack cloth and wipe the entire surface to be painted or varnished. The tack cloth is a piece of cloth dampened slightly with a mix of turpentine and shellac, preferably one that has set awhile, perhaps in a plastic bag or a jar. It's sticky, and will remove sanding dust and dirt. I guarantee you, even if you can't see any surface debris on the piece, you'll see it on the tack cloth after it's been wiped gently over the wood.

Finish Supplies. You'll need more than a brush and your paint or varnish can. At the very least, you'll also need the proper solvent for cleaning up afterwards (read the can to determine whether mineral spirits, denatured alcohol, turpentine, or some other solvent will be required).

While you're examining the can, read the manufacturer's recommendations as to temperature restrictions, drying times, and application techniques. And check out your brush or rag, too. It should be clean and free of dirt.

Try a Test Run. Unless you've used the same finish before, you'd be wise to try it out on a piece of scrap stock first. The chips or samples they show you in the paint store and the picture in the catalog can frequently mislead the eye. Even the contents of the can itself may not be much help; virtually all finishes look different when dry than they do in liquid form in the container.

Apply your chosen finish to the scrap wood, let it dry, and then consider the result. Does it darken the wood too much? Is the color brighter (or duller) than you thought it would be? Now's the time to make a change – and avoid second-guessing yourself later.

Application Techniques. When finishing a flat surface, whether you're using oil-based paints or stain or varnish, keep in mind that you must not allow one portion of it to dry before painting the rest. If you do, a line will probably be quite noticeable. On a large job, complete one section or side at a time.

PAINT- AND FINISHING BRUSHES

The lowly paintbrush: We've known about it since preschool days. Paintbrushes were great fun in kindergarten, too, though for a lot of us they've become less enjoyable as the universe of painting tasks has grown by leaps and bounds. For anyone who lives in an antique, wood-frame house, the paintbrush is rarely out of mind or far from reach.

The paintbrush is, like so many simple tools, more complicated than it seems. The shape of the wooden handle, for example, is comfortable and efficient – and not by accident, because it has evolved over many centuries to its present contoured shape. It suits the working hand, the fingers and thumb holding the broad end (the stock), the other end fitting into the fork formed by the thumb and forefinger.

The paint-absorbing filling isn't merely clamped in the metal ring (the ferrule) that connects the brush to its handle. Before the ferrule is wrapped around the handle and brush, the filling is dipped in a setting compound, often made of epoxy, that binds the bristles together.

Picking the right paintbrush presents almost the same challenge as selecting the right color. Make sure the one you choose suits the paint or other finish you will be using. Among the options here are brushes made from China bristles, synthetic materials, and even ox hair (red handles) and badger fur (with the striped bristles).

Actually, the word *bristles* is sometimes the wrong one. Bristles occur in nature: They are the hair of hogs. But many brushes use other materials, both natural and synthetic.

The best brushes consist of individual filaments that, like a hog bristle, taper toward the end, then split, forming what are known as flags. The flags help hold the paint and to spread it evenly. Some synthetic bristles, in addition to tapering and splitting, are textured as well.

Buying Brushes. I'm no longer surprised at how much the best brushes cost. Having learned a long time ago that for high-quality jobs they are essential, what I'm now surprised by is how long good brushes last and how much easier they are to use than cheap brushes that seem to self-destruct halfway through a job.

Before you buy a brush, inspect it carefully. The bristles should be flexible, but stiff enough that they spring quickly back after you spread them between your fingers. Make sure there are no manufacturing defects, like a poorly attached ferrule or uneven trimming of the brush tip.

A quality brush will, if properly cared for, last from one job to the next. It will spread the paint more easily and evenly, carry more paint from the bucket to the surface being painted, and is less likely to leave telltale bristles behind to mar your perfect paint job.

There are all kinds of brushes to choose from. Among those you're most likely to need are these:

Flat Brushes. When we think of a paintbrush, it is the traditional flat brush that we usually have in mind. It's used to paint all sorts of surfaces with paint or varnish, whether these be walls or trim or objects. Flat brushes come in an array of sizes, from as little as half an inch wide to four and five inches across. The widest are usually called wall brushes, narrower ones varnish brushes.

The proper use of a flat brush involves more than dipping the brush in the paint and brushing it onto the wall. There are a couple of small tricks that make painting a more efficient process.

The grip is important: Grasp the ferrule, the metal band around the brush, between your thumb and fingers. This grip is less likely to cause cramping when you must paint for long periods but, equally important, it disciplines your stroke.

It's like throwing a Frisbee: It's all in the wrist. A gentle back-and-forth swing of the wrist produces even, comfortable strokes.

Don't dip the brush too far into the paint (a third or, at most, a half of the bristle length is far enough). As you remove the brush from the can after dipping it, remove excess paint from the bristle by drawing each side of the brush gently along the edge of the paint can.

Apply the paint evenly. Avoid too much paint: The excess will produce drips and little rivulets that will spoil the even finish. Keep the handle raised above the bristles, so that the paint won't drip into the ferrule. If it does, you'll find it dripping onto your hand, and drops will gradually appear everywhere around you.

Sash Brush. Sash brushes have slightly beveled tips, which makes painting window muntins and other narrow trim easier.

Some brushes also have ends that have been trimmed at an angle to the handle of the brush. Credit some unnamed painter of the past with devising this clever and oh-so-simple solution to painting tricky, angled areas, especially corners. It's still a simple flat trim brush, usually an inch or an inch and a half wide. But the angled tip makes painting edges immensely easier, permitting the painter to see more clearly what he or she is painting, and angling the brush in such a way that it is less likely to apply paint to areas where you don't want it. The sash brush is sometimes referred to as a chisel-edge brush.

Paint Roller. Rollers paint large flat areas like ceilings and floors. They use less paint than brushes do; they spread the paint more evenly than a brush; they make quick work of large, flat areas.

The covers are replaceable and the handles reusable. The nap or fiber on the roller covers varies, and should be matched to the paint you are using (longer fibers for rough surfaces, low-nap for smooth ones; different paint bases and finishes require appropriate rollers, too). The bulky roller does not reach into corners efficiently, so paint the edges with a brush first, then roll into them. Standard rollers are seven inches and nine inches wide, though narrower trim rollers (three inches wide) are also available.

Paintbrush Advice. Paint in long strokes and always keep a wet edge. Keep the light source between you and the surface if possible, and take special care at the edges, corners, and joints you encounter, those being the places where drips and runs are most likely.

Caring for Your Paintbrushes. An investment in high-quality brushes is wasted if they are not properly cleaned and stored after use. So invest the two minutes it takes to do the job right.

Cleaning a brush is made easier if you remove as much of the paint from its bristles as possible. Use up what paint remains on your brush on whatever you are painting. Press the bristles against the inside of the paint can, and lift it up and out as you do: that will squeeze out more paint. Paint away the rest on newspapers.

Next, read the instructions on the can, and use the appropriate solvent. The manufacturers may specify mineral spirits or turpentine for oil-based paint; brushes used to apply latex paint usually can be cleaned with soap and water. The right solvent makes the job easy; the wrong one will probably be no help at all.

Immerse the brush in the solvent. Stir the solvent with the brush, wiping and squeezing the bristles on the sides of the container. If some of the paint has begun to dry on the brush, soaking the brush may be necessary.

Once the paint has been removed from the brush, wash it in warm soapy water in a utility sink or bucket. This cleans the brush of the solvent and remaining paint. Blot the brush dry with a clean rag or newspaper. When storing brushes, hang them up or store them flat so that the bristles don't get bent out of shape.

STRIPPING TOOLS

Stripping off old paint isn't really much fun. It's usually a messy job: Whatever method you use (dry scraping, heat, or chemical strippers), the residue of old paint seems somehow to spread itself all over the workshop. With the proper tools, however, removing old paint can be done efficiently.

The Heat Gun. Heat guns typically have the shape of a gun, with a pistol handle and a switch controlled by your trigger finger. The gun is used

One clever trick that ensures the bristles will maintain their shape is to drill a hole in the brush's handle and suspend the bristles in solvent in this fashion.

GRAIN-PAINTING BRUSHES

Graining and marbling – though widely practiced in the nineteenth century – have long been out of favor. But in recent years, these faux finishes have been rediscovered.

The chief advantage of these decorative techniques is that, for the price of mere paint supplies, you can have the appearance of expensive materials such as marble or handsomely grained mahogany, maple, or other woods. Furniture, trim, even floors, doors, and other surfaces can be given a new visual richness.

The basic techniques are remarkably simple. A base coat of paint is applied to the surface to be finished and allowed to dry. Then a second color is applied, which is then tooled to create the effect of the grains or veins one sees in woods or marbles; in some cases, a third or even more colors may also be used. In the case of verde marble, the base coat is black, the second color green, with white veining added. For a mahogany grain, a base color of a crimson red is largely obscured beneath a glaze of brown. Typically, the base coat is an oil- or latex-based paint, the second coat a tinted glaze. For some effects, charcoal, acrylics, or artist's tube paints may be used.

Graining and marbling are akin to the practices of distressing, in which a second coat of paint (of a different shade or tone) is sponged, stippled, or otherwise "distressed" to give

the painted surface a variegated quality. The key difference is that in graining and marbling the intent is to replicate with some degree of accuracy the appearance of the actual wood or stone. To accomplish that, a variety of tools are needed. A standard paintbrush is generally used for applying the base coat, but a number of specialty brushes and applicators are handy for later steps. Among them are:

Graining Combs. These rubber or metal tools are used to create the illusion of wood grain. While a glaze or top coat of paint is still wet, the tool is drawn through the paint.

Dragging Brush. Also called an overgrainer, this one has horse bristles and can add a striated effect as it is drawn or "dragged" through the paint.

Artist's Paintbrushes. These delicate sable brushes are used for veining and other fine inpainting.

Marbling (or "marbleizing" as the technique is also known) is akin to grain painting. A base coat is applied and allowed to dry, then a glaze of another color is painted on and partially wiped off using any number of a variety of tools, including brushes, feathers, sponges, rags, or crumpled paper. Often a third and even a fourth color may be applied . . . and, thanks to the miracle of paint pigments, a piece of wood is transformed into a piece of stone.

Badger Blender. As the name suggests, this brush is made of badger fur. It's a very soft brush, used for blending coloring with a delicate touch.

Flogger Brush. In contrast to the blender, this brush has quite stiff, long bristles. It's for distressing a painted surface.

Feathers, Rags, Paper Towels, and Applicators. Just about anything you can think of can be used to apply paint – and probably is. Aluminum foil, wood scraps, and sponges are other options. Feel free to experiment.

This eighteenth-century door hasn't looked this good for a long time. But the heat gun, a couple of scrapers, and a heat plate for the flat areas make quick work of a dozen or more layers of paint.

to remove paint (in tandem with a paint scraper), but also will loosen old window putty and tile, as well as soften certain plastics for bending or shaping.

Heating capacity varies from one gun to another. Some have as few as six or seven hundred watts; other have as many as fourteen hundred watts. Some top-of-the-market models have an electronic control mechanism that senses when the gun is running too hot (it detects back pressure) and automatically maintains a constant temperature. The temperatures on most guns are adjustable; the range may range from two hundred and fifty degrees to eleven hundred degrees.

Hold the gun three to six inches from the surface to be stripped. Keep it moving over a small area, back and forth or in a circular motion. When the paint blisters, remove the gun from the area and immediately scrape the softened paint. Often a second pass is required.

The Heat Plate. A near relation of the heat gun, the heat plate consists of a heating element in the shape of a loop. A metal reflector helps direct the heat to the workpiece, maintains the tool at a fixed distance from the surface to be stripped, and protects you from the red-hot element. Some heat plates have built-in scrapers at the toe, others a built-in stand that the tool can rest on while cooling off. When in use, the tool is held by its insulated handle.

The heat plate is best suited to stripping flat surfaces such as doors and panels. As with the heat gun, the heat plate requires a little experimentation. Depending upon how much paint has accumulated on the surface, the plate may need to remain in a given spot for relatively longer or shorter periods of time. When the paint begins to bubble, scrape it with a paint scraper.

There are other stripping options, too. Many chemical strippers are on the market. When using them, be sure to provide plenty of protection, both for yourself and the surfaces nearby. Gloves, safety glasses, and a respirator mask are a good idea; so is having plenty of newspapers handy.

And another thing: If you are stripping paint of a certain age, test it for lead content; most drug stores sell inexpensive testing kits. If there is lead-based paint on the elements to be stripped, be sure to wear a mask when you are scraping. Isolate the job so the entire house doesn't get contaminated. Frequent hand washings are essential, too, as is changing out of your stripping clothes when you reenter the inhabited part of the house. If children live in or visit your home, you would be wise to do the job someplace else altogether as lead is a great danger to them. And very little lead can do a great deal of harm.

The belt sander will also remove paint, both from metal and wood. Be aware, however, that this robust machine will, if you are not watchful, gladly remove more than the surface of paint or varnish. It's a rough and ready tool for tough jobs, not one suited to delicate duty.

PAINTS AND FINISHES

Countless articles and books have been published about the options you have in selecting and applying finishes. I can't pretend to be able to offer you the last word in the limited space available here, but the subject is too important not to address in some detail. I'll try to give you the lay of the land, define some of the key terms (which are so often confused and confusing), and offer a few suggestions.

The reasons for applying finishes to wood surfaces are several. One is to seal the wood, in order to prevent moisture from entering the grain and to protect it from heat, scratches, or even insects. Another goal is to enhance its appearance, adding color, contrast, shading, or even to change its texture. Among your options in finishing wood are stains, varnishes, paints, and rubbed oil finishes.

Stains. As the name suggests, stains are coloring agents that are used to change the color or shade of the wood. In fact, stains are not technically a finish because a simple stain requires a coat (or coats) of varnish or another finish on top to protect the wood.

Stains can highlight the grain, lighten or darken the natural tones, or change them altogether. In general, stains are applied first, and are often followed by sealers or varnishes. Some combination products are sold in which a stain and a sealer are applied to the wood at one time.

There are various kinds of stains that are distinguished by the vehicle or solvent in which the color is suspended. The stain goes on as a liquid, the solvent evaporates, and the stain dries. Linseed-oil based stain is perhaps the classic variety of stain. This grouping tends not to penetrate the wood, but to remain on its surface. Linseed-oil stains are wiped on, become opaque when dry, and mix well with pigments. They're generally applied in a thick coat and allowed to dry until the stain begins to lose its glossy appearance; then the excess is wiped off with a cloth.

Turpentine-based, alcohol-based, and water-based stains are other options. The turpentine-based varieties tend to penetrate into the grain, which means they must be applied quickly and very evenly. Often sprayed on, penetrating-oil stains have the advantage that the next stage in the finishing process can begin within a few hours because they dry quickly. Alcohol stains are usually purchased in an aerosol can; water stains are powdered, requiring mixing.

Exterior stains are chemically similar to oil-based paint but with creosote added to the mix.

Shellac. This is the old standard, though it's used less and less often these days, as advances lead to new, quicker, and easier-to-use finishes. It gets its name from the source of the resin that is its principal ingredient, the lac bug, an insect found in India and other countries in southern Asia.

The principal disadvantage of a shellac finish is that water stains it; another is that alcohol dissolves it. One carelessly abandoned glass and its accompanying film of condensation will produce a water stain that won't go away until the piece is refinished.

Even so, the great popularity of shellac in the past (and among some craftsmen even today) is understandable. In either its white or in its orange form, it's quick and easy to apply with a brush in a series of light coats. Each should be thin in order to avoid drips or runs. I recommend a light sanding between coats and a final coat of paste wax after the shellac has dried thoroughly.

The French Finish. A French polish shines with a mellow, reflective quality that is its greatest appeal – but, since its key ingredient is shellac, it does not protect the wood from heat or moisture damage (again, water-glass rings and the like are a continuing concern). For many pieces of furniture that originally had that finish (or modern copies of such furniture), it really is the appropriate choice. It'll give your arm muscles a workout, too.

French polishes are not all the same, though the basic ingredients are usually a mix of shellac and alcohol (sometimes with boiled linseed oil or a few drops of mineral oil in later coats). The mixture is applied to raw wood with a rag. Wear gloves when applying a French polish.

Coat the surface using light strokes, working with the grain. Some users recommend a swirling motion, as if you were making a series of **O**s in script, but still progressing in the direction of the grain. After the first coat has dried, sand the surface with extrafine sandpaper or steel wool. Many coats are required; with each one, the shine will increase. The more you rub, the more the finish will shine.

Penetrating Oils. These are sold in clear and stain colors, and are easy to apply. They are wiped on and tend to dry quickly and evenly. Penetrating oils are extremely durable and resist both scratching and water damage, because the finish penetrates beneath the surface, sealing and protecting the wood. One result, however, is that the surface itself is left with little sheen or gloss.

These finishes are manufactured in a variety of formulations, some of which have a resin base, some an oil base. Boiled linseed oil and tung oil are common penetrating-oil finishes.

Penetrating oils can be applied with a cloth or brush. Coat the surface thoroughly; after about fifteen minutes (less if the surface is plywood), wipe off the excess. Apply a second coat. There's no need to

This simple set of child's blocks is distinguished mostly by its colors. Made of maple and oak, the blocks are sealed with a glaze tinted with oil pigments. The handsome grain of the hardwood shows through, yet the palette is quite bright enough to please a child.

219

sand between coats when using penetrating oils. If you wish to stain the wood, do that before applying the oil finish. Alcohol- and water-based stains work well with penetrating-oil finishes.

Varnishes. The word *varnish* has become something of a catchall term applied to a variety of liquid preparations that, when applied to a surface, dry to a clear, hard, and often shiny surface. They are good general-purpose clear finishes.

Natural varnishes are made from natural resins suspended in an oil base (typically, boiled linseed or tung oil); the solvent used is turpentine or mineral spirits. A wide variety of natural varnishes are sold for different uses, from marine applications to gymnasium floors to furniture. Exterior varnishes tend to have more oil, those for interior use less. So-called long oil has the richest mix of oil, so its strength is waterproofing, making it perfect for the boatyard; medium oil is very durable, so it's the right candidate for floor finishes. Short oil leaves a hard and brittle finish, suitable for furniture.

Polyurethane is a synthetic varnish. It is durable and dries quickly to a clear and transparent finish. It is sold in a variety of different formulations, both oil- and water-based. Polyurethanes and most other varnishes can be bought in glossy, flat, or satin finishes.

Varnishes are more difficult to use than, say, shellac or penetrating oils. They dry slowly (which means that dust and debris can accumulate on their tacky surfaces as they dry) and the surface tends to bubble. When applying varnish, the room should be warm and as dust-free as possible. Stir the varnish before using it, but don't shake the container, as that will cause bubbles to form.

The brushes, too, must be clean. Overlap your brushstrokes, and apply the varnish in a very thin layer. Don't overbrush. After varnishing an entire surface, go over it once carefully with the tip of the brush. Don't apply more varnish, but smooth the varnish already there in long, even strokes.

When the varnish has dried completely, smooth it using extrafine sandpaper or steel wool. Apply a second coat. After that has dried, you may wish to rub the finish with steel wool or pumice. Apply a paste wax, and buff the finish thoroughly.

Paints. Varnish, oil, shellac, and French finishes are, for the most part, clear finishes. Paint, in contrast, is opaque, and usually contains colored pigments.

The pigments are finely ground solids that are suspended in the base material, which may be latex, oil, or other substances (lead-based paint now is rarely available because of the toxicity of the lead). Paints are sold for use indoors and outdoors (exterior paints are much more durable, resisting fading, chipping, and peeling). Most are sold in a variety of lusters, depending upon whether they dry to a glossy sheen; a semigloss or satin finish; or a flat or eggshell surface. Gloss and semigloss have the virtue that they can be washed and even scrubbed; flat or satin finishes have a soft, understated presence.

Before being painted, raw woods need to be sealed with a primer coat. This seals the wood and prepares a surface to which the paint to follow can bond. The primer used should be matched to the paint to be used; read the instructions on the can or consult your local paint supplier.

Chapter 12.

Workshop Storage

In a perfect world, I'd never waste a moment looking for things. The right wrench would come to hand when I needed it, phone messages wouldn't disappear from my desk, and little tiny set screws would never fall onto the workshop floor. I don't know about you, but my world isn't quite that ideal.

One way to make your workshop life easier – if not quite perfect – is to introduce a high degree of organization. This doesn't mean hiring an engineer with a degree in time-and-efficiency studies, or investing in a thousand dollars' worth of shelves and drawers. Some common sense, a bit of planning, and a couple of hours of work might well save you a month of Saturday mornings – hours and hours that otherwise will be wasted swearing ("Son of a gundog, where is that thing?"), sighing ("Oh, boy, I guess it's lost"), then searching ("It's not in the toolbox or on the top shelf. Maybe it's under the sink . . . or did I use it last in the attic?").

A good system for stowing your tools and storing your supplies will have an added benefit: Wood that's stacked properly stays straighter, tools kept in a secure and suitable spot are safer and less likely to get disuse disease (symptoms: tangled cords, rusty or corroded parts), and there will be fewer breaks, scratches, and other minor damages that occur when hardware is relegated to a "junk box."

Once established, a put-it-where-it-belongs regimen isn't especially hard or time-consuming.

That set of cubbyholes at center was salvaged from an antique desk, now resting atop a simple peg rail. Both are located over the main bench in this workshop, putting tools and supplies out of the way – yet within easy reach – of the workbench.

KEEPING YOUR TOOLS ACCESSIBLE

One of the great advantages of a workshop – as distinct from a toolbox carried to a workplace – is the opportunity to put your tools on what I like to call working display. I don't mean you are showing them off (you probably won't be giving many tours of the workshop anyway). I'm talking about exhibiting your tools to yourself, right there where they are needed, for your eyes to see and your hand to reach out and touch them.

Use Your Wallspace. In a well-planned workshop, there should be a minimum of scrabbling about on the bottom of a toolbox in search of a cold chisel. Instead, put the walls around you to work holding your tools.

The pegboard with bracket approach has been in use at least since the days of Ozzie and Harriet and those cardigan sweaters Ozzie always

Some prefabricated systems on the market are also flexible and sturdy enough for most tools. This one is a step up the evolutionary ladder from the traditional pegboard.

wore. Pegboard may be something of a cliché, but that doesn't make it all bad.

Perforated hardboard is widely available and inexpensive; the pre-fabricated hangers are also commonplace, affordable, and to be found in a variety of shapes and sizes. The hangers do seem to have a tendency to release and drop to the floor and I, for one, think it's over-kill to draw individual tool silhouettes behind each hanger (the hammer goes here, the saw over there, the two-foot level up above . . .). But, hey, if it works for you, do it.

Perforated hardboard can be bought in eighth-inch and quarter-inch thicknesses; use the sturdier stuff if you plan to suspend any power tools from your rack. The board should be firmly attached to furring or one-by battens (screws and washers are a stronger and more permanent means than nails). The furring will provide the space necessary behind the board for hooking the hangers. The battens should be firmly attached to the studs in a wood-frame wall (drywall screws are a good solution) or with masonry nails and construction adhesive to a concrete surface.

There are a variety of somewhat more expensive but improved systems that offer even more flexibility. Most have prefabricated sections that can be mixed and matched to suit any array of tools. Some designs feature hangers that clip firmly in place. Most are designed to be fastened to wall studs spaced at standard sixteen-inch intervals. Shop around, and buy what you like.

A homemade Shaker peg rail keeps tools handy and also appeals to the eye. The edge of the rail is beaded, the pegs let into the rail at intervals.

You also can make your own out of dowel stock. Three-eighths-inch dowel is strong enough for quite heavy tools. Drill matching holes in a strip of one-by stock; angle the holes slightly downwards.

Many tool suppliers and direct mail catalogs sell magnetic strips for wall mounting. They can hold pliers, wrenches, screwdrivers, chisels, and other steel hand tools. Hang one over your workbench.

Hooks attached to the wall or ceiling have their place, too. A push stick hung strategically over a table saw, for example, is easily accessible – and more likely to get used.

Shelves are easy to knock together – no high-art joinery is required here, just sturdy and square surfaces on which to rest planes and hand-held power tools and just about anything else portable.

Commercially available magnetic strips are best suited to mechanical tools with steel or iron elements that the magnet can grip. In this case, the strip is mounted on a piece of one-by-four stock, both to protect the wall behind and to make the tools easier to grasp.

Your fire extinguisher is a low-maintenance item: All it needs is a check of the pressure gauge every now and again to be sure that it is fully charged. If the gauge says "Recharge," get it done, and pronto.

Options from the Kitchen or Office. Keep your eyes open: filing cabinets from the office, lazy Susans from the kitchen, and a multitude of other items designed for specific tasks can be adapted to workshop use. Apothecary drawers and office credenzas also can serve for storage or even as work surfaces.

A perennial trick is to adapt old kitchen cabinets. They may be unstylish in the kitchen, but in the workshop who cares? Solid box cabinets make for safe and secure storage of tools, hardware, and other goods.

As you organize your workshop, don't forget that some of your tools will probably be used not only within the confines of the shop but elsewhere, too. Some of the tools will be trade-specific, designed for use on electrical work or painting jobs or plumbing. You might want to consider designating certain areas or containers for different tasks: a portable tool bag for the plastering tools, an open-topped tool carrier for plumbing supplies and tools, that portable workbench (see page 49) for the odd carpentry task.

Tool Cabinets. Closed cabinets are preferable to open shelves because less dust is likely to penetrate the closed doors (though some will) and coat the tools. They don't necessarily have to be pretty, and can be fixed in place, fastened to a wall, or stowed in a utility area. Or they can be portable, ready to load into your pickup and go to work down the street.

Planes are best stored on their sides, preferably with their blades withdrawn; never, never with metal nearby that could come into contact with the plane irons. A shelved cabinet is ideal for them.

Drawers. Drawers are a good place for small tools and, in particular, for sharp ones. A cabinetmaker's bench, for example, has drawers that suit chisels, scrapers, and other hand-held shaping tools.

A shallow drawer is appropriate for small tools like jeweler's drivers, allen wrenches, drill bits, and saber-saw blades. You might consider installing a drawer in your bench for holding such small items.

TOOL MAINTENANCE

Whatever your storage arrangements, keep your tools clean. After use, remove any sap or resins from cutting tools (kerosene or ammonia will do the job).

A tack rag is handy, too. Dampen a piece of cloth slightly with a mix of turpentine and shellac. It will wipe away oily sawdust from blades, housings, and other parts of hand and power tools. Store the rag in a sealed jar or plastic bag for future use.

Rust is prevented in two ways: one, by keeping the tools dry (that means out of the rain *and* in dry storage areas); and, two, by applying a light film of machine oil wiped on with a cloth. If your workshop is in a cellar, garage, or another damp space, consider buying a dehumidifier to reduce the humidity in the area. However, if your workshop is only occasionally wet and you don't have a dry alternative, try storing your tools in a tight toolbox, perhaps one made of plastic. Add weather stripping, if necessary, and moisture absorbent. For power tools with steel surfaces, a paste wax coating is easy to apply and helps prevent rust.

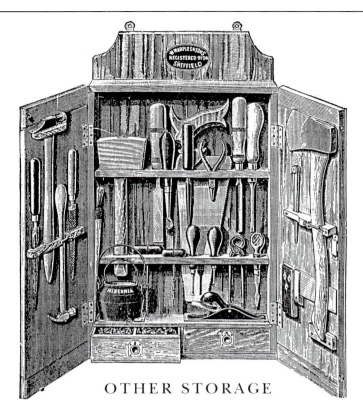

The company selling this particular toolbox gave it the rather grand title of "Gentlemen's Registered Tool Cabinets." It looks very practical to me, registered or not.

OTHER STORAGE

Scrap Storage. Racks or bins are essential if you have more than a handful of odds and ends and offcuts around.

If the ceiling overhead is unfinished, joists or rafters can be turned into storage. Use lag bolts to fasten two or three two-by-fours perpendicular to the ceiling members, and you'll have individual bays for organizing, as well as storing, your moldings and other stock.

Just about any kind of sturdy support will suffice that keeps the stock flat, off the floor, and out of the way.

Hardware Storage. There's only one trick, really. That's to be able to find what you're looking for with a minimum of time and frustration. Easier said than done.

A couple of rules: Apples go with apples, oranges with oranges. Cleanliness probably isn't holy, but it sure is a handy trait.

If you can't look through it (as with clear plastic or glass jars) to identify the contents of a container, label it.

I could go on and on about storing your tools and supplies, but the key consideration is matching your storage facilities to your space and needs. Just keep in mind that the basic rule is to keep it at hand, but not underfoot.

So now you are on your own. You have your shop built (or at least a plan of what you intend). You have your tools at the ready, and maybe even a couple of projects clearly in mind.

So I wish you well in your new space. May all your work be safe and satisfying.

227

JOHNSTON PUBLIC LIBRARY
JOHNSTON, IOWA 50131

I N D E X